WOMEN OF VIET NAM

BY ARLENE EISEN BERGMAN

ILLUSTRATED BY JANE NORLING

EDITED AND PRODUCED COLLECTIVELY BY
SUSAN ADELMAN, ARLENE EISEN BERGMAN,
DIANA BLOCK, PENNY JOHNSON,
JANE NORLING, PEGGY TUCKER

PEOPLES PRESS

A NOTE ON THE SECOND EDITION

This edition of *Women of Viet Nam* is quite different from the first. It was written after South Viet Nam won its complete independence and includes as much information as possible about postwar developments in Viet Nam. The current edition also includes a good deal of new material I collected during a visit I made to the DRV and the liberated areas of South Viet Nam in the fall of 1974.

Special thanks to Le Thi Xuyen, Phan Thi An, Vo Thi The, Bui Thi Me, Tran Thanh Tuyen, Le Thi Thuy, Nguyen Khanh Phuong and the other sisters from the Viet Nam Women's Union who were my hosts, teachers and cherished friends in Viet Nam. I offer you this edition as a modest celebration of September 2, 1975—the first Vietnamese independence day to pass without foreign troops on your land.

Thank you again to Diana Block and Penny Johnson, who helped edit the second edition and to Susan Weiss and Mishaa who helped produce it.

A.E.B.
August 1, 1975

Library of Congress Cataloging in Publication Data
Bergman, Arlene Eisen.
    Women of Viet Nam.

    Bibliography: p.
    1. Women—Vietnam. 2. Feminism—Vietnam.
I. Title.
HQ1749.V5B47 1975 301.41'2'09597 75-28221
ISBN 0-914750-02-X

$2.95 per copy
25% discount for orders of 10 or more.
Special rates available on request.

Published by Peoples Press, 2680 21st Street
San Francisco, Ca. 94110

This book is dedicated to the growing solidarity between women of Viet Nam and women of the United States.

TO EVERYONE WHO HELPED–

Thank you.

Thank you to the women of Viet Nam.

This book grew from the questions, needs and encouragement of women active in the women's movement in the United States. We feel stronger, inspired by the experience of women in Viet Nam. We want to share this strength and inspiration with as many people as possible, particularly women. That is why so many of us worked hard and with joy to create this book.

Thank you to Sharon Hall, who unintentionally launched this project in the spring of 1972, by prodding me to give a talk on the topic as part of a series of protests against the bombing of Hanoi and Haiphong.

Thank you to all the people whose interest and willingness to share their energy and knowledge gave me the confidence to allow the article I planned about women in Viet Nam to grow into a book. Jane Fonda first planted the idea. The early enthusiasm of Susan Adelman, Gail Dolgin, Martha Williams and Terry Karl, all from Peoples Press, committed the Press to make the earliest draft of the book become a reality.

Our editorial/production group includes women who have been active in the women's and anti-war movement for a long time, but none of us had ever taken responsibility for creating a book before. At present, Susan Adelman and Penny Johnson are members of Peoples Press. Arlene Eisen Bergman, a lecturer at San Jose State University; Diana Block, a teacher's aide; and Peggy Tucker, a health worker, are all active in the San Francisco Women's Union. The group met twice weekly for several months, along with Judy Green and Paula Martinet, editing the manuscript line by line, struggling over the political content and clarity of the book. This collective work transformed the process of editing, making it reflect the experience of the women's movement and of all revolutionaries who try to learn from each other and to help each other improve their work. Jane Norling is a people's artist who has been creating beautiful posters, leaflets and murals in the S.F. Bay Area for years. She worked with our group to design the book and create the illustrations which both express and strengthen the meaning of the book. We worked together to plan and paste up each page.

Thanks to the people who freely shared their energy, time and knowledge, making this book theirs as well as ours. Jane Fonda enthusiastically supplied records of both her visits to Viet Nam. Tran Khanh Tuyet, a member of Indochina Resource Center, patiently answered all our questions and struggled to get us to understand Vietnamese culture from her perspective. David Marr, also a member of Indochina Resource Center, spent long hours helping to make the book as historically accurate as possible. Vince Dijanich, a student at San Jose State and Viet Nam veteran, first helped me to clarify the connections made in Chapter 4, "The Politics of Rape," by probing his memory of his tour of duty in Viet Nam—a painful experience for both of us. And special thanks to the Viet Nam Women's Union for taking time to answer the questions we posed.

Many more people read the manuscript at various stages of its development, offered encouragement, and made thoughtful suggestions for improvement. Thank you to Nancy Barrett, Jane Barton, Lincoln Bergman. Miranda Bergman, Deb Bogart, Karla Boyd, Brenda Braham, Cau Thi My Loc, Doan Thi Nam Hau and other members of the Union of Vietnamese in the U.S., Janet Childs, Dee Donovan, Deirdre English, Ann Froines, Nina Gagnon, Vickie Garvin, Sally Gearhart, Arlie Hochschild, Allison James, Barbara Johnson, Laura Klepfer, Magali Sarfatti Larson, Deborah Le Sueur, Ellen Murray, Nha Trang, Irene Paul, Marge Piercy, Margaret Randall, Jill Rodewald, Karen Shane, Judy Schwarz, Susan and other sisters held at the California women's state penitentiary, Tran Tu and the other members of the Association of Vietnamese Patriots in Canada, Lupe Viniegra and Zelima.

Thanks to the people who gave their time and labor towards the technical production of the book: Maisie McAdoo, Errol Hendra, Don Campbell of Honeywell & Todd Lithography. Special thanks to Hal Muskat and Bill Rock whose after-hours work helped the book reach the press on time. Thanks to all the people whose photography and writing we used. They have already been named in the notes.

A personal thanks to Bernardine Dohrn, the woman who first started me thinking about women's liberation back in the sixties; to Meridel Le Sueur, whose love and support began to teach me about women's solidarity and revolutionary optimism rooted in U.S. soil; and to Diana, Jane, Peggy, Penny and Susan who joined with me to create this book.

A.E.B.
June 1974

Photo credits:

Museum of Revolutionary History, Hanoi (p. 46), Liberation News Service (p. 64), Deirdre English and Steve Talbot (p. 145), S.F. Good Times (pp. 149, 221), Viet Nam News Agency (pp. 159, 161, 162, 174, 179, 187), Marc Riboud (pp. 192, 211).

VIET NAM IS ONE COUNTRY

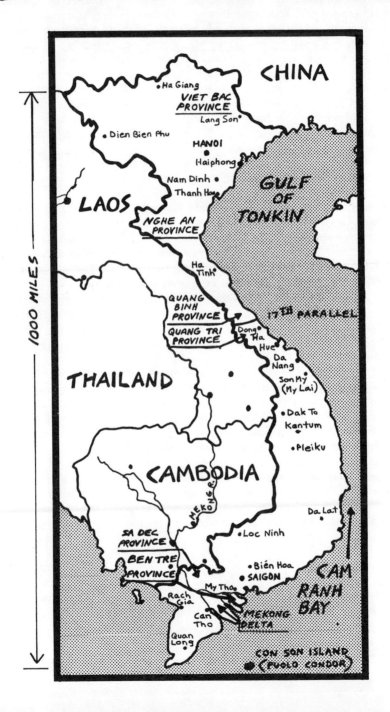

CONTENTS

GLOSSARY

Political geography

Viet Nam: The Vietnamese people, the Geneva Accords of 1954 and the Paris Peace Agreement of 1973 all recognize that *Viet Nam* is one country extending from the Chinese border on the north to the Gulf of Siam on the south. The nation has been temporarily divided into *North Viet Nam* and *South Viet Nam*, separated at the 17th parallel. Today, the government in *North Viet Nam* is the DRV and the government in the South is the PRGRSVN.

DRV (Democratic Republic of Viet Nam): Ho Chi Minh became the first President of this Republic, governing all of Viet Nam until 1954. Since 1954, the DRV refers to the area north of the 17th parallel.

PRG [Provisional Revolutionary Government of the Republic of South Viet Nam]: The coalition government formed in 1969 that adopted the political program of the National Liberation Front. Since April 30, 1975, it has been the sole legitimate representative of the South Vietnamese people. Areas governed by the PRG are also called *liberated areas.*

RVN (Republic of Viet Nam or Thieu Regime): State originally decreed by Diem, 1955, in violation of Geneva Accords. This government controlled a few cities in South Viet Nam and was financed by the U.S. government. After April 30, 1975, it was totally dissolved. Thieu fled the country.

Jarai: People descended from Malayo-Polynesians, living in mountain region of South Viet Nam. One of many national minorities in Viet Nam.

Political organization

cadre: A member of a revolutionary political organization.

ICP (Indochinese Communist Party): Founded in 1930 to organize the fight to abolish feudalism and French colonialism in Viet Nam and to build socialism there.

Lao Dong (Workers' Party): Formed in 1951 in the DRV to continue work of ICP.

PRP (Peoples' Revolutionary Party): Formed in 1962 in South Viet Nam to continue work of ICP.

NLF (National Liberation Front): Coalition of organizations, including PRP, dedicated to overthrowing U.S. domination of South Viet Nam; also referred to as the *Front*.

The Party: When this term appears before 1951 it refers to the ICP; after 1951, it refers to Lao Dong in the North or PRP in the South.

Viet Minh (Front for the Independence of Viet Nam): Coalition of organizations, formed in 1941 to fight against Japanese and French for Vietnamese independence.

Armies

ARVN [Army of the Republic of Viet Nam]: The troops who were trained and financed by the U.S. government to defend the Thieu regime. They surrendered on April 30, 1975.

PLAF (Peoples Liberation Armed Forces): Army organized by NLF.

VPA (Viet Nam People's Army): National army of DRV, originated in 1944 as Viet Nam Propaganda Unit for National Liberation.

militia: People who are not full-time soldiers but are prepared to defend their homes and workplaces militarily.

PRIDE OF BEING WOMAN

Never have I felt as in Viet Nam, in spite of the hard conditions of war, this pride of being woman, since the Vietnamese woman is so much loved and respected by the entire people.

—Cecile Hugel, Secretary General of International Federation of Democratic Women

Phuong lives with her four children, less than fifty miles from Saigon, on land she reclaimed when the United States troops abandoned a base there. Her husband died a few years ago under a thousand-pound bomb. After the GI's retreated from her village, she used to walk two miles a day to the day care center where she left her children. Then she would begin her day as a soldier in the liberation army, setting ambushes for the Saigon troops. In the evening she would return for her children.

Now that there's peace, she still leaves her children at the day care center, but spends her days with a work team in the fields. The team takes turns helping members with the tasks on their land that no one of them could do alone. Until April 30, 1975, Phuong still brought her helmet to the field, prepared for the bombs that dropped occasionally from U.S. planes—planes repainted with the emblem of Thieu's air force.

In this book, you'll meet many Vietnamese women, some like Phuong, and some like Nguyen Thi Dinh, who was illiterate until she was 17, but is now the top leader of the liberation army in South Viet Nam. You'll meet Gam, who at age 16 insisted on joining a guerrilla unit after she saw her best friend raped. And you'll meet women forced to live in cities as prostitutes. Here women testify why they faced torture rather than follow orders given by corrupt men. And here are grandmothers and young children who learn to read at the same time, from stories telling tales of women's strength. You'll also meet Nguyen Thi Binh, Foreign Minister of the Provisional Revolutionary Government of the Republic of South Viet Nam, as well as leaders of the Viet Nam Women's Union and women like Thuoc, a truckdriver in Hanoi.

Through these women and many others, we learn how Vietnamese women—once powerless, timid and invisible—became strong. They have been an essential component of a small, technologically backward people who have amazed the world in resisting the most advanced military power ever unleashed. How have they made progress towards women's liberation in the constant presence of war and death? How do men, citizens of the United States, raised on the best vitamins and mothers' love, become rapists in Viet Nam? How do women maintain their dignity in the midst of starvation and rape? How do they maintain their integrity when, in order to eat, they must become prostitutes, under heavy pressure to straighten their eyes and inject silicone into their breasts? Why did Minh Khai, a famous political leader in Viet Nam, speak for so many women when she said:

Revolution is our way of liberation.

Women in the United States, as in Viet Nam, have been trained to be "numb, numbered, and pegged, bred and conditioned to passivity." [1] The U.S. government has honored fifty thousand "Gold Star Mothers" whose sons died in the Viet Nam War. Seventeen of these mothers have formed a group called "Gold Star Mothers Against the War." [2] These seventeen join with thousands of other women who have begun to hold society, not themselves, responsible for their problems. In the United States, sometimes the task of fighting for a new society seems overwhelming. It's good to learn about women in other places, defying the same monster of destruction with courage and with the certainty that they will win.

This poem, written for an unnamed woman in Viet Nam, introduces us to the strength and pride of all Vietnamese women.

DAUGHTER OF VIET NAM

Wake up, my sister, the nightmare is over,
You live again, sister, you really live;
The searing electric shock, the piercing point,
The brilliant knife; the consuming fire
Have not killed you; heroic girl, your heart, my sister,
Your heart so great, with one drop of blood
It will beat again and it will not beat for you alone.

It will beat for justice, for your native village, for your
 country,
For humanity.
From the regions of death, you have come back to us,
 resplendent
As on the day you went away when the nation called;
You have come back, daughter of glory.
The whole country embraces you
As flesh of its flesh and blood of its blood,
You live again for you have conquered. . . .

 —by To Huu, born in Hue and member of the
 Central Committee of the Lao Dong Party, DRV

This book begins to tell the story of women's liberation in Viet Nam. It starts with the early history of oppression in pre-colonial times. This historical perspective explains why Vietnamese women chose some paths to liberation and not others. It also dramatizes how far and fast they have come towards liberation. The first section ends with an exposure and analysis of the specific ways the policies of U.S. domination affected women in Viet Nam. The second half of this book is a portrait of women's resistance. Using their own words wherever possible, we learn about their work, their political and military activity. The final chapters give us insight into the gains women have made as women in the course of this revolutionary process.

Notes

1. This phrase is from a poem by Marge Piercy, "The Judgment," in *To Be of Use* (New York: Doubleday, 1973).
2. For more on "Gold Star Mothers," see Ann Froines, "Women's Oppression and the Viet Nam War," in *Women on the Move* (University of Oregon, 1973), pp. 231-232.

IMPORTANT DATES

5000 B.C. — Early records of Vietnamese history begin.

111 B.C. — Chinese conquest of Viet Nam.

40 A.D. — Trung sisters lead first national insurrection against the Chinese.

981 A.D. — Chinese expelled from Viet Nam.

1847 — French first invade Viet Nam.

1930 — Indochinese Communist Party (ICP) and Viet Nam Women's Union founded; strikes and armed resistance to French become widespread.

1944-1945 — Famine years; first unit of Viet Nam People's Army formed and general insurrection sweeps the country (August Revolution).

Sept. 2, 1945 — Ho Chi Minh reads Vietnamese declaration of independence from France; days later French launch war of reconquest.

1946 — Constitution of the DRV ratified.

May 8, 1954 — Viet Minh defeat French at Dien Bien Phu.

July 20, 1954 — Geneva Accords recognize Viet Nam as one, independent nation.

1955-1956 — Diem begins terror campaign against Viet Minh and first U.S. military advisors arrive in southern Viet Nam.

Dec. 20, 1960 — National Liberation Front (NLF) forms and calls for general insurrection against Diem in the South.

1960 — Marriage Law passed in DRV, outlawing polygamy.

1961 — Union of Women for the Liberation of South Viet Nam formed.

Nov. 1, 1963 — Coup topples rule of Diem and Madame Nhu in South Viet Nam.

1964 — Gulf of Tonkin Resolution; U.S. begins bombing and sending large numbers of troops to Viet Nam.

1967 — 535,000 U.S. troops arrive by the end of the year.

Jan.-Feb. 1968 — Tet Offensive launched by the NLF.

May 1968 — First session of Paris Peace Talks.

June 10, 1969 — Provisional Revolutionary Government of South Viet Nam (PRG) founded at Congress of Representatives of the South Vietnamese People.

March 1970 — U.S. troops invade Cambodia.

March 1971 — Laos invaded by U.S. troops.

April 1971 — Beginning of U.S. troop reduction.

May 1972 — Quang Tri province liberated and Nixon orders bombing escalation.

Dec. 1972 — Christmas bombing of Hanoi and other densely populated cities. One-third of all the Air Force's operative B-52's are shot down.

Jan. 27, 1973 — U.S., Thieu regime, PRG and DRV sign Paris Peace Agreement.

1973-1974 — U.S. and Thieu continue to violate Peace Agreement.

March 1974 — Fourth National Congress of Vietnamese Women meets in Hanoi.

Fall 1974 — Unprecedented movement in South Vietnamese cities, including Catholic and Buddhist forces, calls for resignation of Thieu.

April 30, 1975 — Flag of the PRG is raised over the Presidential Palace in Saigon marking the decisive victory of the liberation forces.

1.
"ONE HUNDRED WOMEN ARE NOT WORTH A SINGLE TESTICLE"

Even though you sleep intimately on the same bed and use the same cover with him, you must treat your husband as if he were your king or your father.

—from the Confucian marriage manual

It's hard to know how it felt to be a woman in Viet Nam hundreds of years ago, but we can sketch a rough portrait from the historical facts we do know. Bao lives in the late fourteen-hundreds a short distance from the royal capital of Hanoi. She has inherited a well-established national tradition from her ancestors who, for hundreds of years, have rested in the same fields she tills. She lives more than half way around the globe from Europe where, at the same time, thousands of women were executed as witches and men were launching expeditions to conquer the Americas.

Bao is typical of most Vietnamese women. She is a peasant. She goes to the fields every day before sunrise and works in tropical heat until sunset. She is always tired. She knows it is a day's walk to the city where the king lives, but she never has reason to leave her village. As Bao walks to the field from the thatched-roof home she shares with her husband's other wife, she thinks about her husband. When she was 15, Bao married Chanh, who was only ten years old. Bao did not know the child, Chanh, but she married him because her father had ordered the marriage. Chanh's father paid her father two pigs to finalize the arrangement.

Bao understood that her duties as a bride were to work in the fields for Chanh's family. She had expected that when Chanh was old enough they would have sons, to fulfill the duties of ancestor worship. But when Chanh was old enough to father children, he took a second wife who gave birth to a son. Chanh never paid Bao any attention at all.

Bao sings a Vietnamese women's work song to the rhythm of the rice planting:

> *Having to climb up the mountains three times a day,*
> *How could I have retained my beauty and my youth?* [1]

But she stops abruptly as a village notable passes, accompanied by a visiting official. Bao listens suspiciously as they speak the language of the old foreign invaders, Chinese. She has heard that you can see the strange language on paper. She would like to learn to read instead of work in the fields. But Bao knows that only wealthy boys have a chance to learn to read and write. She will work in the fields until her body dies.

No one knows for sure when Vietnamese history began or how long Viet Nam existed as a nation before the Chinese invaded in 111

B.C. Archeologists have found Stone Age relics that were left by humans living in Viet Nam several hundred thousand years ago. A rich Bronze Age civilization, the Dong Son culture, flourished five thousand years before the birth of Christ.

Earliest legends

A popular legend tells that the founders of Viet Nam were a couple: the wife (Au Co) and the husband (Lac Long Quan). He was a dragon suited to living in the plains and on the coast. She was a fairy who wanted to live in the mountains. They agreed to part. Fifty sons followed their father and reigned over the kingdom near the South China Sea and fifty sons followed their mother and governed the northern part of Viet Nam. Before separating, they pledged mutual respect and aid to each other in times of crisis. The equality between husband and wife in this legend stands in sharp contrast to teachings of the Chinese invaders.

Other legends rooted in the remote past show that from the dawn of Viet Nam's history, people had to organize themselves to bring chronic floods under control with an elaborate system of dikes. Some say that slaves built the dikes. Others say they were constructed with communal labor. In any case, there were many tribes before the Chinese arrived—tribes who lacquered their teeth black, as some still do in Viet Nam today. They lived by growing rice in flooded fields. Some were communal and others were chiefdoms that made slaves out of conquered tribes. Some may have been matriarchies—tribes governed by women. [3].

Chinese invaders overturned the communalism and matriarchy of tribal life and imposed a rigid Confucian hierarchy that left an indelible mark on Vietnamese history and culture. The Chinese ruled Viet Nam for a thousand years (until 981 A.D.). Most Vietnamese kings and feudal lords continued to practice Confucian ways even after they expelled the Chinese.

One hundred women are not worth a single testicle.

Since ancient times, Confucian teachers have tried to etch these words in the consciousness of Vietnamese women. In the United States, we still hear: "Women's place is in the home." Proverbs like these reflect and strengthen unequal relationships that subordinate women to men. Throughout Vietnamese history, women have always been the most downtrodden people in the society. As power changed hands from one ruler to the next, the problems Vietnamese women faced also changed—usually they got worse.

Feudalism

Confucianism was more than a religion. It was a mandate for an entire way of life—in agriculture, in family and social life and in politics. The Confucian way in agriculture brought feudalism to Viet Nam. Feudalism is a system in which a small minority of landlords control the economic and political life of everyone else because they control the only means of survival—the land. During the Chinese reign and for much of Viet Nam's later history, all land officially belonged to the king, who gave land grants to noble families and favorites.

The only way for landless peasants to survive was to work for these aristocrats—more or less as slaves. The king allowed communal villages to rent the land not controlled by the aristocracy. In addition to paying taxes, peasant members of the village were periodically required to work on the king's roads, dikes and canals without pay. They also had to do military service. [4] Local notables or leaders controlled every important aspect of village life. Notables organized the rotation of communal lands, had judicial powers to settle local disputes, ran local finances, imposed taxes and demanded forced labor. Of course, only men could be notables—usually the men with the largest land holdings.

The overwhelming majority of Vietnamese women were poor peasants. Although their labor in the fields was essential to the economy, they had no chance to be economically independent. While the Chinese ruled, and for several centuries after, women were not allowed to own land. But, in the sixteenth century, wealthy women gained new rights. A reformist dynasty allowed women to share inheritance with men or inherit an entire family fortune if there were no male heirs. Three hundred years later, a new dynasty took these rights away again. Second-rank wives and concubines never really had any economic rights. And generally, men were the only ones considered capable enough to control the means of economic survival.

Confucian marriage

Marriage itself, particularly polygamy where one man has several wives, was an institution designed to exploit women's labor. Buying a wife or concubine proved cheaper than hiring a servant. Rich landlords collected concubines by purchasing the daughters of poor peasants who couldn't afford to pay their taxes and debts. In some areas, the groom presented his new in-laws with a water buffalo to replace the bride's labor. In effect, women never freely chose their husbands— rather they were sold to the highest bidder. A reluctant bride had two alternatives: either she could devote herself to lifelong service to her father and be celibate or she could commit suicide.

The poor man couldn't afford polygamy. Often, he couldn't afford the bride price for even one woman. A poor woman who was not desired by rich men or who escaped concubinage might marry a member of her own class without elaborate bride price or ceremony. This impoverished peasant couple would share their hardship. The fact that the woman and the man faced nearly equal oppression challenged the Confucian notion of man's inborn superiority. Famine, floods, droughts, plagues, and wars were a constant threat to the very survival of all poor people—especially women. Invariably, during hard times, a daughter would be sacrificed or sold as a concubine, slave or prostitute. At any time, there was little to prevent a mandarin or powerful notable from appropriating the wife or daughter of his tenant.

Upper class wives followed the Confucian marriage manual which taught:

> *Even though you sleep intimately on the same bed and use the same cover with him, you must treat your husband as if he were your king or your father.* [5]

As in traditional wedding ceremonies in the United States, the bride vowed obedience to her husband:

> *She: "I shall never dare to contradict you."*
> *He: "You must obey my father and my mother; you must live in harmony with them, be faithful to me in all things and not try to deceive me."*

To conclude this traditional aristocratic ceremony, the bride prostrated herself twice before her husband, who remained standing over her, nodding his approval. [6]

Throughout her life, the code of the "Three Obediences" negated all possibility for a woman's control over her life. As a child, the daughter owed unconditional obedience to her father. When she married, she transferred her obedience to her husband. Even her husband's death did not free her, for she was then bound to obey her eldest son. Another Vietnamese proverb observes:

> *An officer is one who commands soldiers;*
> *A husband is one who commands wives.* [7]

This rule by men is patriarchy in its purest form. It was stronger among the upper classes. A Vietnamese folksong shows that in peasant villages the word for obedience had more of a connotation of "following" and being "together" than the upper-class meaning of the word which was "submission." The peasant wife sang about following her husband through thick and thin, but made it clear that she would share life's hardships with him, rather than simply submit to his whim:

> *Having pledged eternal love for him,*
> *I will not shun crossing streams and mountains with*
> *   him . . .*
> *In the way of husband and wife,*
> *Depending on each other is essential to guard against*
> *   the adversities of life.* [8]

One of the most basic assumptions of patriarchy is that women belong to men as their property. In order to keep their property secure, Vietnamese men, following the pattern of all patriarchs, rigidly enforced rules guarding their women's chastity. According to the Gia Long Codes, the unmarried woman caught having sexual relations was punished with one hundred lashes. [9] The unmarried mother, even among poor peasants, brought so much shame to her family and village that when exposed, she was forced to undergo a painful abortion and her family had to pay a fine to the village. Apparently, the problem was common enough to be the subject of folksongs:

> *The middle part of my body is swelling up:*
> *Mother, I can no longer stay at home.*
> *If I stay, the village will take away our buffalo as a fine,*
> *Therefore, I have to go away in a hurry.* [10]

The only legitimate function sexual relations could serve for women was to provide their husbands with male heirs. Upper-class Confucian proverbs as well as peasant folksongs urged women to place their chastity above any concern for their own pleasure. The proverb went:

> *Chastity is worth one thousand gold coins.*

The folksong repeated:

> *Once deprived of its sweet stamen,*
> *A flower is no longer desirable.* [11]

The unfaithful wife faced brutal punishment, even though men could have as many wives and concubines as they could afford. In some areas, elephants trampled the unfaithful wife. In others, she had her head shaved and plastered with lime. The laws never mentioned adultery as a crime that men could be punished for committing. The Vietnamese husband could repudiate his wife easily on such grounds as "excessive talking." Repudiation, like divorce, left a woman homeless and propertyless, even though her labor might have supported the household. Women had no parallel rights to repudiate their husbands.

Widows were supposed to remain faithful to their dead husbands. If a woman was caught making love during the period of mourning for her husband, the law said she should be beheaded. [12]

> If you have a son, you can say you have a descendant. But you cannot say thus, even if you have ten daughters. —Vietnamese proverb

Even though daughters worked hard for the family, the father did not acknowledge their worth. Only males could perform the rites necessary for ancestor worship and perpetuate the family line and cult.

Functionary and his following.

Wife and children resent young concubine.

Parents considered female children to be a liability. They believed that the nature of the female soul—more passionate and corruptible than the male soul—made it harder to raise girls. Judeo-Christian myths of Eve as temptress make similar assumptions about women's souls.

Female children had no opportunity to rise above their inferior status. The Vietnamese followed the Chinese system of education which barred women from learning. Even up until revolutionary times, the Vietnamese considered education wasted on women. In feudal society, hardly anyone could advance—men or women—because only the rich could afford the price of an education. In wealthy families, daughters who succeeded in disguising themselves as men managed to get the official Mandarin education.

For centuries, poor women worked in the most menial jobs which, of course, offered no chance for advancement or saving. Women would do jobs that even some poverty-stricken men would hesitate to do: planting seedlings, carrying heavy loads, working on the docks and in small-scale trading.

Segregation within the home mirrored segregation on the job and dramatized women's inferior status. A wife was supposed to walk three steps behind her husband. Richer families divided their homes into different sections reserved for either women or men. A man and woman would not sit together, use the same eating utensils or pass anything directly from hand to hand. Poorer families could not afford separate rooms and while working in the fields, even unmarried women and men could have social contact without shame.

The proverbs spoke of this segregation:

> *What is said in the apartments of women must not leave them and what is said outside must not penetrate there.* [13]

Layers of patriarchy

The patriarch is the father who is undisputed ruler. Vietnamese society itself was built as a series of hierarchies modeled on the patriarchal family. At the top, the Emperor had absolute authority over all. Even the language equated the father's domain with the king's domain. The root word for "family" and for "nation" is the same: *gia*. In the traditional language, the only equivalent for the personal pronoun "I" was *toi*, which meant "subject of the king." A Confucian proverb shows how no one escaped the king's authority:

> *When the wind [meaning king] passes over the grass [meaning the people], the grass has no choice but to bend.* [14]

As in any patriarchy, women carried the worst burden of the Emperor's rule. For example, after the Emperor Le Huyen Tong died, three hundred concubines were imprisoned in his mausoleum to keep watch over his tomb for the rest of their lives. Peasants contemptuously called him "the reclining king."

Mandarins, divided into nine ranks, formed the social layer just below the king. They were the king's representatives and controlled the local notables. Mandarins were an educated elite group of officials who lived on the rents and taxes they exacted from the people in their province, or from salaries they got directly from the king. This proverb reflected women's exclusion from the mandarinate:

> *A woman who meddles in the affairs of court or palace appears as abnormal as a chicken that crows.* [15]

Each mandarin was considered the "father" of the people in his district. A district may have included many villages. Within the village itself, it was the local notable who insisted on direct obedience from the common peasant. Notables collected taxes and kept some money for themselves before they handed over their quota to the mandarins. Notables also drafted soldiers and even kidnapped concubines to serve the mandarins and king.

Weak links in the Confucian chain

Confucianism became weaker, the further south one traveled away from the Chinese border. Confucianism was only brought indirectly to the territory south of Da Nang through the Le Dynasty in the fifteenth century. Vietnamese feudal lords didn't bring Confucianism to Saigon until nearly 1700.

Confucianism was also weaker at the village level, especially among the peasants, than at the national level. The need to coordinate irrigation and flood control through the dike system gave the central government an important function. But the Vietnamese village had a tradition of economic self-sufficiency. It was in the villages that the Vietnamese language survived a thousand years of Chinese occupation. The Vietnamese language reflects a less authoritarian culture than the Chinese. The Vietnamese word for king (*vua*) has the connotation of "protector," one who is closer to the people than the Chinese "son of heaven" who remains aloof from the people.

It was in the villages that a tradition of cooperation and solidarity developed. It was in the villages that patriotism became rooted in the soil—the same soil where the family's ancestors rested. The original notation, *xa,* for the word "village" combined the symbols for the words "land" and "people" and "sacred." Today, in Viet Nam *xa hoi* means "socialism."

Although seventy to eighty per cent of the Vietnamese people today may follow some Buddhist teachings, Buddhism itself did not seriously challenge the patriarchal models that Confucianism established. Buddhism taught precepts for spiritual life, while Confucianism guided political and social life. Mahayana Buddhism came to Viet Nam in the second century A.D., but was considered a "foreign religion" as long as the Chinese were in power.

After the Chinese were expelled, Buddhism became the state religion during the reign of several emperors. Mahayana Buddhists believe that there can be many "enlightened ones," not just one Buddha. But this egalitarian belief did not disrupt the elitist structure around the king because Buddhist clergy enjoyed the privileges previously reserved for Confucian mandarins. [16] During the fourteenth century, after three hundred years of Buddhist reign, Confucianism became the official ideology of the Vietnamese feudal regime. It was at that time that Buddhism took root among the common people and became a support for resistance at the village level.

But even at the village level, Buddhism still helped to maintain women's inferior status. Belief in reincarnation encouraged respect for all life, but also affirmed a fatalistic acceptance of women's inferior role in this life. Only men could be monks and Buddhist nuns had a subordinate position. Buddhists taught that all passion brings pain, but women seemed to pay more dearly for their passions. In the national epic poem of Viet Nam, a Buddhist prophetess tries to comfort Kieu, the leading character, who undergoes incredible suffering. She says: "Grief follows passion, that is the constant law." Buddhism, like Western moral codes, considers sex a lower form of animal activity. The ideal is total detachment from worldly concerns, especially sex. This ideal also applies to men. But women were considered less clean than men. Even today, when a woman is menstruating, she is banned from the Buddhist altar.

The weakest link in the Confucian chain was the strength and determination of peasant rebellion. A tradition of people's resistance and the endurance of centuries of oppression gave women the strength to fight back. Vietnamese women were by no means helpless creatures. Their tradition of resistance, which one woman called "riding the tempest," began at the same time that Christ lived.

Notes

1. These songs are quoted in Nha Trang, "The Traditional Roles of Women as Reflected in Oral and Written Vietnamese Literature (Berkeley: Asian Studies Ph.D. thesis, 1973), pp. 172ff.
2. The information on this legend is taken from Nha Trang's thesis, pp. 244-245, and Nguyen Khac Vien, *Traditional Viet Nam* (Vietnamese Studies #21; Hanoi: Foreign Languages Publishing House, 1969), pp. 18-19.
3. A lot of people who write about Viet Nam say that the Chams formed a matriarchal society. The Chams lived on the southeast coast of Viet Nam, further south than the Chinese went. The Cham kingdom, called "Champa," was independent for fourteen hundred years, until conquered and destroyed by Vietnamese kings in the sixteenth century. Actually, women never had great power in Champa. Although most inheritance was passed on through the mother, the rulers were always male kings and the throne was passed through the father's line. Chams practiced Hinduism, and among the upper classes widows were burned on their husbands' funeral pyres. See Georges Maspero, *Kingdom of Champa*, translated by F. Embree (Yale: South East Asian Studies, 1949).
4. Nguyen Khac Vien, *Traditional Viet Nam*, pp. 28-30.
5. Quoted in Nha Trang, *Traditional Roles*, p. 36.
6. Richard Coughlin, "The Position of Women in South East Asia," (Mimeo: Yale: South East Asian Cultural Report Series, 1949), p. 15.
7. Coughlin, p. 3.
8. Nha Trang, p. 170.
9. The Le Codes were more lenient. They gave fifty lashes. Nha Trang, p. 224.
10. Nha Trang, p. 164.
11. Both are quoted by Nha Trang, pp. 20, 29.
12. Nha Trang, p. 221.
13. Coughlin, p. 7.
14. Quoted by Frances Fitzgerald, *Fire in the Lake* (Boston: Little, Brown, 1972), p. 167.
15. Coughlin, p. 7.
16. Nguyen Khac Vien, pp. 50-53.

2.
RIDING THE TEMPEST

My wish is to ride the tempest, tame the waves, kill the sharks. I want to drive the enemy away to save our people. I will not resign myself to the usual lot of women who bow their heads and become concubines.
—Trieu Thi Trinh, woman who led insurrection against the Chinese in 248 A.D.

The tradition of women's resistance in Viet Nam begins with the earliest attempts to drive out the Chinese invaders. Two sisters led the first national insurrection, forty years after Christ was born. At that time, the one million people who lived in Viet Nam suffered under the harsh rule of a Chinese governor named To Dinh.

The Trung Sisters

One sister, Trung Trac, became a widow when Governor To Dinh executed her rebellious husband. Trung Trac came from a wealthy family, but her mother had taught her two daughters to be strong and independent. Trung Trac and her sister, Trung Nhi, became enraged with the governor's atrocities. They called on the people to follow them in an insurrection against the Chinese. Trac refused to wear the traditional mourning band for her dead husband so that she would not present a demoralizing image to the people she was calling on to follow her.

But before the Vietnamese people would follow women as military leaders, the Trung sisters had to gain their confidence. Trung Trac succeeded in killing a tiger which had been well-known in the region for being an invincible killer. She used the tiger's skin as a parchment for a proclamation urging the people to rise up against the Chinese invaders. Her courage in the face of the killer tiger inspired people to follow her against the Chinese.

The two sisters complemented each other's abilities. Trung Trac was the strategist. Trung Nhi was the fearless warrior. They issued a call to all people to share responsibility for leading the insurrection. From those who came forward, they chose 36 women, including their mother. They trained these women to be generals.

These women led a people's army of 80,000 which succeeded in driving the Chinese out of Viet Nam in 40 A.D. Vietnamese today still enjoy retelling how the Governor To Dinh cut off his hair, shaved his beard and secretly fled the country. The army of the Trung sisters liberated 65 fortresses. After their victory, the people proclaimed Trung Trac, the eldest sister, to be their ruler and renamed her "Trung Vuong" ("She-king Trung"). For the next three years, there were constant battles with the Chinese army. The Chinese had more soldiers, arms and military experience and finally defeated the Vietnamese in 43 A.D. Rather than accept defeat, the Trung sisters chose the traditional Vietnamese alternative to maintain their dignity—they committed suicide. [1]

The Trung sisters are not only Viet Nam's best-loved heroes. The uprising they led also marks the first insurrection in the long process of developing the Vietnamese national identity. The Vietnamese people guarded their national dignity during a thousand years of Chinese occupation by passing on the story of the Trung sisters by word of mouth from one generation to the next. It's difficult to know how much of the legend exaggerates reality but we do know that by the twelfth century, the Trungs had become goddesses with temples built in their honor. Confucian scholars tried to superimpose a patriarchal interpretation onto their legend by giving a greater role to the husbands of the Trung sisters. But peasants and rebellious Vietnamese dynasties restored the Vietnamese version of the legend. Matriarchal principles officially became associated with patriotism when the Tay-Son emperors (eighteenth century) gave two of the lesser female generals of the Trung Army honorary noble titles in a deliberate anti-Chinese gesture. [2]

Today, after so many centuries, stories, poems, and plays about the Trung sisters still glorify their patriotism and courage as women. Phan Thi An, a leader of the Women's Union of the DRV, recently told visitors: "We view it [the Trung rebellion] as an all people's movement under the leadership of women." [3] Every year with the return of spring, on the sixtieth day of the second moon, the people of Hanoi celebrate the anniversary of the death of the Trung sisters. [4]

Women led more than once

In 248 A.D. a peasant woman named Trieu Thi Trinh followed the example of the Trung sisters and, again, took the initiative in leading thousands of Vietnamese in a campaign to get rid of the Chinese. In the course of an argument with her brother, she made the pledge which is still popular in Viet Nam today:

I will not resign myself to the usual lot of women who bow their heads and become concubines.

Women and men fought under her leadership. Before her twenty-first birthday, she had led thirty battles and Viet Nam was again independent. But independence was short-lived. After six months Trieu Thi Trinh's army was defeated. Like the Trung sisters, Trinh committed suicide rather than return to serfdom. After her defeat, the Chinese tried to discredit Trinh. They portrayed her as a monster, denying her integrity as a woman. Among the Chinese, the ideal woman was docile, modest and flat-chested. Chinese portraits of Trinh show her with monstrous breasts three meters long flying over her shoulder as she rides on an elephant and grimly charges an unseen enemy. [5]

Nevertheless, the Vietnamese people continued to retell the story of her rebellion with pride. In a list of the five major anti-Chinese insurrections which occurred before the final expulsion of the Chinese from Viet Nam, those led by women make up nearly half. [6] Vietnamese male patriots, in spite of their privileges as men, have maintained an ideal of women as fighters in order to oppose Chinese domination which was so intertwined with patriarchal domination. This tradition encouraged many anonymous women to follow the famous Vietnamese saying:

When the enemy comes, even the women should fight. [7]

While the Vietnamese woman's place in the home kept her subordinate to men, it also helped to maintain her identity as Vietnamese by isolating her from foreign influence. When the invaders forced men to join their army, the women maintained the Vietnamese tradition in the home. They passed the culture on from one generation to the next in songs they sang at work in the rice fields, as they cared for their children, and in folk dances. By maintaining pride in Vietnamese traditions, the Vietnamese women strengthened national resistance to foreign domination.

In addition to fighting for Vietnamese independence, women also led peasant uprisings against Vietnamese feudal lords. Towards the end of the eighteenth century, Bui Thi Xuan, a woman, became famous as one of the generals of a wave of peasant rebellions that had established a reformist dynasty (Tay Son). She continued to fight after the Tay Sons fell. When the new Emperor Gia Long finally captured her, he ordered that she be trampled to death by elephants—the traditional punishment against women who committed adultery. He fed her heart, arms, liver and lungs to his troops, believing that the remains of this "exceptional" woman would imbue his troops with courage. Today, in Hanoi, there is a street named after Bui Thi Xuan.

Women's culture of resistance

Most of Viet Nam's early records were kept by Confucian scholars. The histories they wrote gave the impression that all women were content to live their lives guided by the rules of chastity and the "Three Obediences." Written histories almost never mention women at

32

all—much less the fact that they may have been dissatisfied with child marriage, polygamy and other patriarchal customs.

But the record of Viet Nam passed on in Vietnamese folksongs tells a different story—herstory. Hundreds of songs composed by women as they worked in the fields echo strong protests. This song was typical of those which ridiculed assumptions of male superiority and demands for obedience:

> We honorable sisters are like a mass of boulders in
>   Heaven.
> How could you youngsters as small as mice think of
>   disturbing us?
> Cursed be you bunch of mice,
> When this rock falls down, your bones will be crushed. [8]

They also protested arranged marriages:

> A young girl is like a piece of silk in a market which
>   doesn't know in what hands it is going to fall. [9]

And they challenged the practice of forcing adult women to marry young boys in order to provide cheap labor for the boy's family:

> Bump! Bump! I took a walk with my husband on my
>   back.
> Crossing a shallow spot, I dropped him by mistake.
> Hey fellow sisters! Lend me a scoop,
> I'll scoop the water and get my husband out! [10]

Other songs rejected polygamy:

> If hungry, you would be better off eating a bunch of
>   sycamore leaves;
> Marry a monogamous man, stay away from sharing a
>   husband with other women. [11]

There were other songs against the sexual repression that maintained women as men's property. They express the probability that the Confucian rules were often broken:

> Chastity is truly worth a thousand gold coins:
> Counting from my ex-husband to you, I have had five men.
> As for lovers that I have had in secret,
> A hundred of them have gathered on my belly as they
>   would in a market. [12]

And:

> Even if I am faithful to my husband, when dead I am not
>   spared from becoming a ghost.
> Being a loose woman, when dead I will be buried in the
>   field just the same.

Some women must have enjoyed open defiance of the rules:

Respecting the rule of fidelity, I have married nine husbands.
Rolling them into balls, I put them in a jar which I then carried on a shoulder pole when I went out.
Accidentally, the supporting basket suspended from the pole broke, and the jar fell to the ground.
The nine husbands crawled out scattering in different directions.

And some songs expressed the protests of widows:

Giving me three cows as offerings later, when I am dead, my son,
is not as kind as allowing me to remarry now that I am alive.

In the nineteenth century a woman poet, Ho Xuan Huong, became famous for her attack on the corruption and hypocrisy of the feudal patriarchy. Her poetry escaped Chinese influence more than any other. [13] She composed her poems in *chu nom*—a language considered vulgar by Confucian scholars. She also played with words, reversing letters in a way that gave a socially subversive dual meaning to many of her lines. Lower-class women must have loved her poetry, because Huong's poems survived for more than a hundred years before they were published in 1914. [14]

Ho Xuan Huong was the daughter of a concubine belonging to a middle-level official. She herself had to become a concubine, presumably because most men were afraid to marry such a talented woman as a first wife. [15] She became a widow soon after her marriage and wrote a poem that denounced polygamy on the basis of the experience she shared with thousands of Vietnamese women:

One wife is covered by a quilted blanket, while one wife is left in the cold.
Cursed be this fate of sharing a common husband.
Seldom do you have occasion to possess your husband, not even twice in one month.
You toil and endure hardships in order to earn your steamed rice, and then the rice is cold and tasteless.
It is like renting your services for hire, and then receiving no wages.
How is is that I have turned out this way,
I would rather suffer the fate of remaining unmarried and live alone by myself. [16]

She exposed the hypocrisy of monks who urged others to renounce worldly pleasures:

> *Before the reverends are big trays of delicacies,*
> *Behind them lurk graceful nuns.*

With these lines, she dared to defend unwed mothers:

> *To marry and have a child, how banal!*
> *But to be pregnant without the help of a husband, what*
> *   merit!*

While the feudal nobility presented themselves as honorable and courageous gentlemen, she focused on their privilege and expressed her contempt:

> *If only I could change my destiny and be a man,*
> *I wouldn't content myself with such feats of valor.* [17]

Women like the poet Ho Xuan Huong and the Trung sisters were clearly exceptional women. But the common women throughout Vietnamese history passed their legends on with pride. Peasant women were by no means simply sorrowful victims of feudal patriarchy. Their songs expressed their anger and also gave strength to their resistance. While polygamy forced women to compete among themselves in gaining the attention of their husband, songs of women's solidarity show that many women learned to cooperate in the face of oppression:

> *Let's leave loyalty to the King for our father,*
> *And filial piety for our mother,*
> *And keep love for ourselves.* [18]

Temple of the Trung Sisters in Hanoi today.

Over the centuries, the heroism of the Trung sisters was repeated daily by the women who endured and grew stronger as they worked in the home to raise families and in the fields to raise rice. Privileged Confucian gentlemen hold manual work in contempt. But those who cannot live off the work of other people, especially peasant women, understand and respect the labor which makes life possible.

Kieu

The hero of the national epic poem of Viet Nam, Kieu, has become a romanticized model of women's endurance in the face of incredible suffering. Nguyen Du, an aristocrat, wrote this poem towards the end of the eighteenth century. Kieu sacrifices her happiness with her fiance and prostitutes herself to keep her father out of jail—the model of filial piety. Most of the poem narrates her misfortunes as a prostitute, concubine, servant and nun. Kieu becomes the incarnation of all who are oppressed in Viet Nam as the author exposes the feudal decay of the eighteenth century.

Nguyen Du portrays Kieu as the victim of an evil society, who, at the same time, defies tradition with her shameless romantic love. After years of separation, suffering and brief episodes of ecstasy, she is finally reunited with her first love. Many Vietnamese today compare the inevitability of the lovers' reunion with the inevitability of the re-unification of Viet Nam. After years of prostitution, Kieu insists on maintaining a "spiritual" relation when she is finally reunited with her original lover:

> *Of love and friendship they fulfilled the claims.*
> *They would forgo one pillow and one mat,*
> *yet they would share the joys of song and verse.*
> *They would drink wine and play a game of chess,*
> *admiring flowers or waiting for the moon.*
> *Their wishes all came true as fate so willed,*
> *and of two lovers marriage made two friends.* [19]

In Viet Nam today, north and south, people everywhere can recite verses from *Kieu* by heart. When playwright Peter Weiss visited the Democratic Republic of Vietnam (DRV), he went to a hospital carved into the side of a mountain to protect it against the bombs. A helmeted woman was on duty at the entrance with her rifle in one hand and a dog-eared copy of *Kieu* in the other. [20] A Vietnamese woman who studies in the United States reports that today women still identify with Kieu and recite lines from the epic when they're sad and mourn their fate. In Hanoi, I joined hundreds of people who filled the Workers' Theater to enjoy a dramatization of the classic. The costumes and set were traditional and very elaborate. The audience, entirely engrossed in the drama, called out warnings to the characters in danger and wept without reserve whenever Kieu suffered another hardship. *Kieu* is not only the national epic poem of Viet Nam, it also ranks as an outstanding classic of world literature.

Kieu's endurance was definitely heroic. But it was a traditional form of heroism that is expected of women: self-sacrifice for family and love. Cam Thanh, a well-known woman author in the DRV, explained the limits of her heroism:

Kieu shows woman in all imaginable humiliation, in all the sufferings that generations of women have endured. Literature was prepared to deplore her fate. But revolution was needed to lift her out of servitude. [21]

Notes

1. You can find mention of the Trung sisters in any history of Viet Nam. Details for this section come from Don Luce and John Sommer, *The Unheard Voices* (New York: Cornell Univ. Press, 1969), pp. 25-26, and an interview between Jane Fonda and Phan Thi An recorded July 12, 1972, in Hanoi.
2. Alexander B. Woodside, *Vietnam and the Chinese Model* (Cambridge: Harvard Univ. Press, 1971), p. 46.
3. Interview between Phan Thi An and members of Asian Information Group, unpublished notes, 1972.
4. Francois Sully, *We the Vietnamese* (New York: Praeger, 1971), pp. 72-73.
5. Mention of Trinh is as common as mention of the Trung sisters. Information here comes from Mai Thi Tu, "The Vietnamese Woman Yesterday and Today," in *Vietnamese Women* (Vietnamese Studies #10; Hanoi; Foreign Languages Publishing House, 1966), pp. 17-18.
6. Nguyen Khac Vien, *Traditional Viet Nam,* p. 27.
7. Mai Thi Tu, p. 17.
8. Nha Trang, p. 217.
9. *Vietnam Advances* (Hanoi) #3 (March-July 1960), p. 15.
10. Xuan-Dieu, "Folksongs of Vietnam," in *Vietnam Advances* vol. 3, #3 (March 1958), p. 20.
11. Nha Trang, p. 232.
12. Nha Trang, p. 228. The next three songs are from the same chapter.
13. Woodside, p. 48.
14. Nha Trang, p. 206.
15. Woodside, p. 47.
16. Woodside, p. 49.
17. This poem is quoted in "Supplement on Women of Vietnam," *Viet Nam News and Reports* #14 (March 5-19, 1973), p. 4. Others by Ho Xuan Huong are found there or in Nha Trang's thesis.
18. Mai Thi Tu, p. 19.
19. Nguyen Du, *The Tale of Kieu,* translated by Huyn Sanh Thong (New York: Vintage, 1973), p. 141.
20. Peter Weiss, *Notes on the Cultural Life of the DRV* (New York: Delta, 1970), p. 120.
21. Weiss, pp. 63-64.

3.
FRENCH MAKE WOMEN THE SLAVES OF SLAVES

France can dream again . . . of not only activity necessary to its commerce, for the development of its industry and creation of outlets for the future, but it can also begin again the noble civilizing mission that has always given it such a high place in the world.
—*Rieunier, French administrator in Viet Nam, 1864*

It took the French armed forces nearly forty years to complete their conquest of all of Viet Nam. They first appeared off the Vietnamese coast in 1847, trying to force the Vietnamese government to accept unfair trade arrangements. They also came to protect Christian missionaries. In 1858, they landed with three thousand troops and officially began the conquest. Peasants fought back and their resistance delayed the French takeover. But the Vietnamese king, who was corrupt and more concerned with peasant insurrections than with French domination, kept signing new treaties, granting more and more territorial control to the French. By 1884, the French stabilized their domination over all of Viet Nam and divided it artificially into three "countries" to make their rule easier.

French colonialists tried to justify their conquest by claiming it was a mission to bring the "benefits of civilization" to Viet Nam. For the Vietnamese people those benefits meant that the price of salt rose five hundred per cent between 1889 and 1907. The average amount of rice each person consumed also dropped nearly twenty per cent between 1900 and 1913. [1] French civilization meant additional suffering especially for women because the French used the feudal patriarchy as a foundation for their colonial regime. Frenchmen did not try to justify the increasing misery of women in Viet Nam. After all, women in France did not win the right to vote until 1945.

French colonists boasted about the money they invested in Viet Nam. But they didn't mention the fact that they invested only in areas that would make an immediate profit which they took back to France. They drained the natural wealth of the land by extracting the metal ores, coal, rubber and rice that belonged to Viet Nam and shipping them to France. They crippled Viet Nam's ability to develop economically by not allowing Viet Nam to trade with any country but France and by forcing Viet Nam to become a market for French goods. The only industries the French set up were a few small-scale businesses manufacturing consumer goods to satisfy the immediate needs of the French settlers and to produce things necessary for their enterprises. While there was no tax on the business operations or incomes of foreigners, taxes that the Vietnamese had to pay increased five times. Seventy per cent of the revenues from these taxes went to pay the police and colonial functionaries, and none went to the benefit of the taxpayers themselves. [2]

France was the birthplace of the slogan "Liberty, Equality, Fraternity." But French policies in Viet Nam assumed that the Vietnamese people were not worthy of the same rights as Frenchmen. In European eyes, this "Oriental race" was expendable. The French kidnapped eighty thousand people to build a railroad to ship their goods to port. Twenty-five thousand of them died. [3] Conditions in the coal mines run by the French were so bad that the French could not get the Vietnamese to work voluntarily in the mines. They had to destroy dikes and flood entire villages in mine areas to make it impossible for the people to earn a living from farming, leaving peasants with no choice but to work in the mines. Still, they had trouble recruiting workers. Fifty thousand men and women died at work in the mines. Desrousseaux, Inspector of Mines, wrote a secret report addressed to the Governor General in 1940:

The peasants will consent to go and work outside their villages only when they are dying of starvation. We must therefore arrive at the conclusion that in order to extricate ourselves from the difficulty of recruiting labor, we must see to it that the countryside is plunged into poverty. [4]

The French policy to "plunge the countryside into poverty" was successfully implemented. The average peasant got poorer and poorer as larger and larger plots of land became concentrated in fewer and fewer hands. Before the French arrived, the maximum amount of land a court official could legally own was barely ten acres. By 1930, the French had two-thirds of the cultivated land in their control. Most of the peasants had no land at all and were caught in a vicious cycle of debt slavery. [5] The French demanded that taxes be paid in cash even though they understood the traditional Vietnamese practice of paying taxes in crops. The few peasants who still owned land had to mortgage it to pay taxes at interest rates that went as high as 3650 per cent. By making the peasants desperate to survive, the French strengthened the hand of the feudal notables and used them to collect taxes and force men into the French army and labor chain gangs.

Many Vietnamese novels and short stories portray the miserable life of peasant women during these times. Until hearing a first-hand account, it's easy to assume that the novels are exaggerated. In one of the most famous documentary novels, *When the Light Is Out,* a desperate mother must sell her daughter to the landlord for one piaster, the same price she must pay to a corrupt official to get an official seal on a document that she needs to pay her tax. [6] The author of this novel was, in fact, documenting real events, but placing them in fictional disguise in order to avoid French censorship.

Slaves in the fields

Nguyen Thi Dam was 76 years old in 1954 when she was interviewed by an Australian journalist. [7] She was living in the Viet Bac region of the Democratic Republic of Viet Nam. Before her people ousted the French, she spent forty years working for different landlords. Her husband died when she was 30, leaving her with a tiny plot of land, two children and a debt to the landlord of fifty pounds of rice and two piasters. The landlord demanded payment of 100 pounds of rice as interest for the first month and another 150 pounds for each month she did not repay the debt. Nguyen Thi Dam recalled:

I tried very hard to get work and collect some rice but every month I was worse off. By six months it was clear I could never pay. So he took our little plot of land. It was very difficult. . . .

She continued and tears welled up in her eyes with the memory:

. . . The only thing to do was to go and work for the landlord. I and the children would be fed but would get no pay. For three years I toiled there and we were all in rags. . . . At the end of three years I could stand it no longer. . . .

She went to look for work in another part of the district, but found nothing, so she returned to her native village and worked for the biggest landlord there.

. . . The work was so hard, I thought I must die. I had to get up at three o'clock in the morning and start pounding rice. It was work enough for two or three people. . . . After that, I had to go to the fields and it was so dark I would have lost my way except for holding the buffalo by the tail. It was dark again by the time I finished ploughing in the evening and had to follow the buffalo home again. For that, there was a bowl of rice and a little salt daily for myself and the children. . . . Sometimes I would steal a little fish paste—hide it between my thumb and forefinger—and lick it while eating rice. At night I had to clean up the house and if the landlord wasn't satisfied he would take his whip to me. . . . Myself and the children wore rice sacks. . . . I had to carry the manure out to the fields, plough, do weeding, harvesting and everything from three in the morning till ten at night. Once when I begged for something to buy clothes, at least for the children, the landlord brought me twenty-seven pounds of rice. He put it on the floor and said, "This is what you have earned. And I give it to you. But as I have to feed your children, I must take it back." And he took it away again. . . .

She described how the landlord ate the best quality rice, fish and chicken:

He would invite Japanese or French notables about once a month for banquets and the villagers had to come and help decorate the house. He had concubines too, but their life was no better than ours. They were starved and whipped. . . .

When her daughter was 16, the landlord severely humiliated her for not gathering enough weeds.

He wrenched off all her clothes and flung her head-first into the fish pond. . . .

After nine years, Nguyen Thi Dam left and went to work for another landlord who treated her slightly better. In their precious moments of free time, she and her children strained themselves to clear a patch of jungle. But to get from the tiny shack where she lived to her jungle patch she had to use a path a hundred yards long which led through the fields of the rich landlord she had worked for before. On the pretext that her buffalo ate his grass, the landlord seized the land that she had cleared along with the crop.

After losing her land again, she returned to her husband's village and tried renting land. But the rent was so high, there was nothing left to eat. Her daughter died:

She needed rice, but I could give her none. There were no clothes even to bury her in. . . . She had scarcely known a moment's happiness in her life. She was beaten by landlords before she even knew who they were. . . .

Her son died of starvation the following year, 1944. Finally, the French bombed her shack, killing her granddaughter.

This old woman celebrated the signing of the Geneva Accords in 1954, when the French agreed to leave Viet Nam. A few months later, she witnessed the execution of the landlord responsible for her misery and her child's death. With the revolutionary government in power, she also received a plot of land, a buffalo to share with another family, a three-room house and five good planks for a coffin. This allotment brought her final security and was a great relief to her since one of the biggest fears of old people in Viet Nam is to be buried naked without a coffin. Nguyen Thi Dam ended her story:

If I have difficulty working the land, they [the Peasant' Association] send someone to help me. For the first time in my life I eat well . . . all around me people are happy. We have schools here. . . . But things are just beginning. You come back and visit us in a year's time and you'll see some changes.

Madame Dam's story is not unusual. Most Vietnamese peasants were either landless or had so little land, they had to borrow just to begin the season's planting. A sharecropper had to rent a buffalo at the price of twenty per cent of his crop. So it became common for share-croppers to hitch their wives and children to ploughs instead of renting buffalo. In 1943, a Vietnamese agronomist observed:

They hitch to their shoulders ropes padded with pieces of torn matting lest the ropes cut into their flesh. Because of the weight to be pulled, they are unable to keep their balance and must use a bamboo cane to lean on. [8]

Women in plantations, mines and factories

The French were proud of their profitable rubber plantations. Most of the labor on these plantations came from indentured servants who were recruited from the poorest peasant regions. Conditions were so brutal that recruiting agents drugged peasants in order to get them to sign up. The plantations became known as "hell on earth" and workers who tried to escape were tortured to death. The figures in Table I underestimate the number who died supplying French industrialists with rubber because they only include those who officially signed con-tracts. [9]

TABLE I

Plantation	Years	Total number of workers employed then	Number who died
Dau Tieng (Michelin)	1917–1944	45,000	12,000
Loc Ninh & Minh Thanh (Cexo)	1917–1945	37,000	10,000
Terres Rouge	1917–1945	198,000	22,000

By 1945, the French couldn't recruit enough rubber workers through their normal means of deceit. The liberation movement of the Viet Minh had become too strong. So the French converted the planta-tions into prison camps and arbitrarily arrested people when they needed more workers. Any complainers were shot on the spot as Viet Minh. By this time, sixty per cent of the workers were women. The French designed a special torture for pregnant rubber workers called the "upside down pot." The victim was forced to dig a hole and lie face down with her stomach in the hole as the overseer beat her. Eight out of ten women miscarried.

A folksong expressed the grim reality:

> It's easy to go to the rubber plantations,
> But hard to return from there.
> Men left their hides, women their bones. [10]

French colonists also boasted about bringing industry to Viet Nam. In fact, the French destroyed a lot of native handicrafts and infant industry. While thousands of Vietnamese wore rice sacks, French-owned factories produced textiles for export. A Frenchman named Dupre owned a huge textile factory in Nam Dinh. He began with only six hundred workers in 1900, but by 1937 fourteen thousand worked for him—mostly women. [11] Mrs. Hoang Thi Yen began working for the "wolf boss" when she was 12 years old. Her mother landed the job for her by bribing an intermediary. Yen recalls:

It was in 1920. Officially the factory's workday was fifteen hours. For most of the women workers, who lived at some ten kilometers' distance from it and who went to work on foot, it was, in fact, a day of eighteen to nineteen hours. I left home before dawn only to come back late at night, broken by fatigue. I could never sleep as much as I needed to or even wash myself, there being no Sundays. My mother washed my clothes and supplied me with meager cold meals—a ball of rice with some sesame, parched and crushed together with salt—which I ate in secret at the mill, for no breaks were allowed during work time.

Dupre paid women only three-quarters as much as he paid men. All his workers received fines for tardiness, absenteeism, talking, dozing, taking meals during work hours, breaking yarn and breaking shuttles. The workers even had to pay for spare parts and repairs on the machines. Overseers had only contempt for the women at the mill and competed with each other in manhandling the workers. Beatings were commonplace. Hoang Thi Yen continued her description of her life as a textile worker:

I got married at 18 and became a mother at 24. I gave birth to four children, but two of them died for want of care. Each time I was delivered by a village midwife at my own charge. The factory had an infirmary with a single lying-in bed for some five thousand women workers. To get into it, one had to give presents to the nurses. There was no maternity leave and every woman had to find someone to replace her during her absence when she was in childbed. Many a prospective mother, compelled to go on working, gave birth to her child at the foot of the machines. After childbirth, young mothers would hurry back to the factory for fear they might lose their jobs. It was the same thing with the sick. The Wolf Boss specified in one of his circulars that the sick who could not come to work should send in their resignation.

There were no safety precautions at the factory. Compensation for the numerous maimings was unheard of. Mrs. Yen explained why they accepted such outrageous conditions:

That was horrible. But one had to live. What we feared was neither ill-treatment nor accident. It was the loss of our jobs.

The French policy of destroying the subsistence peasant economy worked to make people totally dependent and desperate. When Dupre's workers threatened to strike, he taunted them:

Listen to this: to recruit 100 dogs is difficult, but I have only to raise a finger and 1000 coolies of your race will come and replace you.

In factories, women's wages were consistently less than men's. In 1930, the average daily wage for a male worker was 1.50 piasters and for a female worker it was only .31 piasters. By 1936, during the Depression, the average wage for a man dropped to 1.13 piasters and to .17 for the average woman! [12]

1886: Political prisoners held by French

Increased poverty intensified the humiliation of women. In a famine year, a man could buy a slave girl or concubine for a few pounds of rice. The French commercialized sex and transformed thousands of traditionally modest women into prostitutes. But it's important to remember that these same prostitutes were very skilled at sabotage. According to Bernard Fall, prostitutes took credit for one-third of all the French posts destroyed by the Viet Minh. [13]

Ho Chi Minh, the most important leader of the Vietnamese independence movement against the French and U.S. invaders, focused one of his earliest articles on exposing the sadistic treatment of Vietnamese women by the French. His 1922 article protested the rape of several women and an eight-year-old girl. He urged in the same article that their "Western sisters in France" join a campaign to ease the suffering of women in Viet Nam. But it was to be a long time before women in the West could identify with the problems of women under colonialism.

The Vietnamese patriots who protested French policies often found themselves in prison. Cynical French administrators, in fact, made jokes about having "three prisons for every school." In 1924, out of 600,000 school-age children, only 62,000 boys and 10,000 girls (three per cent of female children) were enrolled. By 1945, ninety per cent of the women of Viet Nam were still illiterate and only a handful were in universities. [14] French administrators cared even less for women's health than they did for their education. Thirty per cent of the women who died lost their lives in childbirth. The infant mortality rate was thirty to forty per cent. [15]

Famine: two million dead

For decades, French policies had reduced the people of Viet Nam to a perpetual state of desperation. But they were responsible for unprecedented tragedy in Viet Nam during World War II. The French administration, which was friendly to the Fascists, collaborated with the Japanese invaders. The French and Japanese confiscated and burned rice for fuel, forced peasants to plant export crops like jute instead of rice, raised taxes and raided villages, stealing all of their valuables. These policies were decrees of mass murder in the countryside where people were already living at a bare subsistence level. Two million Vietnamese people starved to death between 1943 and 1945!

People continued to work even when they were eating only roots and covering themselves with only banana leaves or mats made from hay. Others lay out in the market area waiting to die in the hopes that some kind-hearted person would notice them and bury them. One survivor wrote:

My village sank deeper and deeper into the morass of hunger and cold. Every day some two dozen people died. Some died digging up their potatoes in the fields; some died on the roads while out begging; some went down to the river to fish and fell into the water. . . . [16]

Parents forced themselves to deny their children food, knowing that if they divided the available food between themselves, they had a chance to survive. If they divided the food equally among the entire family, no one would have enough to live. And if only the children were fed, they would soon follow their parents to death anyway since they couldn't survive on their own. A French official named Vespy wrote:

There are old people and there are children. There are men and women, shrunken under the weight of their poverty and suffering. Their bodies are nearly all naked and their bones jut out shaking. Even girls who have already reached puberty and whom one might expect to show some embarrassment are in the same condition. Now and again they stop to close the eyes of those who fall never to rise again, or to strip off any piece of rag which is left behind on their bodies . . . one feels ashamed of being human. [17]

That same year, in August 1945, a general insurrection swept the country. On September 2, 1945, Ho Chi Minh issued Viet Nam's declaration of independence from France.

Early feminism

The August Revolution in 1945 was the climax of political ferment which had begun generations earlier. Between 1905 and 1906, while in prison, an unusually well-educated woman used her own blood to write a poem in Chinese calligraphy recording the crimes of the French against the prisoners. She ended with these words:

All women should be united in the struggle against the French colonialists in order to survive.

Today, the calligraphy of this unnamed martyr is displayed in the Museum of Revolutionary History in Hanoi. There is little other written record of the role women played in the many peasant rebellions against the French. But we do know, for example, that in 1907, a woman innkeeper named Nguyen Thi Ba poisoned to death two hundred French soldiers who were occupying her district. [18] The innkeeper's feat was no doubt part of a pattern of defiance and sabotage waged by women throughout the countryside.

In the cities, on the other hand, political activity focused on gaining access to education. Most of the women involved were daughters of

48

middle-class families and the educated elite. French money subsidized the first women's periodical, a weekly called *Women's Bell,* in 1918. Its editor, a widow, proposed that women should be allowed enough general education to be able to improve the performance of their duties as wives and mothers. The question of equal rights for women was not considered. The editor's strategy assumed that by educating women, their dignity would be ensured. There was no notion of developing political power for women—a strategy which would have forced them to confront French colonialism. Each issue of the magazine cost 40 piasters. The annual rice harvest of the average peasant in 1931 was valued at 128 piasters. [19]

By 1919, the French opened up the educational system to women who could afford it. Within ten years, traditional educators published nearly thirty new textbooks for women designed to protect women from being corrupted by the "romance" rampant in the standard texts. During that decade, about eight per cent of all Vietnamese women were in school. Reforms in the city created a literate group of women that nearly equaled the number of prostitutes created by the impoverishment of the countryside.

By 1926, some of these educated women organized, and cautiously proposed more radical changes. In Hue, Dam Phuong founded a local group called the Hue Women's Labor-Study Association. She invited Phan Boi Chau, a well-known revolutionary nationalist, to give the principal speech at the Association's opening ceremony. His speech was moderate on women's issues and discreetly anti-French. In 1927, this ex–Confucian scholar wrote a textbook for women which proposed the elimination of some patriarchal rules. He urged women to join the struggle for independence by "marrying Viet Nam." He wrote, "This husband is more than 3000 years old and yet doesn't look old." [20] By 1929, after some years in French jails, Phan Boi Chau understood that feudalism, the traditional patriarchal family and French colonialism were all tied together. In an essay on "The Woman Question" he urged that women form collectives to share labor and educate each other. He also suggested that women follow the tradition of Trieu Thi Trinh (248 A.D.) and reject marriage or else be sure to marry a "comrade" not a "husband."

The stated goal of the Women's Labor-Study Association was:

To build for women a sense of self-development by means of new occupational skills and within the boundaries of both Eastern and Western virtue and intelligence.

The Association organized women's classes in cooking, sewing, weaving and other skills considered acceptable for women. But they also made a soft-spoken call for women to reject the "Three Obediences" and to travel. By 1929, eighty-seven women were on the paid membership list, but there were many more followers. Dam Phuong traveled to set up similar associations in other cities and established contacts in Saigon and Hanoi.

In 1929, there was an upheaval within the Hue Women's Labor-Study Association. A woman named Nhu Man became the editor of the Association's journal and challenged the strategy that viewed skills classes as the means toward liberation. Her editorials urged that political organization for equal rights should be the focus of the Association. Like Ho Xuan Huong's poems a hundred years earlier, Nhu Man's articles attacked arranged marriage, rules about chastity and occupational restrictions. She proposed socialism as a solution. Her articles may have been a bridge between urban middle-class women and the thinking of revolutionary leaders like Ho Chi Minh, who had written articles in Paris as early as 1922 which called for women's liberation, independence and socialism. One thousand copies of her journal were printed.

French repression against the Association began for the first time in 1929. The Association remained isolated and unknown to thousands of peasant women like Mrs. Dam and factory workers like Mrs. Yen. By 1931, the French took over the organization and its pro-French chairperson endorsed the traditional four Confucian virtues for women. The Association soon disappeared. Meanwhile, the misery of the majority of lower-class women and their own traditions of resistance gave birth to a new women's organization. It's possible that the most far-sighted members of the original Association followed the lead of Nhu Man and took part in the new women's union.

The birth of the Women's Union

In 1929, a woman named Minh Khai had to leave home because her parents demanded that she not go out at night. Her father was a railroad worker and her mother a small trader. They feared their daughter would bring scandal to the family. Minh Khai couldn't explain to them that she spent her evenings doing political work—organizing people to challenge French colonialism and feudal patriarchy. She was a member of one of the revolutionary groups that followed the leadership of Ho Chi Minh in uniting to form the Indochinese Communist Party in 1930. The Indochinese Communist Party (ICP) set two basic goals: (1) to fight against French imperialism to gain national independence, and (2) to fight against feudalism to gain land for the peasants.

The ICP incorporated the struggle for women's emancipation into its fight against feudalism and colonialism. Experience showed that

Minh Khai

women's emancipation was impossible under colonial rule, and that it was essential to the revolutionary process. Ho Chi Minh often said:

Women make up half of society. If women are not liberated, then society is not free. [21]

Minh Khai and other women affiliated with the ICP founded the Viet Nam Women's Union the same year the ICP was founded. It was the first national women's organization ever to exist in Viet Nam. Many of the leaders of the Women's Union were also members of the ICP. They enthusiastically supported ICP policy, which assumed that women needed their own separate organization in order to concentrate their energy on the struggle for women's rights. They worked to include all working women in their organization and others who were not part of the constituency of the trade union and peasant organizations. In 1930, heavy French repression forced the Women's Union to be a clandestine organization.

Their demands reflected the needs of peasants and women who worked in the factories:

Reduce rents and interest rates!
Equal wages for equal work!
No dangerous work for women!
Two months fully paid maternity leave!
Down with forced marriage!
Down with polygamy!
Abolish the habit of holding women in contempt! [22]

These demands took the form of slogans in hundreds of demonstrations and strikes which challenged the French colonial administration in 1930 and 1931. In March 1930, strikers at one of the central rubber plantations disarmed the local French soldiers and felled trees to erect roadblocks. Women who had been raped by French Foreign Legionnaires blinded the rapists with a mixture of ashes and lime. In spite of incredible material sacrifices, the workers at Nam Dinh textile mill struck for three weeks. Peasants supplied strikers with whatever aid they could and joined demonstrations demanding workers' rights and land for the peasants.

In two provinces, Nghe An and Ha Tinh, French repression incited the peasants to arm themselves and force the local functionaries to flee. They set up peasant associations to take over local administrative functions, creating an embryonic form of revolutionary government in a territory of a hundred thousand inhabitants. The original Nghe-Tinh Defense unit included forty women out of a total of 120. For the first time in Vietnamese history, lands were redistributed to women, and women took part in public meetings and political education classes, gaining control over their lives. The peasant administration, called the Nghe Tinh Soviets, fell after several months of intensive bombings and shellings by French troops. Although they had power for only a short time, the Nghe Tinh Soviets made a deep impression on Vietnamese women, moving large numbers of women to join the Women's Union and the anti-French resistance. [23]

French administrators responded to the revolutionary challenge with brutal repression: summary executions, arrests, tortures, life terms at forced labor, and death sentences. Nguyen Thi Ngia, an activist in the Soviets, was only 23 when the French arrested her. They tortured her for information about where other revolutionaries were hiding. She cut off her own tongue, rather than betray her friends. Before the French executed her, she wrote:

I'm going to die and I wish all the sisters who remain will continue the struggle until the revolution succeeds and women gain equal rights with men.

Many leaders escaped arrest thanks to the protection of peasant women who hid them in their homes. Women cadres had to find subtle and discreet ways to organize other women. Members of the Women's Union organized mutual aid societies for weddings and funerals—because social gatherings were the only form of legal group activity. At these gatherings, Union members would find the most active and energetic women and recruit them into the Union, which was an underground organization.

Women in the United States have been very open about their personal lives within the women's movement. Sharing stories of their personal herstory and pain gives them strength. But women in Viet Nam, during most of the anti-French resistance—and in the Saigon-controlled areas before April 30, 1975—could not even know each other's real identity. They met at night, in darkness, with their faces hidden, using aliases and leaving meetings separately, one by one. This anonymity has been an essential protection. If one member is arrested and tortured, she has little information to reveal. Also, village life and a tradition of resistance have provided the conditions for a certain solidarity among Vietnamese women. They don't experience the same isolation that separates women in the United States from each other, because they haven't lived under capitalism which thrives on competition among people.

The only period when the French allowed the Women's Union to function legally was during the time of the Popular Front Government in France: 1936–1939. The Union openly organized the Democratic Women's Association to oppose Japanese and German Fascism and to demand democratic rights for women. They organized reading groups to spread patriotic literature, held rallies of thousands of women, and gained some civil rights. Women led strikes against market taxes and at the Hong-Gay coal mines, Nam Dinh Textile Mill and the Hai Phong spinning mill. At the Hai Phong spinning mill, the boss was forced to grant the workers a fifty per cent wage increase, allow a ten-minute break in each work shift for women to suckle their babies, stop corporal punishment against women and set up a medical center in the factory for ailing women.

On May 1, 1938, five hundred women joined a mass rally in Hanoi. Representatives from the Women's Union spoke from the rostrum, voicing women's aspirations for democratic rights and their grievances against arranged marriages and double standards. The speakers explained the specific ways fascism oppressed women. This mass activity was really pioneer work in political action for women. It was the last major activity before the Vichy government took over in France and the Japanese invaded Viet Nam, instituting new repression.

Between 1940 and 1945, the ICP prepared to take political power from the French. They formed the Viet Minh, a coalition or front of many groups which united to expel the French and Japanese from Viet

September 2, 1945: Ho Chi Minh reads Vietnamese Declaration of Independence from France.

Nam. The Women's Union organized the Women's Association for National Salvation, which became part of the Viet Minh. The Association's membership was secret, but women managed to mobilize for open demonstrations against high taxes, against the Japanese confiscation of the rice crops, and against the press-ganging of men into the pro-Fascist army—a form of kidnaping which the colonists legalized. Beginning in 1943, women faced with starvation picked up sticks and pitchforks to arm themselves against the French and Japanese who ordered them to plant jute instead of rice.

Women in the Viet Minh

Ha Que, the current President of the Viet Nam Women's Union, described how the women organized to attack a Japanese gunnery and recover their rice:

We organized teams for demonstrations. We never came at the same time. But we came at different times from different directions so that the enemy didn't know how many people we had, how strong we were. We made them confused and worried about where all the women were coming from. We were all over the town. We set up committees to take the rice away, some to stop the Japanese soldiers, some demonstrated in front of city hall, some cared for those who might be wounded. [24]

Although the Women's Association for National Salvation was illegal, its activities were supported by most Vietnamese people. The famine and other French/Japanese atrocities convinced more and more women that their only means of survival was to join the revolutionary movement.

Anh Tho, now a poet and leading member of the Writers' Union in Hanoi, was one of many women who joined the struggle at that time. She told me why:

My mother was one of five wives. She was the first wife but suffered a lot because she could not give birth to a son . . . some of the concubines would be expelled from the house if they didn't give birth to sons. They would starve. Mothers would throw their children into the sea and then jump in after them.

I was deeply moved by the sight of children with eyes blurred from starvation, just sitting listlessly. Sometimes when I opened the door, I would see 5 or 7 people collapse, corpses in heaps . . . .

I loved to make poems but my father didn't think I had the capacity. He held me in contempt and didn't let me study past the primary grades. The best way of making a poem at that time was to act—to make the revolution. Because of the hard life of polygamy, we made the revolution. There was no choice. I joined the Viet Minh because of their women's liberation program. . . ."

Some women, like Anh Tho, formed collectives to purchase arms and transport weapons. They opened inns and restaurants to finance the movement. They served as liaison, protected other revolutionaries, agitated among the enemy soldiers and served as spies.

Women participated in the earliest armed actions against the French. By 1945, the first all-woman guerrilla unit was formed by Ha Que, now President of the Viet Nam Women's Union and member of the Central Committee of the Lao Dong Party—the governing party in the DRV. Over one million women participated actively in the anti-French Resistance. During the war years (1946-1954), the Women's Union grew to include several million members. Several women's groups who had stayed apart from the Union—religious groups, for example—joined the new Union in 1946. The new Union mobilized women into the war against the French, and protected women's rights. Part II of this book includes a more detailed account of these activities.

Independence in the North—Betrayal in the South

By August 1945, people throughout Viet Nam joined the general insurrection that expelled both the Japanese and French fascists. The entire nation was freed. People in villages from the Chinese border in the North to the Gulf of Siam in the South began to elect their own local government—People's Councils. On September 2, 1945, Ho Chi Minh spoke for all Vietnamese people as he read the formal Declaration of Independence from France. The Emperor Bao Dai, who had cooperated with the French, abdicated and fled from Hanoi. Ho Chi Minh became the President of the Democratic Republic of Viet Nam—the new independent republic that represented the entire nation.

The French fought back. In 1950, they set up an artificial country whose capital was Saigon and reinstated Bao Dai as Emperor. By 1954, Bao Dai and his Prime Minister, Ngo Dinh Diem, represented very few Vietnamese but called themselves the official representatives of the "State of Viet Nam." After a nine-year war, the unity and determination of the Vietnamese people, combined with a dedicated and competent leadership, succeeded in the decisive defeat of French colonialism. It was also a defeat for the U.S. government which was paying for 78 per cent of the French war effort by 1954.

After the French defeat at Dien Bien Phu, representatives from the Democratic Republic of Viet Nam, the "State of Viet-Nam," France, the Soviet Union, the People's Republic of China, Cambodia, Laos, the United Kingdom and the United States met in Geneva. The Geneva Accords recognized Viet Nam as one sovereign, independent country. The Accords arranged for the temporary partition of the country to facilitate the withdrawal and disarming of troops on both sides. Viet Minh troops withdrew to north of the 17th parallel and French troops to the south. Article Six stated:

The military demarcation line is provisional and should not in any way be interpreted as constituting a political or territorial boundary.

The Accords promised that free elections of a new government for a reunified country would take place in 1956. The U.S. was the only member of the conference who refused to sign the Accords, but did pledge "to refrain from the use of force to disrupt the Agreements."

The United States began violating the Geneva Accords before the ink on them was dry. In September 1954, the South East Asia Treaty Organization (SEATO) unilaterally put South Viet Nam under its "protection." In November, the U.S. began sending aid directly to the Diem regime. By February 1955, U.S. General O'Daniel took over the training of the South Viet Nam Army—ARVN's predecessor. That same year, Diem "dethroned" Bao Dai and declared himself head of state of the "Republic of Viet Nam." In 1956 instead of holding the free elections promised in the Geneva Accords, Diem set up concentration camps and began a campaign of terror against all who demanded enforcement of the Accords. Nevertheless, hundreds of thousands of people demonstrated in Saigon for the Geneva Accords and against Diem.

President Eisenhower kept Diem in power by financing and training his army. Ike sent the first U.S. soldiers to Viet Nam in 1956. In his book *Mandate for Change,* he explained why no elections were allowed:

I have never talked or corresponded with a person knowledgeable in Indo-Chinese affairs who did not agree that had elections been held . . . possibly eighty per cent of the population would have voted for the Communist Ho Chi Minh. [p. 34]

The government of the Democratic Republic of Viet Nam in the North persistently urged Diem to open negotiations for reunification and warned him of the dangers of enslavement to United States domination. The people in the North began the tasks of reconstructing the war-torn country, creating a socialist society, and moving towards women's emancipation.

Meanwhile, in the South, the people faced mounting problems under a new form of foreign domination: U.S. neo-colonialism. Diem stayed in power by bribing officials with U.S.-supplied dollars and by arresting and executing as much of his opposition as he could catch. The *Pentagon Papers* provide overwhelming evidence that the U.S. government created and manipulated the Saigon regime. But even American officials understood that their puppet government could not be successful. In 1960, the U.S. Embassy in Saigon made a special report "On the Internal Security Situation in Viet Nam":

The situation may be summed up in the fact that the government has tended to treat the population with suspicion or to coerce it and has been rewarded with an attitude of resentment and apathy. The basic factor which has been lacking is a feeling of rapport between the government and the population. The people have not identified themselves with the government. [25]

Madame Nhu, Diem's sister-in-law, increased women's distrust for that government when she founded the "Women's Solidarity League." It was a paramilitary organization presumably dedicated to gaining women's rights. In fact, the purpose of the League was to mobilize women to persecute those who fought for Vietnamese independence. Women who wanted their husbands to keep jobs in Diem's bureaucracy had no choice but to join the League.

In March of 1959, Diem declared a "state of war" against the Vietnamese Communists—"Vietcong"—defined by Diem as anyone who opposed his dictatorship. On December 20, 1960, the National Liberation Front was formed as a political organization that united the following groups: the Radical Socialist Party—a party representing patriotic intellectuals; the Democratic Party—a party representing independent businessmen who opposed foreign control; the People's Revolutionary Party—representing workers and peasants; organizations representing trade unions, youth, women, peasants, students, writers and artists; the Patriotic Buddhists Association; Association of Catholics Devoted to God and Fatherland; Association for the Moral Renaissance of Hoa Hao Followers; the Movement for Autonomy of the Tay Nguyen Nationalities; and others.

They issued a manifesto which explained that the NLF had formed to meet the desires of the Vietnamese people to overthrow Diem's regime and to liberate the nation from U.S. control. They organized the People's Liberation Armed Forces (PLAF) as a regular army. Most Vietnamese joined the struggle on the side of the NLF and rejoiced when a coup overthrew Diem and Madame Nhu. The day of the coup, November 1, 1963, is still a national holiday in South Viet Nam. By 1964, the NLF was close to its goal. The U.S.-approved Saigon regime that replaced Diem was crumbling.

Massive numbers of U.S. ground troops and bombers came to the rescue. By the end of 1966, about a half-million American men were on Vietnamese soil. The genocidal policies of the U.S. government brought new misery to the people of Viet Nam—especially the women.

Notes

1. Tam Vu and Nguyen Khac Vien, *A Century of National Struggles* (Vietnamese Studies #24; Hanoi: Foreign Languages Publishing House, 1970), pp. 40–45.
2. Tam Vu and Nguyen Khac Vien, p. 65; also quoted in Ngo Vinh Long, *Before the Revolution* (Cambridge: MIT Press, 1973), p. 63.
3. Tam Vu and Nguyen Khac Vien, p. 47.

4. Ngo Vinh Long, pp. 116-117.
5. Details of this section and many more can be found in Ngo Vinh Long's book, pp. 8-89.
6. Ngo Tat To, *When the Light Is Out* (Hanoi: Foreign Languages Publishing House, 1960; original edition 1930).
7. Nguyen Thi Dam's testimony comes from Wilfred Burchett, *North of the 17th Parallel*, 2nd edition (Hanoi: Red River Publishing House, 1957), pp. 119-124.
8. Ngo Vinh Long, p. 46. Long writes that in all of Cochin-China, there was not one peasant who was not in debt.
9. These figures plus other details on life on rubber plantations come from Long, pp. 112-113.
10. Mai Thi Tu, p. 25.
11. Vu Can, "With the Nam Dinh Weavers," in *Vietnamese Women* (Vietnamese Studies #10; Hanoi: Foreign Languages Publishing House, 1966), p. 194. The testimony that follows from Mrs. Yen comes from pp. 198-202 of this article.
12. Jean Chesneaux, *The Vietnamese Nation* (Sydney, Australia: Current Book Distributors, 1966), p. 141.
13. Bernard Fall, *Street Without Joy* (New York: Schocken, 1972), p. 141.
14. Chesneaux, p. 131.
15. Burchett, *North of the 17th Parallel*, p. 217.
16. Tran Van Mai, "Who Committed This Crime," in book by Ngo Vinh Long, pp. 219-276.
17. Ngo Vinh Long, p. 133.
18. Anonymous, "The Woman Inn-keeper at the Southern Gate," *South Vietnam in Struggle* #232 (January 20, 1974), p. 6.
19. The information for this section on early feminism comes from the following sources: Nha Trang, Ph.D. thesis, pp. 252ff., and David Marr, "The 1920's Women Rights Debates in Viet Nam," unpublished paper, 1974. Details on the value of the piaster come from Ngo Vinh Long, pp. 124-125.
20. Marr.
21. This quote is repeated in nearly every document written about women in the Democratic Republic of Viet Nam.
22. Unpublished correspondence by Viet Nam Women's Union, Hanoi, October 29, 1973, addressed to this author.
23. Information on period 1930-1931 from Tam Vu and Nguyen Khac Vien, pp. 98-101, and from unpublished correspondence by Viet Nam Women's Union. The rest of the history of the Women's Union is also from the unpublished correspondence.
24. "History of the Vietnamese Women's Movement" *Viet Nam Report* #9 (April 1975) p. 9.
25. *The Pentagon Papers,* New York Times Edition (New York: Bantam, 1972) p. 72.

4.
THE POLITICS OF RAPE IN VIET NAM

This is my rifle [GI holds up M-16]
This is my gun [puts hand at crotch]
One is for killing
The other for fun.

—*training exercise in U.S. Army*

On August 2, 1965, during a raid on Hoa Vang District and north of Dien Ban District, in Quang Nam Province, GI's gathered hundreds of women in the courtyard . . . and took turns raping them. Among the victims were many old women of seventy and teenagers of ten or twelve. [1]

People around the world have heard about the massacre at Son My Village—sometimes called My Lai—on March 16, 1968. In that district, U.S. troops killed as many as five hundred civilians within a few hours. But it is not well known that before the massacre, troops of the Third Airborne Brigade, 82nd Division, raped hundreds of women. [2] It may be hard to believe reports like these but they become irrefutable when the GI's themselves begin confessing:

When we went through the villages and searched people, the women would have all their clothes taken off and the men would use their penises to probe them to make sure they didn't have anything hidden anywhere; and this was raping, but it was done as searching. [3]

Sp/4 Joe Galbally of the American Division reported:

We went through the village; it was about an eight-man patrol. We entered a hootch [peasant home]. These people are aware of what American soldiers do to them, so naturally they tried to hide the young girls. We found one hiding in a bomb shelter in a sort of a basement of her house. She was taken out, raped by six or seven people in front of her family, in front of us and the villagers. This isn't just one incident; this was just the first one I can remember. I know of ten or fifteen such incidents at least. [4]

No one should dismiss these crimes as "natural but unintended and inevitable consequences of war," because not all warriors are rapists. There are virtually no verified reports of rape committed by NLF or North Vietnamese troops. To understand rape in Viet Nam, we must return to the U.S.

Getting away with it

Ralph Garofalo is a psychologist who treats rapists at the Center for Diagnosis and Treatment of Sexually Dangerous Persons, Bridgewater, Massachusetts. He implied, in his own crudely sexist manner,

62

that men will commit rape if they think they can get away with it:

Yet on the balance, the rapist is not an exotic freak; in some cases his behavior is merely an extreme manifestation of the normal male sex drive. I don't think there's a man worth his salt who hasn't seen some chick walking by and wanted to screw her. The crucial distinction is that normal men find a socially acceptable outlet for their desires, while the rapist loses all sight of moral and legal considerations. [5]

In Viet Nam, the U.S. Military Command made rape "socially acceptable"; in fact, it was unwritten, but clear, policy. Systematic mass rape was a policy implemented by consistently covering up reported rapes and by making it clear to GI's that they had no real need to fear punishment. Of course, this policy was never socially acceptable to the Vietnamese people, but they had no voice in the U.S. media.

Garofalo's equation—"the normal male sex drive" equals sexual aggression—is, in reality, a myth. It's a myth created by this violent society where individuals can only profit at others' expense. It's a myth that men are trained to live up to. In this way, sexual aggression becomes the rule, even though it's not a biological imperative. Sexual aggression reinforces itself by keeping women in a subordinate position—dependent on men for protection. When people accept another myth—that women are naturally weak and passive—women become easier prey for men and are less likely to rebel against the entire system of oppression.

Assertions that women are naturally passive form part of an elaborate mosaic of myths which proclaim women's inferiority. These myths persist in one form or another because they're convenient rationalizations to justify and maintain economic exploitation of women. For example, the assertion that "serving as wife and mother is the highest fulfillment of all women's natural needs" implies that all women should be satisfied and happy leading "private lives" as housewives. But housework is monotonous menial labor which serves a public function—women's labor in the home supplies the economy with billions of hours of free labor—labor necessary to produce and maintain the nation's work force. Employers' profits would be a lot lower if they had to pay even minimum wage for all the hours of work done by the wives of their employees—work which makes it possible for these employees to be available and efficient at the job.

Employers in an economy based on profit also need a pool of unemployed people, or reserve labor force, whom they can easily hire and fire to do temporary jobs, low-paying jobs, undesirable jobs, and strikebreaking. Housewives form the ideal constituency of the reserve labor force because they're available for work outside the home and they often have useful skills. Belief in myths that "women's place is in the home" makes it less likely that women will challenge their boss when he lays them off or pays them poorly. Ideas about "women's place" or that "a woman can't be happy unless she's serving a man" combine in a strong social pressure that forces many women not to "take men's jobs" or to earn as much as a man. This subordination of women is also given as a flimsy compensation to poor and working-class men. These men are systematically denied access to the basic source of power in the United States: control over the profitmaking resources of the nation.

Other myths turn reality upside down to hide or justify white men's privilege. It's a lie that most rapists are Black men lusting after white women. Historically, white men regularly raped Black women to terrorize them into submission and to produce more slaves. Today, the majority of rapes do not cross race lines. An accurate reading of publicity about the rapes of white women by dark-skinned men really exposes the racism of the courts and the media, which try to use Third World men as scapegoats for women's oppression.

In short, the rape which was rampant in Viet Nam was bred in the United States where it is not a problem of natural biology or psycho-pathology or a breakdown of law and order. It is part of a carefully woven net of capitalism, racism and sexism that traps all oppressed people—but devours women.

Producing men

As soon as a young boy learns to speak in the United States, or perhaps earlier, he begins to learn that "girls are not as good as boys." He sees men with power and women with none. He learns that "being a man" is something to be proud of. Male pride is nurtured by its oppo-site—female adoration and helplessness. Ideals of manhood in our society require that the young boy learn to stunt his emotional growth. "Crying is for girls." They require that a young man be aggressive, competitive, brave, even cruel. They teach that "you can tell the men from the boys by how many women they've conquered." They teach that "all women secretly want to be raped."

They also teach that a woman's helplessness and gratitude to her "savior" makes a man into a hero. Susan Griffin, in an article called "The Politics of Rape," points out that chivalry is a "male protection racket." The rapist may force a woman to depend on the "knight" for protection. But the "knight" also takes advantage of her by disguising his own sexual aggression in more socially acceptable forms. Excessive courtesy and contempt are two sides of the same coin. [6] The same Marine who "salutes a lady" may refer to a common woman as "Susie Rottencrotch."

As a boy approaches manhood, the demands to prove himself a *man* escalate. Variations on the games of "I-dare-you" or "chicken" are endless. It's impossible for any boy to escape the influence of friends, home, school, TV, and movies. The model is either John Wayne or James Bond. John Wayne is the "strong silent type." Psychologists write:

On the screen, he doesn't feel comfortable with women. He does like them sometimes—God knows he's not "queer." But at the right time and in the right place—which he chooses. And always with his car/horse parked directly outside, in/on which he will ride away to his more important business back in Marlboro country. [7]

John Wayne in real life is a staunch supporter of Richard Nixon and is proud to glorify the adventures of the Green Berets in Viet Nam. James Bond's image is a variation on the same theme. He treats women like sales items. He's cool, detached, independent and non-feeling. He kills with ease. Perhaps he is dead inside but externally he's lively and charming. Not all men identify with the John Wayne/James Bond image of manhood. Some are driven crazy by it. Some fight it. Third World men have their own models of masculine superiority like Superfly. But in varying degrees, there exists a bit of the male superstar in every man raised in the United States.

Many white middle- and upper-class men have a chance to disguise their Wayne/Bond desires in a cloak of polite manners. They got draft deferments and proved their manhood in college sports and sororities and later in aggressive business deals. But the national habit of "proving yourself a man" was a convenient tool in the hands of draft boards and military recruiters. They tried to convince draftees, most of whom were Third World and white working-class men, that to resist the draft was cowardly and unmanly. Doing your duty by serving your country in Viet Nam became another proof of manhood.

Of course, many who were drafted and served understood that their dignity had nothing to do with fighting in Viet Nam. They went because they faced the choice: join the Army which "is after all a job and promises to teach you a skill" or go to jail. A Black reporter in Viet Nam did a survey in 1970 of Black enlisted men and found that seventy per cent of them named Malcolm X as their hero. Sixty-four per cent believed their fight was in the United States, not in Viet Nam. Thousands of men were thrown in stockades and brigs because they challenged the military machine. Since 1963, a half-million GI's received discharges "under less than honorable conditions." In 1972, Black soldiers received twenty-one per cent of all Bad Conduct discharges and thirty-three per cent of all Dishonorable discharges. [8] Black men took the lead in rejecting the pressure to perform as dictated in Viet Nam,

Times Square, New York City

and a number of white men, especially those coming from poor urban families, joined them.

In spite of the harsh penalties, two hundred thousand men became fugitives rather than go to Viet Nam. As early as 1964, Malcolm X urged Black men not to fight Uncle Sam's wars, but to fight for Black liberation. In 1965–1966, SNCC, the most militant civil-rights organization, popularized the slogan "Hell No We Won't Go," and by 1967, the anti-draft movement incorporated thousands of people, both Third World and white.

But many of those who most identified with the John Wayne/James Bond image of manhood voluntarily enlisted in the U.S. Armed Services. Those who joined the Marines present the most extreme cases:

When I look back on it I can see that I wanted to go to war because like most little guys, we were the product of seeing battle, John Wayne and all that kind of thing and you think it's cool. And then you want to go and see what it's all about and be a hero. That was in my mind when I got over. I wanted to be a hero.

He continued:

And I always wondered, like if I didn't go if it was just because I was afraid to go. . . . It may seem foolish . . . after I got to Viet Nam and was in contact, I realized how foolish I was—to think, you know, that my reason was to find out, "Am I gonna chicken out?" [9]

Another Marine explained that his friends said "Join the Marines if you want to be a man"—"so I did." [10] Going to Viet Nam, for many young men, became a kind of initiation rite—a way to earn a place in this society as a man. Many said that they had to prove that they could face death "without shitting in our pants."

Training

Before going to Viet Nam, GI's may sit through some hours of indoctrination classes which teach that they will be fighting, perhaps dying, for democracy in Viet Nam. But even the trainers must know that only those soldiers who are totally blind to reality can take the line seriously after a brief time in Viet Nam itself. In fact, by 1970, only fourteen per cent of the Black soldiers and twenty-one per cent of the white soldiers believed that they were fighting to build democracy in Viet Nam. [11] The kind of training new recruits undergo shows that the Pentagon has discovered that if you can't motivate men to fight for an unjust cause, you can motivate them to fight to assert their racial and sexual superiority.

Once in training, all GI's, whether volunteers or draftees, face a total onslaught from the he-man-making machine. The Army totally isolates new recruits from the outside world for the first eight weeks of basic training. They shave their heads. They uniform and drill their bodies. They assault their identity. Drill instructors call them "sweetie, shithead, fatboy, creep or faggot" until they prove themselves as men by becoming killers who seem to enjoy killing. A drill instructor in San Diego yelled to a platoon that wasn't clicking its heels loud enough:

You want to march on your toes like you have a bunch of high heels on? OK ladies that's just fine, put your arm up like you're holding a purse. Now get on your toes and repeat after me [switching to a high falsetto] "We're a bunch of girls and we can't march." [12]

Vets remember that if they referred to other GI's as "guys," they were ridiculed: "We don't have any guys in this army, Sweetie, only *men.*" If the new recruit mistakenly called his M–16 a "gun," he had to recite the ditty that opens this chapter about the difference between a rifle and a gun. If he didn't thrust his bayonet into the dummy with enough spirit, they called him a "pussy." If he was repulsed by graphic recommendations on cutting out someone's guts, they told him to "go home to mama." The brutalization process skillfully manipulated ideas which are full of contempt for women. To be a man, a GI had to hide his humanity and become more or less schizophrenic, depending on how much he really believed his indoctrination. Trainers had the advantage because they could convince the recruits that brutality was a matter of survival. A vet recalled:

When you made mistakes, they screamed, "You're not going to live three minutes over there, you idiot." And I believed them. [13]

After four weeks of basic training and harassment, the recruit gets a chance to prove he is *somebody,* the chance to prove himself on the rifle range. Now, instead of being only a victim of brutality—the brutality of his drill instructor—he can become an agent of brutality. The enemy target was the "gook." Drills focused on a "hostile and inferior race" as the enemy and not on hostile ideologies.

White drill sergeants could easily draw from an infinite variety of white supremacist myths which reflect and reinforce the oppression of Third World people inside as well as outside the United States. Since the earliest days of slave trade, white men's prosperity has depended on the denial of Third World people's right to self-determination. Racism is built into the imperialist system so that Asian, Black, Latin and Native American people face systematic discrimination in jobs, politics, the schools, the courts and in housing.

Third World women carry the triple burden of racial, economic, and sexual oppression. For example, a Black woman usually gets the lowest-paying jobs and often can only survive with the aid of Welfare. But the Welfare Department tries to dictate every intimate detail of her life—even forcing her to sign papers authorizing her own sterilization. The white real-estate industry forces Black people to live in ghettoes. But when Black people *choose* to live with each other and are proud of their culture, racist politicians call them "fanatic separatists" or "culturally deprived." White police occupy and terrorize Third World communities in the ghettoes of the U.S. in much the same way that U.S. troops occupied Viet Nam.

"Mere Gook Rule"

Killing in Viet Nam came easier to the killers who thought their victims were not quite human: "gooks, dinks, slopes"—with slanted eyes and maybe "slanted pussies." Many ignorant men looked forward to finding out how it would be to "screw" a woman who was the subject of so many racist jokes about her vagina opening cross-ways. Few spoke of the Vietnamese as people. They were just numbers in body counts. Corporal John Getmann, 3rd Marine Division, explained the racism of the system:

When somebody asks: "Why do you do this to people?" your answer is, "So what, they're just gooks, they're not people. It doesn't make any difference what you do to them; they're not human." And this thing is built into you, it's thrust into your head from the moment you wake up in boot camp to the moment you wake up when you're a civilian. And it's a very hard thing to try to forget about it. It's about the only way I can put it, it's—they make you want to kill. Their whole thing is killing. You're not to question, you're not supposed to ask why. If you're told to kill, you're to kill. [14]

When a GI tried to stop several buddies in the process of raping a Vietnamese woman, they brushed him aside with, "What are you worried about? She's only a gook!" The jargon of Army lawyers expresses the same racism. The MGR—or "Mere Gook Rule"—is the unwritten law that nearly guarantees an American soldier his freedom if charged with raping a Vietnamese woman. [15]

The attitudes and training of recruits to the People's Liberation Armed Forces, the military organization of the NLF, stand in stark contrast. Recruits receive a political education designed to make them understand these basic principles: (1) Why do we fight? Because we are oppressed and want to lead a decent life free of foreign oppressors and feudal exploiters. (2) For whom do we fight? All peasants, workers and oppressed people throughout the world will benefit from our victory. (3) We, the poor and exploited, should have the power in society and be proud of our work. (4) Victory is certain.

It is PLAF policy to give peasants, who have been traditionally held in contempt, a sense of dignity and strength. One regimental political officer explained:

We reject the concept that the masses are simply "cannon fodder" who will blindly follow their leader. . . . We want people who know exactly why they do what they do, who act together when the occasion demands, but each of whom is a separate being bringing his/her own experience, intelligence to bear on the concrete problems to be solved. This makes unity a creative, living concept and not just a slogan. [16]

After fifteen days of political education, the recruit receives a gun. But the education continues in the form of daily sessions in which all activity—including what officers do—is discussed and criticized. The soldiers are evaluated according to standards that have nothing to do with the assertion of manly or racial superiority:

Complete identification with the people in any area where our troops are stationed or operating is an absolute imperative and anyone in-

volved in the slightest violation of the "why and for whom" concept in relations with the people would be severely criticized. We are a people's army, devoted to helping the people themselves successfully carry out their revolution.

The test of Viet Nam

Once in Viet Nam, most GI's became numb to the killing and developed an elaborate cynicism to shield themselves from doubt and guilt. A vet named Kirk reported:

I didn't feel it [killing] was traumatic. I mean, I was, you know, you're ready for it, you know, you see TV, movies all your life. You know what to expect.

Kempton, another vet, even found pleasure in killing:

Yeah, I wanted to kill, I really did. . . . I ran out there with my rifle and I was just all smiles from here to there . . . mentally it was like a good time, a good party, you know, like this is party time, let's get going. That's the way I felt. [17]

Technology made it easier for some to kill. GI's reported how pulling the trigger became automatic and required no thought. But many soldiers maintained a sense of humanity and killing brought them to a state of moral crisis. Some cried. Some went mad. Many killed only when it was absolutely necessary for their own survival. As the war dragged on, resistance to participating in the slaughter gained momentum. Soldiers wore buttons with peace signs, with guns pointing to the earth, and with slogans: "No Vietnamese ever called me nigger." Mutinies made headlines, but there were thousands of men who quietly withdrew from the military effort. Many turned to heroin, especially those stationed in the rear. Others felt sorry, but were ashamed of these feelings:

I felt sorry. I don't know why I felt sorry. John Wayne never felt sorry. [18]

The GI jargon thickened their shield of cynicism. White phosphorus, which continues burning flesh until it hits bone, was called "Willie Peter." They called 2000-pound bombs "daisy cutters." They called torture by electric shocks from a field telephone "Bell Telephone Hour." They named their tanks: "Cong Au-Go-Go," "WETSU" (We Eat This Stuff Up), and "Saigon Tea." The 12th Air Commando Squadron at Bien Hoa was responsible for defoliating miles of Vietnamese land. Their proud motto was, "Only you can prevent forests!" [19]

INTRODUCING "THE KINGSMEN" U.S. ARMY
Assault Helicopter Company

SPECIALTIES:

Combat Assaults (Day & Night)
LRRP, Ins. & EXTR
Emergency Ammo Resupply
Flareship & Phyops
Emergency Medivacs
VC, Extermination
People Sniffer & Defoliation

SIDE LINES:

Worlds Greatest Pilot
International Playboy
War Monger
Renowned Booze Hound
Social Lion
Ladies Man

PROVIDING: Death and Destruction 24-Hrs. a Day. If You Care Enough To Send The Very Best, Send KINGSMEN.

LIVE BY LUCK
LOVE BY NATURE
KILL BY PROFESSION

DEATH ON CALL
WIRE Griffin SAN FRANCISCO 96383
C Btry 4th Bn (ARA) 77th Arty

Calling cards of units in Viet Nam

A Japanese reporter described a moving scene where cynicism was combined with the emotional invalidism of James Bond. During a search-and-destroy mission, GI's would generally invade villages and homes, destroying lives and anything that could support life. It took one GI only a few minutes to wreck everything a poor peasant owned. As he threw away the family rice supply and was about to hurl the only remaining jar to the ground, a young woman pleaded with him through her tears, "Please stop, it's a special relic from our ancestors." He stopped, but only long enough to remark, "What a pretty girl!" and then resumed his destruction. [20]

Rape as terrorism

Rape is not a crime of passion; it is an act of aggression. [21]

From the distressingly long list of cases, it's impossible to know the exact personal motive of each rapist. But the general motive for rape as the military policy of an aggressive army is clear. Terrorism is a classic counterinsurgency tactic against people's war. Rape is a classic act of terrorism which not only serves the political function of intimidating a rebellious population, but also allows the rapist to reassert his manhood. A conscious policy of counterinsurgency made rape in Viet Nam standard operating procedure aimed at terrorizing the population into submission:

I saw one case where a woman was shot by a sniper, one of our snipers. When we got up to her she was asking for water. And the lieutenant said to kill her. So he ripped off her clothes, they stabbed her in both breasts, they spread her eagle and shoved an E tool [entrenching] up her vagina, and she was still asking for water. And then they took that out and used a tree limb and then she was shot. [22]

Sp/5 Don Dzagulones, Americal Division, testified to the torture of villagers thought to be sympathetic to the NLF. Most of the prisoners were women, children and old men:

They brought in a woman prisoner who was alleged to be a spy. They continued the interrogation in a bunker and she wouldn't talk. I don't think she even gave them her name. So they stripped off her clothing, and they threatened to rape her, which had no effect on her at all. She was very stoic. She just stood there and looked at them defiantly. So they threatened to burn her pubic hairs . . . she caught on fire and went into shock . . . they gave the medics instructions to take her to the hospital under the pretext of being in a coma from malaria. [23]

On September 16, 1966, soldiers of the 25th Infantry Division stationed in Ben Luc and Go Den (Long An Province) rounded up two hundred women and took turns raping them. That same month, fishermen from Cai San and Cai Con found the naked bodies of ninety-seven women floating in the river. [24]

Rape as revenge

The Marines, "Leathernecks," have a battle psalm:

Yea, though I walk through the valley of the shadow of death,
I will fear no evil;
'Cuz I'm the toughest mutha in the valley. [25]

But soldiers in Viet Nam were afraid. They were also frustrated. They took this fear and frustration out on the people, especially the women. GI's were unnerved by the fact that they couldn't distinguish between the "enemy" and civilians. Booby traps caused the majority of casualties and a good deal of the deaths in Viet Nam. Any Vietnamese, even a child, could set a booby trap. Most booby traps are arranged so that the victim acts as his own executioner. They're traps for "boobies," for fools. [26] GI's responded with hatred:

I hate gooks . . . and of course the only way you could determine who hated them the most was how many times you beat them or killed them or raped them or something like that. [27]

The NLF also challenged the GI's by setting ambushes. In conventional war, the aggressor sets the time and place of battle and the victor is the one with the most firepower. But NLF guerrillas refused to allow American invaders the option of initiating battles. The U.S. soldier never could be sure when the enemy would strike. He was

highly visible. His opponent was invisible. Sensing that most civilians were sympathetic to the NLF, the American GI was constantly aware of his vulnerability.

Sometimes, liberation soldiers would demoralize GI's by deliberately making them feel like helpless objects. They would speak to the foot soldiers, "grunts," in English over loudspeakers about U.S. battle plans that the grunts hadn't been briefed on. Nervous GI's understood that the PLAF could have just as easily shot them as spoken to them. One Marine reported:

This NVA soldier goes "Good Morning, Marines." A lot of shit they did just to fuck up your head. I mean, they must have had a chance before that to really zap someone. They did this shit just to scare the fuck out of you. . . . Everyone fucking flies out of the trenches with their rifles. They're expecting attack. Fucking gook is probably laughing his ass off in the bushes. [28]

Humiliated GI's took revenge by humiliating women:

One thing that was more or less a joke . . . and it would get a laugh every time from somebody, was if we were moving through a village and there was a woman present. Her clothes, at least the top half were just ripped [off]. I've seen that happen and done it several times. . . . It only takes one hand to rip those kind of clothing. [29]

L/Cpl Thomas Heidtman continued to explain that after a woman's breasts were exposed, she would be shoved aside into a ditch and in John Wayne style, "We'd just keep going."

45,806 GI's died in combat in Viet Nam. Another 47,000 died from "non-hostile" causes. Three hundred thousand were wounded in action. Some GI's did not recognize that they had been ordered to invade Viet Nam by the President of the U.S. They blamed the Vietnamese people. One GI paraphrased the thoughts of a rapist before he mounted a terrified Vietnamese woman:

. . . you dirty bitch, you killed Wilson and you killed Weber and Cox and Rotger and Bell and you got me out here and look what my buddies are doing. I hate this war and it's your fault I'm here. [30]

Women suspected of fighting for the liberation forces were called "Vietcong Whores" and would be subjected to "gang bangs" whenever captured. Vets testified to raping women after they were dead. Troops of the 11th Armored Cavalry used an automotive grease gun to rape a dead woman and joked that they had "packed her full of grease." [31]

When he felt his manhood threatened, the GI would also treat his ally, the ARVN soldier, with incredible brutality. For example, after receiving consent to ride in a U.S. truck, a legless ARVN soldier touched the leg of a Marine in gratitude. The Marine recalled:

The little slope grabbed me by the leg. And I had been in the country long enough to know that most of them are queer. They hold hands and stuff. And this sort of irks most Marines and soldiers. And we're told that it's a Vietnamese custom, when you're friendly you should hold hands. So they try to hold a lot of guys' hands. So they end up getting beat bloody. The guy grabbed my leg. So I got mad. I wasn't in a good mood that morning and I whacked him. And my buddies grabbed his crutches. And I said, "Go!" So we took off. We threw his crutch in a rice paddy and went another 150 yards and threw the other crutch and then out he went. He was screaming and crying and begging us. "Out you go." We all had a good laugh about that. [32]

Some rapists were not intentionally applying a policy of terrorism or revenge. Some had just been trained to think that this horror was fun. A soldier named Eriksson witnessed the kidnapping of Pham Thi Mao, 18 years old, by four GI's. They took her from her village so that she could service them on a five-day reconnaissance patrol in Bong Son Valley. They forced her to carry their baggage and after they ate and rested, the sergeant announced that it was "time for recreation." All four repeatedly raped her and then resumed their patrol. When night fell, they raped her again and then shot her. [33]

Perhaps the most barbaric rapes were those specifically intended to destroy future generations. In the course of a sweep of Mo Cay District, Ben Tre Province, early in 1971, GI's raped to death five school girls. [34] Torturers also deliberately thrust sticks with sharpened ends, broken Coke bottles, and electric bulbs into the vaginas of captive women to make it impossible for the victims to bear children. [35]

"It was the rape that made me see the true face of the war"

A Vietnamese woman from a middle-class Saigon family is now in Canada working with the Union of Vietnamese in Canada, a group that has supported the liberation struggle. Until about 1970, she had supported Thieu and the Americans. It was the rapes that made her change her mind.

In some societies, women who have been raped are outcasts. The policy in the liberated zones of Viet Nam is to treat women who have been raped as victims of American aggression. Revolutionary cadre actively fight against the traditional shame and prejudice against women who have been raped. Vietnamese women often transform their shame into fighting energy. Le Thi Hong Gam, a heroine of the PLAF, became a guerrilla when she was 16. She insisted on being allowed to take up arms after witnessing the rape/murder of her best friend. By the time Gam died in combat, at age 19, she had killed 26 enemy troops. Other women respond to rape with their own individual acts of resistance. The *New Yorker* magazine, April 15, 1972, reported the practice of "deranged war widows deliberately squatting to relieve themselves in front of hotels where Americans stay." Some women may silently guard their hatred and join the struggle at a later time.

Huyn Thi Kien explained why she joined the struggle to expel the American invaders:

I'll tell you another incident I saw. A woman was going to give birth in about two weeks. During a raid, GI's forced her back into a room and tried to rape her but she resisted. So the five GI's tied her to the bed and raped her to death. After that, they used their bayonets to pluck out the fetus. And they laughed. . . . In my case, as a woman and a peasant in the South, I only worked very hard to live. When I witnessed these savage crimes of the GI's with my own eyes I felt very strongly. In order to defend my own life and the lives of my family, I had no other way but to join other women and to fight back. [36]

The Women's Committee to Defend the Right to Live was a strong mass organization in Saigon and other cities. A well-publicized dual

The banner reads: "U.S. Imperialists Out of Viet Nam."

rape of a mother and daughter became the incident that initially sparked the women to organize the group in 1970. Forming the organization, in itself, was a particularly heroic act. All organizations that called for peace were illegal in Saigon. Just two weeks before its public founding, ex-President Thieu announced that he would "beat to death" anyone who spoke for peace.

The Women's Committee to Defend the Right to Live began with four demands: immediate withdrawal of all American troops; ouster of Thieu from government; the formation of a new coalition government; and respect for the dignity and civil rights of women. They have staged demonstrations, boycotts, strikes in the marketplace, and other mass activities to campaign for their goals. Many of their members, including their founder, Madame Ngo Ba Thanh, were imprisoned for years. Madame Thanh, a lawyer educated at Columbia University, was finally released from prison after several years of international pressure and months of hunger strikes. After her release, she rejoined her sisters in the Women's Committee to Defend the Right to Live in fighting for the release of other political prisoners and for the enforcement of the Paris Peace Agreements. They took leadership in the political movement that joined in the final liberation of Saigon on April 30, 1975.

When Johnny comes marching home

Since 1961, nearly six million men have returned as veterans of war in South East Asia. Many more know vets as brothers, sons, lovers, co-workers, and students. Tens of thousands of veterans have joined an organization called Viet Nam Veterans Against the War (VVAW). They have taken the leadership in many anti-war activities. They also have helped many vets begin the difficult process of challenging their own racist and sexist attitudes in rap groups and other forms of counseling. An editorial headlined "Free Our Sisters" in the newspaper published by the San Francisco chapter of VVAW recognized GI responsibility for rape in the following way:

Rarely do we comment on the courage it takes for our sisters to walk in the streets, where they are open targets for any men who so desire. How many of our sisters get raped in our streets and what are we doing about it? Our attitude is one of silent support for the rapist.

So, even though the system we live under is the main culprit for the oppression of women, we also have a responsibility to our sisters. We must try to understand what our sisters are going through. How women also would like to feel independent the way men do, but all the cards are stacked against them. We have to rally to their cause, which is the full emancipation of women. [*The Veteran*, Spring 1973]

But the commitment of VVAW is only a small beginning. We can only speculate on how deep and ugly are the scars inflicted by a "tour of duty" in Viet Nam. In a war where the invaders could gain no territory, they could only show "progress" by making the body count as high as possible. When these soldiers come home, what happens? There are no reliable statistics showing how many cases of wife beating, child abuse, rape, murder and suicide are committed by Viet Nam veterans. But there has been a lot of experience with "Post Viet Nam Syndrome" (PVS). Symptoms of PVS include guilt, emotional numbing, insensitivity, mistrust of society and organization, alcoholism, drug abuse, violence, rage, sexual aggression and sexual impotence.

All men learn to suppress their emotions, especially emotions of sympathy. Men and women alike learned to live with statistics of body counts, and reports of war atrocities. We have all been brutalized and numbed by U.S. government policy in Viet Nam. In Viet Nam itself, the emotional mutilation process is accelerated and exaggerated. Vets explain, "You learn not to have friends . . . you don't want to get too close to anybody, 'cause it might kill you." Other vets reported initial traumas when they first killed somebody, but later pulling the trigger became a habit, a reflex. [37]

When these men return to a non-combat situation, they deliberately insulate themselves from emotion-laden situations, fearing they might lose control and have their combat "instincts" return. They fear that if they unlock their emotional vaults for any one reason, all their accumulated fears and anguish will pour out. This fear creates enormous problems within families and other social relations. One vet confessed:

If I am fucking and a girl says "I love you," then I want to kill her . . . [because] if you get too close . . . you get hurt. [38]

These vets are cracked-mirror images of an entire society suffering from Post Viet Nam Syndrome—a national crisis embodied in the brutality of our prisons and mental hospitals, in the cynicism of Watergate and the bankruptcy of the economy. In contrast, the Vietnamese women who survived and fought against all the barbarism U.S. society produced, give us a vision of the potential for human renewal.

Notes

1. Committee to Denounce War Crimes of U.S. Imperialists, "Crimes Perpetrated by U.S. Imperialists and Henchmen Against South Viet Nam Women and Children" (Viet Nam: Gai Phong Publishing House, 1968), p. 13. (In the following notes this pamphlet will be cited as "Crimes.")
2. "Crimes," p. 14.
3. Quote from Sgt. Scot Camil, First Marine Division, cited in VVAW, *Winter Soldier Investigation* (Boston: Beacon Press, 1972), p. 13.
4. *Winter Soldier Investigation*, p. 46.
5. *Newsweek*, August 20, 1973, pp. 67–68.
6. Susan Griffin's article, "The Politics of Rape," was originally published in *Ramparts* (1971), but has been reproduced by many women's organizations.
7. Jack Balswick and Charles Peek, "The Inexpressive Male," in *Family Coordinator*, October 1971, pp. 363–368.
8. Results of this survey by Wallace Terry II, "Bring the War Home," in anthology edited by Clyde Taylor, *Viet Nam and Black America* (New York: Anchor, 1973), pp. 200–222. Discharge and other statistics of resistance by GI's from pamphlet published by VVAW/WSO, "Amnesty" (1973), p. 4.
9. The quote is from an ex-Viet Nam Marine whom the author calls "Tidwell" in Norma Juliet Wikler, "Vietnam and the Veterans' Consciousness" (UC Berkeley,

Sociology Department, Ph.D. thesis, June 1973), pp. 52-54.

10. Wikler's thesis, p. 71.
11. Wallace Terry II, p. 205.
12. Quoted by Wikler, p. 81. Other insights into what happens in training come from my own informal discussions with vets, especially Sp/4 Vincent J. Dijanich, Co. "E," 502 Infantry, 101 Airborne Division.
13. Quoted in Wikler, p. 82.
14. *Winter Soldier Investigation,* p. 5.
15. See "This World," *San Francisco Chronicle/Examiner,* (Sunday) March 21, 1971, p. 7.
16. This quote and other details on PLAF training come from Wilfred Burchett, *Viet Nam Will Win* (New York: Guardian Books, 1970), ch. 2, "Making of a Soldier," p. 19.
17. Both quotes are from Wikler, pp. 196-200.
18. Robert Jay Lifton, *Home from the War* (New York: Simon & Schuster, 1973), p. 121.
19. Don Pratt and Lee Blair, *Salmagundi Vietnam* (Vermont: Charles E. Tuttle Co., 1971), p. 33.
20. Katsuichi Honda, *Vietnam: A Voice from the Villages* (Japan: Committee for English Publication of Vietnam: A Voice from the Villages, 1967), p. 20.
21. Boston Lesbian Feminists, "Vietnam: A Feminist Analysis,", in *Rough Times,* vol. 2, #8 (July 1972), p. 6.
22. *Winter Soldier Investigation,* p. 14.
23. *Winter Soldier Investigation,* p. 118.
24. "Crimes," pp. 13-15.
25. Pratt and Blair, p. 144.
26. Charles J. Levy, "ARVN as Faggots," in *Transaction,* vol. 8, #12 (October 1971), p. 23.
27. My Lai vet quoted by Lifton, p. 189.
28. Levy, p. 26.
29. *Winter Soldier Investigation,* p. 28.
30. Lifton, p. 54.
31. *Winter Soldier Investigation,* p. 94.
32. Levy, p. 21.
33. "The Crime on Hill 192," in *South Viet Nam in Struggle* #50 (December 20, 1969), p. 7.
34. Nguyen Thanh Son, "Wicked Schemes," in *Women of Viet Nam* #2 (1972), p. 17.
35. "Crimes," p. 7.
36. Huyn Thi Kien interview with Anne Dockery and Karen Kearns, "I Wanted to Spit in Their Faces," *Liberation News Service* #328 (March 24, 1971), p. 7.
37. Both of these reports are from Wikler, pp. 190-194.
38. Lifton, p. 271.

Liberation forces did not fire on GI's wearing this button.

5.
MASS
PRODUCTION
OF
PROSTITUTES

The half million GI's in Viet Nam were looked upon not as defenders of freedom but as consumers. Sex was the biggest product.
        —*Richard Boyle, author of* The Flower of the Dragon

At the height of U.S. troop occupation, there were four hundred thousand prostitutes in South Viet Nam, nearly one for every GI. This is twenty times as many prostitutes as the combined total of women doctors and professionals. These prostitutes are the end product of a process that began when Diem started rounding up his opponents and forcing them into concentration camps in 1956. A Harvard professor who advises the State Department explained why the U.S. tried to "empty" the countryside of Viet Nam of its people, as a "solution to popular wars of national liberation":

Time in South Viet Nam is increasingly on the side of the [Thieu] *government. But in the short run, with half the population still in the countryside, the Viet Cong will remain a powerful force which cannot be dislodged from its constituency so long as the constituency continues to exist.* [1]

By 1973, as a result of forced urbanization, bombings, and defoliation making the land barren, peasants had swollen the population of Saigon to over four million. In 1954, the entire population of Saigon was only four hundred thousand.

"Grab 'em by the balls and their hearts and minds will follow."
—U.S. Marine commander describing rural pacification program

The United States Senate Subcommittee on Refugees estimates that between 1965 and 1973, more than ten million people were forced to flee their villages. Before 1966, some of these people may have fled their homes because they believed U.S. propaganda about the evils of the NLF. But by mid-1966, with the establishment of "free fire zones" —rural areas where all living matter was considered targets for U.S. firepower—as well as search-and-destroy missions, defoliation and the arrival of armored personnel carriers mashing rice fields, there is no doubt that nearly all were fleeing the U.S. invaders.

At the same time that artillery and bombing raids against the people in the countryside escalated, U.S. policy makers stepped up a psychological war campaign. Blizzards of leaflets fell on villages. At first, they had pictures of blackened fields of rubble with the caption: "If you support the Vietcong, your village will look like this." Other leaflets, perhaps written by experts who understood that the villagers were sisters, brothers and parents of "Vietcong," dispensed with all mention of politics. Here is the full text of one such leaflet:

[Headline] Here Is the Giant B-52 Bomber [with picture].
[Text] Friends, you have experienced several terrible bombing raids, sowing death and destruction. The area where you are living will be bombed again, but you will never be able to know at what time it is to happen. The aircraft will fly extremely high, and you will not possibly be able to see or hear them. They will sow death among you but not tell you first. Hurry up and leave this region in order to save your life. Use this leaflet or the Pass Permit of the nationalist government to approach the nearest government outpost. The people and the army of the Republic of Viet Nam will greet you happily. [2]

Chemical defoliants and bombs have destroyed sixty per cent of the arable land in South Viet Nam. By making the countryside unlivable, U.S. policy makers hoped to be able to get Vietnamese peasants to renounce the liberation struggle and obediently follow the Saigon-based regime. But conditions in the refugee camps and cities only succeeded in winning more support for the liberation struggle. Refugees were not simply forced to change addresses. They were plunged into a totally alien and hostile environment. Thousands were corralled into barbed-wire enclosures with no land to till, no rivers to fish, no schools or sanitary facilities. After untangling enormous red tape, refugees may have gotten one pound of rice and eight piasters a day for the first sixty days in the camp—when corrupt officials didn't pocket it. With inflation, a small grapefruit or tiny bunch of bananas cost five hundred piasters. [3]

Counter-insurgency experts made a concerted effort to settle refugees around U.S. bases and along major highways to discourage "enemy attacks." An American reporter gives us this image of these barren "New Life Villages":

Around American bases . . . there had grown up entire towns made up of packing cases and waste tin from canning factories—entire towns advertising Schlitz, Coke and Pepsi a thousand times over. The "food," "shelter," and "jobs" that Westmoreland had promised came to this: a series of packing case towns with exactly three kinds of industry: the taking of American laundry, the selling of American soft drinks to American soldiers and prostitution for the benefit of Americans. [4]

Even after the signing of the Paris Peace Agreement in January 1973, and in direct violation of the Agreement, Thieu continued to force refugees to settle in areas where he thought he could control them. [5] Articles 2 and 3 of the Cease Fire Protocol guarantee the rights of freedom of movement and residence to all South Vietnamese civilians, and Article 5 calls for the removal of all devices that hamper the population's movement. But Thieu ordered:

Arrest and detain those persons who incite the people to leave those areas controlled by the government in order to go into communist controlled zones or vice versa. If they protest, they will be shot. [6]

In some areas, Thieu did not allow the people to work in their own outlying fields for fear they might come under "communist control." [7] Nevertheless, in spite of the tight security, thousands of people managed to escape the camps or take them over. Before leaving, they often left slogans painted on the walls like: "Hang the Americans and the American puppets." [8]

The final act of the refugee drama came in the spring of 1975. As ARVN crumbled and abandoned the cities, thousands of people seemed to be fleeing from the liberation forces. A few, who had grown rich serving Thieu and the U.S., fled with suitcases full of money in order to preserve their privileged way of life. Most fled because they expected the cities to be bombed by Thieu's air force or because fleeing ARVN troops took them hostage. Others fled because they were the victims of a systematic psychological warfare campaign that the CIA's Colonel Lansdale first began in 1954. The *Pentagon Papers* show that for 20 years, the CIA and Pentagon have been weaving an elaborate web of lies and "dirty tricks" designed to make the South Vietnamese people hate and fear the "Viet Cong."

When the total liberation of South Viet Nam was imminent, the U.S. used this psychological, as well as physical, coercion to evacuate thousands of Vietnamese from the country. U.S. government propaganda headlined "Terrorized Refugees Flee Communism" in an attempt to justify years of U.S. aggression. A few of those who left were high-level Thieu officials who might have been punished by the PRG. But most of the people who left were forced evacuees who would have preferred to stay had they been given an informed choice. This forced evacuation was in direct violation of the Paris Peace Agreement. The Provisional Revolutionary Government of the Republic of South Viet Nam (PRG) has stated that all forced evacuees are welcome to return to Viet Nam without fear of reprisals.

Spirals of dependency and corruption

Unemployment, inflation and corruption are terms which hardly begin to describe the Saigon-controlled economy where more than four million former peasants had no work; where the piaster, which was once equal to one cent, in the end barely valued one-fourth of a cent; and where Thieu's Under-Secretary of the Ministry of Revolutionary Development—responsible for the Pacification Program—was a pimp. The economy was totally dependent on American money. Revenues that the Thieu regime got from taxes were less than one per cent of what the U.S. spent in South Viet Nam on military aid.

This dependency created a spiral of corruption and increased dependency that killed native industry and invested any available cash in luxury goods to sell to Americans, to prosperous pimps and prostitutes, and to Saigon's generals. Scrap metal—the remains of U.S. planes and other war materiel—made up ninety per cent of the exports from the Republic of South Viet Nam. In 1967, there were four hundred opium dens in Saigon. Three years later, there were three hundred thousand. Indochina, with the encouragement of the CIA and Air America, became the hub of international heroin traffic. The CIA bought the loyalty of many Vietnamese officials with the proceeds from this booming trade. [9]

Officially, the Thieu regime maintained that prostitution, like heroin, was illegal. But a Saigon official candidly explained:

The Americans need girls; we need dollars. Why should we refrain from the exchange? It's an inexhaustible source of U.S. dollars for the State. [10]

"Saigon has become an American brothel." —Senator Fulbright

In Saigon, there's a street named *Tu Do,* which means liberty. According to two Frenchmen who spent several years in Saigon:

Ask any Vietnamese and she or he will tell you, "Take liberty street, that means take the liberty to do absolutely anything!" [11]

Tu Do was the main street of the red light district. There were more than two hundred agencies known to recruit young girls from the provinces to serve in the twenty-one thousand bars, hotels and whorehouses in Saigon. The prostitute scene in Saigon has fascinated American journalists who often give the impression that women have "profited" from U.S. troop occupation. But some describe the grim reality:

There is a woman who directs a group of deaf and dumb prostitutes—most of them 14 and 15 years old, some even younger. They cluster nightly at the corner of Tu Do Street nearest the Continental Hotel, usually just before curfew hour. . . . At this time of night, there are prostitutes—among them some who I have watched grow old and tight-faced in the last ten years—standing at street corners all over town hoping to be picked up by late cruising customers. At this hour too, pimps haul their girls around on the backs of motorcycles and offer them at bargain prices. [12]

At the height of GI occupation, some prostitutes may have become rich by Vietnamese standards, but all were subject to brutal exploitation. One veteran who had been stationed in Pleiku said that in "Sin City," which appeared within three months after the base was built, a room in the whorehouse—actually a tent—would have fifteen or twenty beds. He remembered: "They got 300 piasters a lay." Three hundred piasters were officially equal to three dollars, but with black market prices, it came to about one dollar. If the prostitutes tried to get more money, U.S. Military Police would declare their establishments off limits. Similar "strips" appeared wherever there were U.S. bases. The strip at Phu Loi, however, operated only during daylight hours because the NLF controlled the countryside in that area at night. [13]

Among the four hundred thousand prostitutes, there were many varieties, each suited to the different needs of her clients. In provincial outposts, some provided multiple services as indicated by the following sign: *"Car Wash and Get Screwed."* Since many white GI's wouldn't

go with women they had seen with Black GI's, some prostitutes learned American habits of discrimination. A GI could "rent-a-wife" by the day, week or month. These marriages were outright slavery where the woman became servant and sex object. Many GI's preferred to rent wives because the faithful wife was less likely than the prostitute to catch and pass on V.D. In Viet Nam, GI's sometimes lived in luxury previously reserved for high colonial administrators:

Like I had, ah, it sounds kinda strange, but I had a houseboy and at first I had a girl to come in and she'd shine my shoes and make my bed, do my laundry, just anything entailed in taking care of my house for a grand total of $7 per month. [14]

The varieties of pimping were also infinite. In Chi Hoa Prison, a small city of ten thousand prisoners within Saigon before liberation, there was an infirmary room where certain "nurses" sold their charms to the richest prisoners. They were part of the prison staff. The prison administration—the same ones responsible for the systematic torture of political prisoners—took a substantial cut of the "nurses' fees." [15]

As GI's left Viet Nam, the prostitutes remained, trapped in a cycle of heroin addiction and poverty. The most attractive ones serviced the fifteen thousand U.S. "civilians" who remained in Viet Nam as advisors to Thieu's army and police until all U.S. personnel were forced to leave by the victorious liberation forces. But most prostitutes lived on the brink of starvation.

Thieu made a display of breaking up some prostitution rings, but his real purpose was to gain control of Saigon's most lucrative businesses. The pattern of women's degradation continued, however, as illustrated in an article which appeared in a Saigon newspaper. It exposed the practice of kidnapping young girls from the countryside, especially from refugee camps, and selling their virginity for $250 to $300. Mrs. "Boiling Water Six," who ran the operation until April 1974, kept the girls shut up in secret caves and had them beaten when they screamed for help. The girls were summoned from the caves only long enough to give their favors to foreign and Vietnamese businessmen and U.S. advisors. The girls' abductors originally enticed them to leave the countryside by offering them respectable jobs in textile factories and rich people's homes. The girls believed the promises because they were made by women posing as charity ladies. [16]

Seduce and destroy missions

A Vietnamese proverb speaks of the lotus:

The lotus lives in the mud, but does not have its stench.

In Viet Nam, prostitutes were often thought of as "lotus," and maintained their "moral fragrance" by finding ways to aid the liberation struggle. Demonstrators demanding peace and withdrawal of American troops always knew they could count on receiving refuge in the prostitutes' quarters after the Saigon police broke up their demonstrations. The U.S. Army once discovered a cache of explosives inside Bien Hoa Air Base which had been smuggled past the gate by women who appeared to be prostitutes. Who knows how much of the chronic sabotage inside U.S. bases was done by women thought to be prostitutes?

Probably the most valuable contribution that prostitutes have made towards the liberation of Viet Nam has been the information they have gained and passed on to the liberation forces. GI's with little respect for women would talk freely to these women. Those prostitutes who gathered around bases kept careful track of all supplies coming and going, and often had the opportunity to pace off the exact dimensions and layout of supply depots, storage areas, recreation areas and communications centers. More than one woman soldier in the People's Liberation Army was discovered to have valid gate passes giving her access to U.S. bases.

GI jokes tried to cover their fear. Tales of "seduce and destroy missions" were rampant. They recounted the dangers of being disarmed by Saigon whores. But in reality, it was nearly impossible for GI's to conceive of enemy women as "soldiers." To them, PLAF women could only be "whores," servants or playthings for the PLAF troops. U.S. reporters perpetuated the myth that these women were camp followers, so most readers of the U.S. press remained ignorant of the role of women in the PLAF as fighters.

The average U.S. foot soldier did not want to be in Viet Nam. He might count off the days he had left to serve on a picture of a nude woman divided into 365 parts. As each day passed, he colored in another section of the body. [17]

On the other side, as a soldier in the PLAF, a Vietnamese woman resolved to continue fighting until the last American aggressor left Viet Nam and her people were free. When she rested between battles, she had no interest in visiting "Sin City." She might spend her free time reading from the national epic poem *Kieu*. And she knows Ho Chi Minh's last words by heart:

> *We must keep firm our resolve to fight the U.S. aggressors*
> *Until total victory.*
> *Our mountains will always be.*
> *Our rivers will always be.*
> *Our people will always be.*
> *The American invaders defeated,*
> *We will rebuild our land ten times more beautiful.*

National mutilation or "removing natural Asian defects"

Ho's words fell on the deaf ears of Saigon surgeons trained in the United States to help the war wounded. These doctors went, instead, into the lucrative business of reshaping the bodies of Vietnamese women to conform to American standards of beauty. According to an article in the *New York Times:*

Dr. Ban will convert what he refers to as "natural Asian defects" within an hour. (He has a team of five doctors.) He also said, "By removing a woman's complexes we give her confidence and transform her psychology. It's a lot of fun." [18]

Thousands of Vietnamese women have undergone the ordeal of cosmetic surgery to be more appealing to their customers from the USA. Rounder eyes, breasts expanded with silicone, noses reshaped with silicone, hips padded with silicone—all brought a higher price from GI " johns," and became a necessity for the livelihood of many Vietnamese prostitutes and bar girls. The article continued:

The fashion doesn't stop there [at eyes and breasts]. In their eagerness to imitate Europeans, some Vietnamese want bigger noses, dimpled cheeks, cleft chins . . . even fatter fingers. A pioneer in the operation is Mrs. Nguyen Cao Ky, the glamorous wife of the former Vice President. . . . Cosmetic surgery is still a risk, contends Dr. Thai Minh Bach who has performed the operation often, but says that he spends half his time patching up the mistakes of other surgeons.

Many of the Vietnamese women who worked as waitresses or walked the streets could not afford to Westernize their bodies. But they did wear tags with their "western names." *Xuan*, which means "spring" in Vietnamese, became "Ann." *Phuong*, which means "flower," became "Fran." Some GI's complained that prostitutes stole from them. But more would joke about how they could bribe a woman to bed with a can of "hair spray" which was really spray starch. Few of the women could read English labels. [19]

In addition to new names and cosmetic surgery, the Americans have also brought to Saigon topless restaurants and CIA-sponsored cultural magazines with editorials like: "What is happiness? No such thing exists. Only acceptance is real. To accept, that's all." [20]

The roller derby, seen on an American military TV station, inspired Le Huu Tai, a millionaire, to set up a skating rink where people skated to the rhythm of hard rock sounds:

Certainly you can see this is a civilized way of life. It gives the impression of the American way of life, and certainly the American way of life is civilized. This contributes to civilization here. [21]

But most Vietnamese believe that Le Huu Tai is a traitor. They're repulsed by the "American civilization" as they have seen it in Viet Nam. Millions of people preferred to live in bomb shelters in the countryside, far from the corruption of Saigon. Thousands who lived in the occupied cities maintained their dignity by making the streets unsafe at night for any member of the occupying army, by demonstrating, by striking, by all forms of resistance. After the signing of the Paris Peace Agreement, more and more people tried to return to the countryside, even at the risk of being shot by Thieu's police.

In early 1974, more than a year before the PRG took power in Saigon, a member of the Viet Nam Women's Union told Jane Fonda:

You mustn't be discouraged when you see the situation in Saigon today. We will have an enormous job [of cleaning it up], but I know from our experience that it can be done. [22]

Her optimism had a solid foundation. The Political Program of the NLF in 1960 and the Program of Action of the PRG adopted in 1968 both affirmed the commitment to:

Combat the U.S.-imported slavish and depraved culture and education, which are impairing our people's fine cultural traditions. . . .

On April 1, 1975, as the campaign to liberate the South was nearing its end, the PRG issued a ten-point policy for governing newly liberated areas. The policy banned all agencies that promoted the alien culture which degraded women.

As soon as Saigon was liberated, a ban was placed on prostitution and PRG women cadre launched an enormous campaign to find housing, food and new skills for the thousands of unemployed. In some districts, the people took over abandoned villas left by fleeing U.S. advisors and turned them into dormitories and re-education centers for women who had been prostitutes. Students and other young people took the initiative in cleaning the streets and painting over signs and billboards that insulted women.

Twenty years ago, women in the North undertook a similar task. The Viet Nam Women's Union was able to eliminate prostitution entirely within two years after the French left and to integrate 30,000 ex-prostitutes into the new society. Today, women in the South have begun to apply the lessons of their Northern sisters to ensure an independent dignified life for all women.

Notes

1. Samuel Huntington, "The Bases of Accommodation," *Foreign Affairs,* July 1968, pp. 652-653.
2. Quoted by Earl Martin, "Refugees in Viet Nam," *Indochina Chronicle* #25 (June 11, 1973), p. 6. This publication and Ngo Vinh Long's "Refugees: Thieu's Other Political Prisoners," *Thoi Bao Ga* #38-39 (August-September 1973), are both excellent sources of information on refugees in Viet Nam.
3. Luce and Sommer, p. 170, and Ngo Vinh Long, "South Viet Nam's Economy," *Thoi Bao Ga* #19 (December 1971), p. 2.
4. Fitzgerald, pp. 352-353.
5. Joseph Treaster, "Saigon's Transfer of Refugees Is Protested," *New York Times,* March 24, 1973.
6. Quoted by Earl Martin,
7. *Christian Science Monitor,* January 29, 1973.
8. Earl Martin, p. 7.
9. Information on the opium dens is from Fitzgerald, p. 385. Frank Browning and Banning Garrett exposed CIA involvement in heroin trade in "New Opium War," *Ramparts,* May 1971. Since then an entire book has been written on the subject by Alfred McCoy: *The Politics of Heroin in South East Asia* (New York: Harper, 1973).
10. Quoted by Thanh Nam, "In the Shadow of the American Embassy in Saigon," *South Vietnam in Struggle* #164 (September 11, 1972), p. 2.
11. Jean-Pierre Debris and Andre Menras, *We Accuse* (Indochina Mobile Education Project, 1973), p. 4.
12. *New Yorker,* April 15, 1972, pp. 52-54.
13. Jonathan Schell, *The Village of Ben Suc* (New York: Vintage, 1967), pp. 108-109.
14. Veteran Kallis, quoted in Wikler, p. 136. Other information in this paragraph comes from Wikler, pp. 136, 170, and from many other reports by Viet Nam veterans about prostitution.
15. Debris and Menras, p. 73.
16. *Dien-Tin* (Saigon newspaper) ran a series of articles on this operation for the first two weeks of April 1974. Thanks to Tran Khanh Tuyet for translating and summarizing them for me.
17. Debris and Menras, p. 73.
18. *New York Times,* May 21, 1973.
19. Blair and Pratt, p. 137.
20. Ann Froines, "The Cultural War: Smack, Pimps and Coca-Cola," *University Review,* April 1972, p. 19.
21. *New York Times,* July 1, 1973, p. 4.
22. Jean Horan interview with Jane Fonda, in *Off Our Backs,* vol. 4, #4 (March 1974), p. 4.

6.
ATTACK ON FUTURE GENERATIONS

When you carry your child nine months in your womb, bear it in labor
with death all around you, only to find that the monstrous weapons of
imperial technology have assaulted you even there, you carry the war
deep inside you.
   —*Sheila Rowbotham, author of* Women, Resistance and Revolution

Many people are numb to the statistics that testify to the grim facts of
genocide and ecocide in Indochina. War makers encourage people not
to allow themselves to connect these cold statistics with the real suffering of women, children and men in Viet Nam. But it would be unreal to
discuss the oppression of women in Viet Nam without remembering the
U.S. government's attempts to destroy the Vietnamese people as a
race.

Scorched earth and Zippo brigades

   More than half of the territory of South Viet Nam has been sprayed
with a defoliant called "Agent Orange." "Agent Orange" contains di-
oxin—a chemical unrivaled in its power to deform the unborn babies
of pregnant women who ingest it, even in tiny amounts. It is truly rare
earth in South Viet Nam's countryside which was not sprayed with defoliant. U.S. planes directly sprayed more than ten per cent of the
South Vietnamese population with this chemical. In Hanoi, the
Institute for Protection of Mothers and Children has found that expec-
tant mothers exposed to "Agent Orange" have six times more chromo-
somic breaks than survivors of Hiroshima. [1] They give birth to babies
with flippers instead of arms and legs, babies without tear ducts,
babies with kidney defects, babies with brain damage and pointed
heads.
   During the heavy carpet bombing in bothNorth and South, U.S.
aircraft timed their raids to take the greatest toll of lives. They attacked
factories during shift change, population centers during meal times or
while people slept, churches during mass, schools during class hours,
and marketplaces while they were crowded with shoppers. Most of the
victims were women and children. The men were away at the front. [2]
   Women living in "free fire zones" had to endure incessant attack.
They reported:

In some areas, helicopter gunships hovered overhead ready to strafe
any moving individual. In others helicopters circled all night, their
powerful searchlights illuminating the terrain ("So bright that you can
see a needle on the ground"), uninterruptedly strafing the pathways so
that movement was impossible. B-52's joined the assault. . . . "Each

morning, when we wake up, we don't know whether we are living until we open our eyes." [3]

In the South, "Zippo Brigades" left surviving women and their families homeless. L/Cpl Thomas Heidtman, 1st Marine Division, testified:

He [the company commander] said, "We're going to have a zippo inspection right now." And I would say approximately two-thirds of the entire company had Zippo lighters. We held them up, lit them, demonstrated that they were filled, would burn. Then put them away. He smiled and let it go at that. We went out. I would say at least fifty per cent of the villages we passed through would be burned to the ground. There was no difference between the ones we burned and the ones we didn't burn. It was just that where we had time, we burned them. [4]

What they didn't burn, they flooded. The Pentagon has admitted that after deliberately bombing dikes, Phantom jets would seed clouds with silver and lead iodide. According to an article in the *Los Angeles Times,* May 19, 1974, U.S. military experts claimed that they intended to make the "Ho Chi Minh Trail" impassable. But the fact is that thousands of people lost their homes in floods.

Separations and involuntary divorces

For the Vietnamese, the family has been at the center of their survival as a people. The history and wisdom of generations is present in each generation and passed on in a continuous flow of life. The disruption of this flow is a serious threat to past and future generations. Women, as bearers of the next generation, have been special targets of repressive, pro-U.S. regimes, since the earliest violations of the Geneva Accords. Diem's troops arrested and tortured women whose husbands had regrouped to the North and forced them to sign forms divorcing their husbands. These women had to remarry within a stipulated time as proof of their "sincerity." Diem's armed agents would seek out these woman, and, if the women hadn't found new husbands, they would rape them on the spot. Sometimes the men would invite the troops who had encircled the village to take turns in mass rape. [5]

Madame Nhu, Diem's sister-in-law, became powerful by serving American interests in Viet Nam. It's ironic that at the same time Diem's troopers were forcing village women to divorce their husbands, Madame Nhu was trying to present herself as a crusader for women's rights by outlawing polygamy and divorce. But her loyalties were to Catholic doctrine, not to women.

In spite of Diem and his successors, family bonds remained strong. During the years that the U.S. forced the partition of the North and South, loyalty to distant family members became a militant defense of one's political principles. One Southern woman echoed many when she refused to denounce her revolutionary husband who was living in the North. When the police insisted she denounce her husband, she told them:

I could not denounce my husband. He is in my heart. If you want me to denounce him, kill me and take out my heart. [6]

But nearly every Vietnamese family, northern and southern, has endured painful separations and losses—with so many away fighting or killed. Liberation Army members are volunteers. Their families missed them but were also proud of them. The majority of Thieu's million-man army were conscripted against their will. Thieu also deliberately kept families torn apart, within the South, in an effort to prevent people from leaving the areas under his control. He hoped his policy of "shooting on the spot" anyone who tried to flee to "communist-held areas" would enable him to maintain his constituency.

Thieu used terror to get family members to betray each other. For example, he arrested the sister-in-law and brother of Madame Binh, Foreign Minister of the PRG. U.S. interrogators tried to get the couple to sign statements denouncing Madame Binh. When they refused, their child was taken away and is presumed dead. [7]

"The North and South are kith and kin"

This is the slogan painted on the arch at the south end of the Ben Hai River at the 17th parallel—the temporary demarcation line between North and South.

When I was in the North in the fall of 1974, it seemed like half the people present at most meetings were Southerners. They had gone North in 1954 when the Viet Minh regrouped. They fulfilled their obligations under the Geneva Accords and they expected to return home within two years when reunification was promised. Instead, many of them had not seen their families in twenty years. One of them was Vo Thi The, a national leader of the Viet Nam Women's Union in the North who had once taught literature in Hue. She explained to others:

I turn suffering into hatred to fight for the reunification of our family. I'm determined to sacrifice all my personal life to the service of the revolution. Our whole people are inspired to fight, struggle for reunification to be able to live under the same roof. Members of all our families are in both North and South. [8]

This poem, written by a woman in the North, long before the total liberation of the South, anticipated how her family would be reunified and future generations protected:

WINTER MONSOON

I lie here listening to the winter monsoon
Wail in the night and I think of you.
Little daughter dear,
Have you gone to sleep or lie you there awake?
Who is looking after you my child?
Who picks up your blanket
when you drop it in your sleep,
your plump fingers exposed to the cold?
How I crave to hug you, and kiss your lips,
and put my cheek against yours
and caress your shoulders,
Oh my little daughter.
Without you how the bed looks forlorn!
Can there be in this world
more grieved mothers?
In your letter you said, "I dreamt of you, mother."
No, my child, it won't help to dream,
Let us be back together,
By destroying the enemy.

The U.S. attempted to partition Viet Nam permanently by pounding the land on both sides of the 17th parallel with enough bombs to make it unlivable. Vo Ninh Village in Quang Binh province, about thirty miles north of the 17th parallel, was a typical target. When we visited there, our host apologized for the makeshift conditions— thatch and mud huts. She explained that people had only recently emerged from living in underground tunnels and caves.

U.S. planes dropped 94 bombs per person on our village—not including pellet bombs which were too many to count . . . . Nevertheless, we continued to help our kith and kin in the South, no matter the consequences. We kept the roads repaired so the supply lines stayed open.

In a farewell toast to us, a member of the Quang Binh Women's Union executive committee celebrated the signing of the Paris Peace Agreements which ended the bombing of the North and added:

American women must know that our sisters in South Viet Nam are the other half of our bodies, so we are still aching.

That was in September 1974, seven months before they could celebrate total victory.

The kidnapping

In April 1975, the U.S. government airlifted between eight and ten thousand children from Viet Nam. They were carelessly loaded into cargo planes, unsafe for human transportation. On April 4, 1975, more than 150 children died when one of the cargo planes crashed.

President Ford, in a display of humanitarian concern, personally welcomed the next planeload of children. On April 7th, the *San Francisco Chronicle* reported that fifteen thousand U.S.-supplied anti-personnel bombs were dropped on the coastal cityof Nha Trang. And more babies arrived in San Francisco.

Between April 21 and April 25, hundreds of asphyxiation bombs, CBU-55's, made in the U.S., were dropped on the Xuan Loc area. These ultra-lethal bombs, banned by international conventions, cause instant death by suffocation to any living thing within a 750-foot radius. On April 25th, the *San Francisco Chronicle* announced that the wife of a retired U.S. Army colonel would care for 100 handicapped Vietnamese children. She claimed: "They would have been killed by the communists because they are unacceptable in a communist society."

Nothing could be further from the truth. In Hanoi, a U.S. reporter heard:

We have struggled and sacrificed for thirty years so that our children's generation could live in peace. This kidnapping is another form of genocide against the Vietnamese people. [9]

The motivating force behind "Operation Babylift" was military politics, not humanitarianism. In the spring of 1975, the world watched panic-stricken ARVN soldiers trampling civilians in order to escape liberation forces. This spectacle convinced nearly everyone that Thieu's end was near. But the U.S. Ambassador in Saigon, Graham Martin, and President Ford clung to the hope that if Congress granted $700 million in emergency aid to Saigon, the tide might change.

Polls showed that seventy-eight per cent of the people in the U.S. were against any further intervention in Viet Nam. Congress balked at supporting a loser. In a last ditch effort to rally support for a bankrupt policy in Viet Nam, Ford and Martin engineered "Operation Baby-lift." Even corrupt Saigon officials objected to the plan. But Thieu's Welfare Minister finally consented and explained why:

He [the U.S. Ambassador] stressed that this evacuation along with the millions of refugees abandoning Communist-controlled zones will help create a shift in American public opinion in favor of the Republic of Viet Nam. Especially when these children land in the U.S., they will be subject to television, radio and press agency coverage and the effect will be tremendous.[10]

This politician knew that most of the children were not orphans. Anxious Saigon mothers sometimes placed their children in orphanages to protect them from the shelling. Others left children temporarily in the care of orphanages because they could not afford to feed them at inflated Saigon prices. Some of the children lived with their parents but got picked up arbitrarily by U.S. adoption agents. Some of the children did lose their parents in the war but should have stayed in Viet Nam where there is a long tradition of community care for orphans.

Despite the best intentions of adopting families in the U.S., adoption became one more insult to the people of Viet Nam—a denial of their national traditions and integrity. There are no orphanages in the DRV. Relatives, friends and neighbors raised the children who lost their parents. During Christmas, 1972, when Nixon sent B-52's to bomb Hanoi, hundreds of children lost their parents overnight. The Vietnamese politely turned down offers from friends all over the world who wanted to adopt the children. Instead, the children's neighbors adopted them, so the children would not have to leave their home streets, let alone their native country.

Organizers of "Operation Babylift" claimed they were rescuing children fathered by Black GI's from the racist hatred of the Vietnamese people. But Viet Nam is not a racist society. There were many children in Viet Nam fathered by Senegalese or Moroccan troops who

Le Van Dang lost both parents and his arms in a B-52 raid on Quang Tri. He is a hero because he taught himself to write.

fought for the French. They have grown up in the DRV enjoying the same rights as any Vietnamese citizen. It is also important to note that many of the children thought to have Black GI fathers were, in fact, members of the dark-skinned national minorities native to Viet Nam.

Many of the families in the U.S. who adopted the children sincerely believed they were acting in the best interests of the children. They were, however, blind to the reality in the U.S. where all non-white children must face constant racist oppression. "Operation Babylift" officials claimed that every child was already adopted before leaving Saigon. But volunteers at the receiving center in the U.S. Army Presidio, San Francisco, described a scene that resembled an auction block. One AID official told a reporter that the babies were "adoptable, exportable and ready to move."[11] Some adoption agencies made a lot of money moving them.

"Operation Babylift" ended with the liberation of Saigon. The kidnapping was the final atrocity in a long line of atrocities committed against the Vietnamese people. The U.S. government has responsibility for returning the children to their homeland. The best way to care for the children would be to contribute to healing the wounds of war in Viet Nam as stated in Article 21 of the Paris Peace Agreements.

Reunions

The President of the Women's Union of Quang Tri, Tran Thi Hong, welcomed us to South Viet Nam. Quang Tri became the first liberated province of South Viet Nam on May 1, 1972 and she explained the significance of their victory:

It was a dream fulfilled to drive the enemy out of our land and smash his scheme to divide our country at the Ben Hai River.

When Quang Tri was liberated, family and friends in the 23 villages— villages which were arbitrarily separated by the 17th parallel—were reunited.

Each time the PRG liberated an area, it followed a strict policy of "national reconciliation and concord"—a policy that facilitates the reunification of families and friends. To implement this policy, the PRG encourages those men who were drafted into Thieu's army (ARVN) to return to their villages without fear of reprisals. Returning ARVN soldiers settle on new plots of land, allotted to all Vietnamese, and are given building materials and seed to begin a new life. Families and community members accept them as long as they join in the task of rebuilding the war-torn country.

Immediately after Danang was liberated on March 29, 1975, more than one hundred thousand ARVN troops returned to their native villages. In May, the PRG predicted that within six months after total liberation, all people in the South would be able to return home.

Within days of the liberation of Saigon, Southerners who had been living in the North also began to return home. For the first time in twenty years, post, telephone, and roads linked Hanoi and Saigon. Trains and buses, loaded to capacity, headed south carrying thousands of eager people in search of their families. Trains and buses made the return trip full of Southerners who wanted to visit the North, curious about life there. By May 17th, there was a three-week waiting list for people wanting to make the journey.

Le Thi Thuy, who had been living in Hanoi for twenty years, was one of the first to return to Saigon. She is a native of Saigon, and went North in 1954, leaving her three- and four-year-old children with relatives. While she lived in the North, Thuy became a leader of the Viet Nam Women's Union—often speaking for Vietnamese women at international gatherings. Now she is home, working with her Southern sisters. Perhaps she is reunited with her children who became adults while the family was separated. The U.S. government claims that women like Thuy are "North Vietnamese cadre invading the South." But they are, in fact, Southern activists going home.

Notes

1. Dinh Nan Thang, "American Bombs and Defoliants," in *Women of Viet Nam #4* (1972), p. 11.
2. U.S. genocidal policies have been carefully documented by many authorities—both Vietnamese and Western. In his book, *Nuremberg and Viet Nam,* General Telford Taylor, U.S. Chief Counsel at the Nuremberg trials, argues that the U.S. is guilty of war crimes in Viet Nam. The book was published in New York by Bantam, 1971.
3. Quoted by David Hunt, "Organizing for Revolution in Viet Nam," *Radical America,* vol. 8, #1-2 (January-April 1974), pp. 39-40.
4. *Winter Soldier Investigation,* p. 26. For a detailed account of the total destruction of one Vietnamese village by the U.S. Army, see Jonathan Schell's *The Village of Ben Suc* (New York: Vintage, 1967).
5. Wilfred Burchett, *Viet Nam Will Win,* pp. 119-120.
6. "History of the Vietnamese Women's Movement." *Viet Nam Report #9* (April 1975) p. 9.
7. Jean Pierre Debris and Andre Menras. "The Policy of Slow Death." *Tricontinental #84* (1973) p. 12.
8. Kathleen Gough Aberle. "An Indochinese Conference in Vancouver." *Bulletin of Concerned Asian Scholars,* vol 3 #3-4 (Summer-Fall 1971) p. 4.
9. Unpublished letter from reporter, Linda Garrett, who was in Hanoi, April 28, 1975.
10. Letter of former Saigon Welfare Minister to ex-Premier Khiem. *New York Times,* April 7, 1975.
11. Reported by Steve Talbot, *Internews* (radio), April 12, 1975.

7.
WOMEN
IN CAGES

Before my arrest, I was, in fact, a mere civilian, a housewife. After my imprisonment I felt I should do something to contribute to the struggle of my people.
—Ding Thi Huong, who became a member of the Union of Women for the Liberation of South Viet Nam after six years in prison

There were at least a quarter of a million political prisoners in Thieu's jails in South Viet Nam. Nearly half were women. Some were arrested because they rejected the sexual advances of Thieu's soldiers. Some were arrested because they got caught up in indiscriminate round-ups. Some, like Ngo Ba Thanh, were arrested because they campaigned for peace. Some were arrested because they supported the Provisional Revolutionary Government.Hardly any of these women had trials and none had definite sentences.

Politics in a police state

Regardless of the situation at the time of arrest, there was only one basic reason why these people remained in jail—systematic terror and police-state tactics were the only way Thieu maintained his power as long as he did. By June 1974, people in Saigon-controlled areas faced the worst famine since 1945. Even high-ranking bureaucrats living in Saigon had to spend more than half their salaries on rice alone. The cost of living doubled between the time of the signing of the Paris Peace Agreement in January 1973 and the liberation of Saigon, April 30, 1975. People saw Thieu as the man responsible for the continuing separation of their families, for rampant disease and plague, for the packs of rats that invaded even the rich neighborhoods of Saigon, for corruption and heroin addiction, for the betrayal of the country. *Dan chu* is the Vietnamese word for democracy—literally, the sovereign people. Vietnamese people living under Thieu's so-called democracy changed the word to *dan chui*—meaning, the insulted people. [1]

Financed and supported by the U.S. government, Thieu continued to flaunt every article of the Paris Peace Agreement until his resignation. [2] His Air Force bombed PRG areas, his troops made forays into those liberated areas, and he refused to allow a free political contest in South Viet Nam. He knew that enforcement of the Paris Peace Agreement would quickly end his rule. The Agreement recognized two governments and two armies in South Viet Nam—the Thieu regime and the PRG. The Agreement also recognized "three political forces"—the Thieu regime, the PRG and the neutral Third Force—and stated that a National Council of National Reconciliation and Concord would include representation of all these forces. The Agreement gave the Council the responsibility for implementing the Paris Peace Agreement, achieving national reconciliation, insuring democratic liberties and, most important, organizing free elections in South Viet Nam in which:

The South Vietnamese people shall decide themselves the political future of South Viet Nam through genuinely free and democratic general elections under international supervision. [3]

The Third Force might have been an important key in breaking the deadlock between Thieu and the PRG through political rather than military means. But Thieu consistently denied the existence of an independent Third Force and insisted that the Third Force places at the Council be filled in equal numbers by him and the PRG. The Third Force was, in fact, an independent political tendency which stood for peace in Viet Nam, opposed Thieu, but had not joined the PRG. It was made up of a combination of urban people—students, intellectuals, Buddhists, Catholics and even civil servants within the Saigon regime who have grown increasingly hostile to U.S. intervention. Beginning in 1972, Thieu systematically arrested and tortured Third Force spokespeople and supporters in an attempt to prevent them from forming a coherent political organization.

Nevertheless, a number of leaders of the Third Force did emerge. Madame Ngo Ba Thanh provided a model of courage and persistence in opposing Thieu, and became a leading representative of the Third Force. She is a lawyer with degrees from the University of Strasbourg and Columbia University. Thieu first arrested her for being the founder and chairperson of the Women's Committee to Defend the Right to Live. She belonged to the urban upper class but during the two years she spent in prison she identified closely with peasant women and the urban poor who were her sisters in jail. In Chi Hoa Prison, she defied authorities with nightly "news broadcasts" and information bulletins to her fellow prisoners. Guards could only silence her by transferring her to Bien Hoa Prison and keeping her isolated. She and other members of the Women's Committee to Defend the Right to Live withstood brutal torture. But she told well-wishers who attended her court appearance:

Don't feel pity for us. As bad as we are treated in prison, we're freer than any of the functionaries of the Saigon regime. [4]

The Paris Peace Agreement provided for the release of all political prisoners. Thieu reclassified Ngo Ba Thanh, along with countless others, as a "common criminal" in order to get around his treaty obligations. She protested with an extended hunger strike, lasting months. Mounting political pressure finally forced Thieu to release Ngo Ba Thanh in late 1973. Although under constant surveillance and police harassment, Thanh joined with others who led the growing Third Force movement that contributed to Thieu's final downfall.

Days without sunlight, nights without fire

With ninety-two per cent of his budget coming from the U.S. and two million people unemployed, Thieu's power depended entirely on U.S. support. There were twenty-four thousand U.S. military personnel in South Viet Nam disguised in civilian clothes. Most of them "advised" Thieu's police and military apparatus after the signing of the Paris Peace Agreement. [5] The Thieu regime had 1.1 million men in the army, and admitted to having at least 120,000 policemen. There were four categories of police, plus hundreds of thousands of part-time informers who were regularly forced to give information to the police.

In Saigon, there was a policeman on every corner who spent his entire day stopping people at random and checking their ID cards. Anyone out after curfew was arrested. Every night thousands of police fanned out through Saigon to do house-to-house searches. Every household had a brown book in which each person in the family was listed by name, sex, job, and ID card number. When the police entered the house after curfew, everyone was brought out, and subject to arrest if those present didn't match the list in the brown book. Once arrested, the victim had little hope of being released until she or he signed a confession. This was the period when most of the tortures took place. Through torture, the police tried to get a confession and the names of other people who were "communists." Fred Branfman, an ex-AID functionary, insisted that "without this torture, the Thieu regime would fall." [6]

The torture was carried on so systematically and on such a mass scale that it was impossible for Thieu to hide it. [7] Debris and Menras, two Frenchmen jailed for two years in Chi Hoa, reported the special torture techniques reserved for women. They named Duong Van Chan as the man who ordered that live eels be inserted into the vaginas of women students, including the woman who was Vice President of the South Viet Nam Students' General Association. Young women were invariably forced to stand naked for hours in front of masked interrogators. The tormentors undertook endless intimate "examinations"; ran lizards over women's bodies; used cigarettes to inflict burns on nipples and methodically burnt off public hair; uncapped coke bottles, shook the contents vigorously and then inserted the bottle into the vagina; and took pleasure in rape, especially of virgins. [8]

Those who survived interrogation faced the continuous horror of conditions calculated to execute the prisoner slowly, over months, even years, of time:

> Living in two-meter cages, colder than rock hollows,
> Days without sunlight, nights without fire.
> Breathing nothing but a smell of human feces.
> Lying on muddy wooden boards,
> Fighting with rats,
> Keeping company with earthworms and crickets.
> Eating uncooked rice mixed with petroleum,
> Rotten salt-fish smelling of tainted flesh . . . [9]

There were special prisons for women—Phu Tai and Thu Duc—where thousands of women had to make army uniforms and mosquito nets in exchange for a bowl of rotten rice each day. In 1969, for the first time, women were taken to the infamous prison island of Con Son, also called Puolo Condor. They went on the boat which shuttles between Saigon and the island, traveling with the rats in the hold, chained on the floor perpetually damp with excrement, like the Africans in the old slave ships. [10]

In the face of torture, starvation, rats, vermin, disease—treatment that has crippled, maimed, and mutilated minds and bodies for life—women inside these jails became living models of the infinite capacity and possibility for human beauty and resistance. Every morning, prisoners were supposed to salute the Saigon flag, but many chose, instead, to face beatings and torture. A proverb etched on the wall in one cell begins to explain why these people were willing to sacrifice so much to maintain their dignity:

> The mountain is only so high, the river stops.
> Our capacity is without limit.
> The stars can move.
> Our will is unshakable.

In private, a prisoner recited the preferred version of the last sentence:

> The Americans can get to the moon,
> but they can never get past the determination
> of the Vietnamese people. [11]

At Con Son, prison guards beat many women for singing a liberation song on December 20, the anniversary of the founding of the NLF. One of them, Hien Luong, wrote this poem, celebrating the defiance of the sisters who had been brutalized:

SONGS THAT CANNOT BE SILENCED

Sing! Let us sing out,
Sing out again so our hearts may burst into flame
And our burning blood may finally melt these chains.
So that in the depth of the blackest night
The sun shines forever.

Here they come with their sticks
In the glacial silence
In the bolted cell
Their bloodshot eyes rivet on us
They hurl threatening words,
"Who's the bitch who had the nerve to sing?"

Mute rage engulfs our hearts
Our retort:
A willful silence.

After vain threats and questionings
Blows rain down.
So much flesh is torn
Over all the body, so much pain!

Then, my sister,
You stood up proud
Rising above the pack of killers
"Down with terror! Down with the brutes!"

Hand in hand,
Shoulder to shoulder:
A human wall
Will not give way.
Scarcely have they turned on their heels
Our laughter bursts out more brightly
Our voices rise more sweetly
More harmonious together
With a stronger beat
Defying the impotent rage of the guards.

Such power in such frail bodies—
Does it come from magic?

The next day, reprisals.
Aged mothers,
Little sisters, barely thirteen years old,
Beaten with the rest
Just for having sung.
"Who led the singing?"
Answer: a willful silence.
Cornered between the wall and the hard ground
They fell unconscious.
Awakening,
Into their ears glides the sweet lullaby of an elder sister
Like the voice of the native village.
Suddenly, on your trembling lips
Blooms the rose of a first smile
That no chains nor shackles can imprison! [12]

Minh

Minh was 22 years old when Jane Fonda interviewed her in Hanoi during the summer of 1972. She was there for medical treatment. Minh told why she had joined the NLF:

We have come to learn that we cannot be happy until the U.S. troops withdraw from Viet Nam and until we can determine our own lives.

Her job was to hide soldiers. She had been captured by Thieu's police three times, three times tortured, and three times she had managed to escape.

She told how Saigon soldiers forced her mouth open, poured soapy water down her throat until her belly got very swollen and then jumped on her stomach. During her interview with Jane, Minh suddenly bolted for the door. The other women in the room ran to her side and tried to calm her. She began to fight like an animal, very powerfully, and flail her arms. Finally, they had to pin her down to the ground where she continued to struggle. Then she began to pant, heavy like a large animal, and her voice, deep and angry, began to repeat the same thing over and over again very rapidly. Jane reported:

I will never forget the sound of her voice. I looked up and everyone in the room was crying and I asked what was happening. And they told me she was reliving the torture. They said she had these seizures regularly, every day, sometimes five times a day. I asked what she was saying and they told me, crying in admiration, that she was saying, "It doesn't matter what you do to me, I will never speak. We shall be free. It doesn't matter what you do to me, I shall never speak. We shall be free... [13]

Huyn Thi Kien also refused to talk when she was tortured. With the help of friends, she escaped to Hanoi, where she received an artificial leg to replace the one her torturers cut off. She explained how she was able to defy the torture:

I thought very hard and decided that I would rather die than let my comrades get arrested and be killed because of my information. . . . [They cut off one leg and after a month, she received word that they were planning to do the same to the other. The night before she knew she would be interrogated again . . .] I thought very hard about the terrible thing that would happen to me the next morning. I thought many things. I thought about how I joined the struggle to liberate the families and myself, my brothers and sisters and the villagers and the country in general. I thought that if I died, many others will live and fight for the cause I have followed. I was determined to keep my loyalty! "I cannot be bought off by the enemy, I cannot say anything about my comrades, I cannot betray the country. I would rather die." Thinking these things, I fell asleep, and in my mind I was ready to face anything. [14]

The next morning, mistaking her faint for death, her torturers did not completely sever her leg. A sympathetic prison nurse saved her and helped her to escape.

Mind vitamins

Some people did eventually talk—unable to endure torture indefinitely. But neither Minh nor Kien are "super-women." They represent hundreds of women who maintained their defiance in the face of torture because they gained unlimited strength from feeling themselves part of the struggle of an entire people. Every act of resistance became a "mind vitamin"—the prisoners said *thuoc bo*—for the rest. At Chi Hoa prison, the women had to be beaten unconscious before the guards were able to transfer them to Con Son. The rest of the prisoners protested with a hunger strike. [15] Another prisoner explained how unity among the prisoners made resistance possible:

We never started a hunger strike alone, separately. By the tens, by hundreds, and sometimes the whole prison went on strike. We even refused to drink. . . . That's what they were afraid of, the obstinate will, not of one, but of the whole collectivity . . . if need be, ready to die in support of their demands. To let a whole prison die would rouse public opinion, they would get into trouble from their bosses, since their job was not to do away with detainees, but to "convert" them. Especially as we always took care to present apparently harmless demands at first. . . . But the main thing was to compel them to give up to prove that they were not masters here. [16]

Women like Minh and Kien dedicated their lives to the national liberation of their people, refusing to compromise, because they knew this was the only way to survive. They maintained their resolve because they were sure of victory. This certainty made them know that their death, if it became inevitable, would not be wasted. They knew they would be avenged and they could not conceive of betraying either the memory of other fallen comrades or the struggle of those who fought on until total victory.

But most of the women in prison didn't talk because they had no information to divulge. They, in fact, had not taken an active part in the liberation struggle before their arrest. Peasant women who remained politically naive, more privileged bourgeois city women, and revolutionary women shared a common fate in prison. Prison became a school where jailers taught the barbarous nature of imperialist rule and inmates taught each other that the only way to remain human was to join with other prisoners, putting their principles before their personal self-interest.

The prisoners also found ingenious ways to hold literacy and technical education classes. A woman who had been in Phu Tai prison wrote about how they used the time in prison to make themselves more capable revolutionaries. She wrote:

The teachers were chosen among those of higher education . . . some of them had been to the seventh or even eighth grade. The earth floor was at the same time the "desk" for the teacher, the "blackboard" and "copybook" for the students. By turn we kept vigilance while the others studied . . . literature, history and mathematics. . . . We collected small pieces of paper from cement bags, boxes of sweets, cigarette packets thrown away by guards. As pencils, we used small sticks of bamboo; as for ink, we used soot mixed with water. The paper thus gathered was used for those of lower educational level. Most of the others used the floor. . . . It's not easy to describe fully the beatings and torture we were subjected to when small pieces of paper bearing the dates of May 19 [Ho Chi Minh's birthday] and September 2 [Independence Day] were discovered.

Once Mrs. H. was raped by torturers' dogs. Before dying, she gave to her neighbor a piece of cement-bag paper which had been

*cleaned for the fifth time. (We had decided that a piece of paper would
be unusable only after its seventh cleaning.)*

*... What we knew we taught to others. Anyone could be a teacher
and a student. There were regular examinations. At the end of a school
term, we passed to a higher grade. After seven years in Phu Tai, we
averaged the fourth grade, including those who did not know a single
word when they first came to prison. ... The beast-like American imperialists have tried all means to deceive us, for instance, by offering
better conditions to study in the U.S. if we married them. We rejected
their offer and continued our study in jail. ...* [17]

There were more than three thousand women detained in this prison.

Women in prison, living in rags without even a shred to clean
themselves during menstruation, found ways to comfort each other.
Their solidarity, combined with the atrocities of the wardens, and the
humanity of the NLF cadre in prison, convinced many women to join
the liberation forces while in prison. Their determination to be free became legends to inspire the growing strength of their sisters
everywhere.

Now, all the prisoners are free!

In the spring of 1975, as Thieu's army and police fled each newly-
liberated province, prisoners freed themselves, often with the help of
the local population. In some cases, Thieu's guards had received pan-
icky orders to liquidate all the prisoners. But, instead, many guards
aided in the release of the prisoners as an expresion of their support for
the new government. After the liberation of Saigon, prisoners freed
from Con Son Island Prison received a special heroes' welcome. They
have renamed the island "Vo Thi Sau"—after the youngest woman
prisoner ever executed there. With the Americans gone, the luxurious
home of U.S. Deputy Ambassador Lehman became the headquarters of
the Prisoners' Committee. This organization, which was once illegal
because it campaigned for prison reform, is now helping ex-prisoners
regain their strength and return to normal life.

Seventy per cent of the freed prisoners have TB. One hundred per
cent of the women contracted gynecological infections while in prison.
Some of those with the most severe medical problems are recovering
their health at the new center the PRG has organized in Dalat. This
central highlands city, a tourist resort built by the French, is famous
for its beauty and pleasant climate.

On April 29, 1975, one of them, Nguyen Thi Chau, was released
from Chi Hoa Prison when the guards fled. She had been tortured because she refused to denounce Ho Chi Minh. Now she is the President

of the People's Revolutionary Committee that governs 250,000 people in the 10th Precinct of Saigon. She joined the thousands of newly-independent South Vietnamese people who will heal their wounds as they build a new society.

Notes

1. Debris and Menras, *We Accuse,* p. 4.
2. For details of the violations of the Cease Fire Agreements check: Indochina Resource Center, Breakdown of the Vietnamese Ceasefire: The Need for a Balanced View" (pamphlet; Washington, D.C., 1974), and "The Paris Agreement on Viet Nam: One Year Later," *Indochina Chronicle* #30 (January 21, 1974).
3. These provisions are in Chapter IV of "Agreement on Ending the War and Restoring Peace in Viet Nam," signed January 27, 1973, in Paris by foreign ministers of USA, RVN, DRV and PRG.
4. Details about Madame Ngo Ba Thanh are from Debris and Menras, *We Accuse;* Indochina Peace Campaign, "Women under Torture," pp. 7-8; and "An Inhuman Court Session," *Women of Viet Nam* #2 (1972), pp. 15, 16, 31.
5. Statistics on Thieu's budget are from Guy Gran, "American Welfare Abroad—Aid to South Viet Nam," *Indochina Chronicle* #24 (April 8, 1973), p. 7. Details on U.S. personnel serving Thieu from "U.S. Civilians in S. Viet Nam," *Tricontinental News Service,* vol. 2, #3 (February 13, 1974), p. 17. Information on unemployment from "In the Cities," *South Viet Nam in Struggle* #229 (January 1, 1974), p. 3.
6. Fred Branfman, "Indochina Today: What 50,000 Americans Died For," *Liberation,* September-October 1973, pp. 10-11.
7. For detailed documentation of torture, see Don Luce, *Hostages of War* (Washington, D.C.: Indochina Mobile Education Project, 1973); Indochina Peace Campaign, "Women under Torture" (Santa Monica, 1973); *In Thieu's Prisons* (Hanoi: Foreign Languages Publishing House, 1973). However, the most vivid and understandable account comes from two men who spent two years in Thieu's prisons—Debris and Menras.
8. Debris and Menras, pp. 55-56.
9. Lines from a poem by an ex-prisoner, Nguyen Dan Trung: "Cries of Hatred from the Hell of Chin Ham," *News from Viet Nam* #6 (May 15, 1973), p. 2.
10. *In Thieu's Prisons,* pp. 75-81, and Debris and Menras, p. 37.
11. Debris and Menras, pp. 46-47.
12. Debris and Menras, pp. 47-48. A slightly different translation of the same poem is found in "Women under Torture."
13. Quoted in the script of the slide show *Women of Viet Nam,* by Nancy Dowd and Jane Fonda (mimeo, 1973; available from IPC).
14. Huyn Thi Kien, "I Wanted to Spit in Their Faces," *LNS* #328, pp. 7-8.
15. This occurred in November 1969 and was reported by Debris and Menras, p. 21.
16. Quoted by Nguyen Khac Vien, "With the Survivors from Saigon's Prisons," *Tricontinental News Service,* vol. 2, #3 (February 13, 1974), p. 22.
17. "Women under Torture," pp. 22-24.

8.
PEOPLE'S WAR IS WOMEN'S WAR

I am Minister of Foreign Relations and the head of the delegation representing the PRG at the Paris Conference, but I am also, and this to me is the most important post of all, Vice President of the Union of Women for the Liberation of South Viet Nam.

—*Nguyen Thi Binh*

Foreign troops, from France and the United States, and native Vietnamese people have battled on the same soil but they have fought different wars. The French and U.S. troops each fought a war of invasion, to maintain their colonial and imperial power. The Vietnamese people fought for a better life, for land for the peasants, for independence and reunification of their country.

Faced with more than a half-million U.S. soldiers trampling over South Vietnamese soil, with the most sophisticated intelligence gathering machinery in the world, with computers, electronic battlefields, chemical defoliants and millions of tons of bombs—one may wonder how the Liberation Army grew stronger and how its leaders avoided capture. The woman who commands the PLAF, General Nguyen Thi Dinh, recently disclosed that, in fact, she had been arrested several times. But her captors had no idea who she was. Once, sometime after 1965, when ARVN soldiers arrested her, many villagers—aware of her real identity—all went at once to the jail, insisted that she was their relative, and vouched for her political loyalty to the Saigon regime. She was released. [1] The only way for a small, poor country to defeat a large, technologically advanced country is to mobilize, educate, organize and arm the whole population to resist. For these reasons, the Vietnamese call their war "A People's War" and a just war. [2]

In 1951, Ho Chi Minh gave these instructions to the soldiers fighting the French:

We fight for the people. But we are not the "saviors" of the people. We have the duty to serve the people. All soldiers must gain the trust, respect and love of the people. You must conduct yourselves in such a way that when you have not yet arrived, people are waiting for you, when you arrive, people will help you, and when you leave, people will regret your departure. To accomplish this, the army must assist and love the people. Each soldier must be a propagandist by his or her own deeds.

A generation later, during a gathering celebrating the signing of the Paris Peace Agreement, Le Duan, one of the top leaders of the DRV, repeated that their commitment to the people was responsible for their victory:

We fight and we win not because we are endowed with steel skin and copper bones, but because we are human beings, real human beings.

*We are Vietnamese who are moral, loyal, patient, strong, indomitable,
but filled with compassion.* [3]

The first section of this book explains why women joined in this
People's War. Their reasons depend on when they joined, where they
lived and on their individual experiences. Some, like Vo Thi The,
fought on after 1954 to reunify the country so that their families could be
together again. Others, like Le Thi Hong Gam, were enraged by the
rape of their sisters and saw that the only way to stop assaults on
women was to get rid of the U.S. troops and to convince the Saigon
army to come over to the people's side.

More joined to avenge the deaths of people they loved. Thousands
joined local militia forces to defend their villages rather than be herded
into concentration camps. When peasant women realized that bombs
would fall on their homes whether or not they were resisting, they
inevitably decided to raise their chances for survival by joining the
liberation struggle and learning to operate anti-aircraft weapons. One
woman in the South joined the liberation struggle because she heard
that the police were planning to arrest and torture her to discover the
whereabouts of her brother:

*At least if I was going to get tortured, I might as well have done some-
thing so the pain was worth it.* [4]

Dinh Thi Huong spoke for many women who joined the liberation
forces after the horrors of false arrest and prison. [5]

People's War is also women's war because most women are poor
peasants and getting rid of feudal injustices is a primary goal of
People's War. The August Revolution of 1945 overthrew the feudal
state at the same time as it began the war of independence against
France. Whenever the people's army drove the French out of a new
region, the first thing they did was to confiscate French land and re-
divide it among the peasants. Vietnamese revolutionaries knew that
their struggle would be a protracted one because they needed many
years to wear down the strength of an enemy which initially had much
more power. They needed strong bases of resistance that could sustain
the war over generations. These bases or "liberated zones" are free
from feudal and colonial domination. This is how the Vietnamese
explain the functions of the liberated zone:

*The liberated zone plays the role of a strong rear-base of people's war.
It's a place for the armed forces to reorganize, train and rest. . . . It is
furthermore the starting point of attacks launched by liberation forces
against the enemy's refuges. It not only satisfies all the material requirements of the front, but is also the source of revolutionary enthusiasm for our armed forces and population. . . .* [6]

By continuing to meet as many of the people's needs as is possible, given the hard times and priorities of war, the liberation forces were constantly growing. One woman, who came from a very poor refugee family in the South, wanted to go to school, but couldn't afford the fees charged by Thieu's government. She joined the PRG because she knew that in the liberated territory she could receive a free education, equal to that which any man would receive.

Another woman also joined the National Liberation Front to escape the burdens of feudal patriarchy. She explained:

I considered my serving the Front an escape from all the hardships I endured while I lived with my mother-in-law before I joined the Front. She behaved very harshly towards me. It was also an opportunity for me to care for the people's welfare and happiness. That is what I liked most. [7]

Since 1954, the entire northern part of Viet Nam, the DRV, has been a liberated zone. Women there have made enormous strides towards their liberation. Women in the North felt strongly about protecting their homes from American bombers and defending what they have built since independence. They provided firm support for their sisters fighting in the South, while continuing their struggle in the North in whatever ways were needed.

No civilians

People's War is also women's war because women's participation is essential for its success. The concept that every citizen is a soldier and must be trusted is a tried and tested tradition. It was first used to defeat the Mongol invasion in the thirteenth century. During the People's Wars of this century, again, there are no civilians. A peaceful village one day may become a combat zone the next. The front is everywhere and everyone is involved in the fight.

For example, several years ago, an 88-year-old peasant woman was enraged by the atrocities of the foreign troops invading her village. She insisted that NLF cadre teach her how to trigger land mines. She waited six months for the opportunity and eventually killed two U.S. soldiers. Other GI's captured her, but they released her when she convinced them she was just an innocent grandmother. She became known as "Heroine Eighty-Eight." [8] Other old women smuggle rice or arms to younger women soldiers. Children deliver messages, students demonstrate, and invalids also have a role. Kien, whose leg was cut off during torture, now works in a liberation hospital. No one is unemployed.

Liberated zones and the territory of North Viet Nam may not have been subject to ground invasion, but both faced the daily battle with invading bombers. General Giap described the "ground against air" war as a new kind of People's War where everyone fights the enemy's air and naval forces, works to ensure communication and transport, engages in production, and fights to defend the North while serving the front in the South. [9] The Women's Union launched the "Three Responsibilities" Drive in the North in 1965 which specified women's indispensable role in this "New People's War." The Three Responsibilities were for production, the family and serving the front, fighting if necessary. In the course of this campaign, women have learned new professions and taken over key management roles in the economy.

The decisive victory of the Vietnamese people that forced the U.S. government to abandon all attempts at controlling South Viet Nam is impressive evidence of the strength of People's War. The goals and policies of People's War work to free women from feudal patriarchy and imperial oppression. The success of People's War requires the participation of everyone—especially women. We shall now see how in the process of working, demonstrating or bearing arms to free Viet Nam from foreign rule, the Vietnamese women have also begun to free themselves from their traditional oppression as women.

Notes

1. Nguyen Thi Dinh told this story to Jane Fonda and Tom Hayden in an interview April 19, 1974. They reported the interview in informal conversation with this author.
2. Much of the information for this chapter comes from the classic statement on People's War in Viet Nam by General Vo Nguyen Giap, *The Military Art of People's War* (New York: Monthly Review Press, 1970).
3. Both are quoted by Tran Van Dinh, "The Viet Nam People's Army," *Indochina Chronicle* (Washington, D.C.) #31 (February 28, 1974), p. 3.
4. Jane Barton, "Women POWs in South Viet Nam," in IPC pamphlet "Women under Torture."
5. Kathleen Gough Aberle, "An Indochinese Conference in Vancouver," *Bulletin of Concerned Asian Scholars,* Summer–Fall 1971, p. 8.
6. Pham Cuong, "In the Liberated Area," in *South Viet Nam: From NLF to PRG* (Vietnamese Studies #23; Hanoi: Foreign Language Publishing House).
7. Quoted by David Hunt, "Organization for Revolution in Viet Nam," *Radical America* vol. 8, #1–2 (January–April 1974), p. 140.
8. Story of "Heroine Eighty-Eight" told (in informal conversation) by Jane Barton, medical worker who lived in South Viet Nam for two years.
9. General Vo Nguyen Giap, "Revolutionary Armed Forces and People's Army," *Viet Nam Courier* #3 (August 1972), p. 14.

9.
LEARNING
TO
FIGHT BACK

The first days I felt ill at ease—marching in step, lobbing grenades, taking aim with my rifle, hitting the ground. . . . But as soon as I saw the American planes come back, my timidity left me.
                                        —Anh Vien, South Vietnamese peasant woman

Men whose power rested on feudal and colonial institutions have the primary responsibility for the subordination and passivity of women. Revolutionary leaders worked hard to convince people—especially the timid ones—that: "There is nothing inevitable about poverty. You are poor because you live under an unjust system." [1] But even as people take power to change the system, there's no automatic, 24-hour transformation in women's lives. It's been difficult for Vietnamese women to develop confidence in their ability to take initiative, to fight back, to do "men's jobs." The struggle for survival provides the initial push and momentum for the learning process. "Turn your hatred into energy" has been the guiding principle of the Vietnamese resistance. Women in particular have an enormous store of old hatred and new energy.

Beating the drums

Hatred becomes effective fighting energy as people overcome their fear. Small first steps make larger ones possible. In 1960, for example, after six years of Diem's terror campaigns, the National Liberation Front understood that a total assault on Diem's troops would require an impossible display of courage on the part of unarmed peasants. In the Mekong Delta, one of the first things cadres asked all villagers to do was to beat drums to create a fighting atmosphere and a sense of unity.

Many of the peasants were so frightened of Diem that they locked themselves in their homes before they would beat their drums. When Diem's officials did not respond to these unorthodox provocations, the NLF won its first small victory; and people gained enough confidence to leave their homes for meetings. The size of the meetings grew until all the villagers began to think of themselves as a collective force capable of defending itself.

At meetings, they had careful discussions of the nature of the enemy—trying to assess his power and vulnerability realistically. Foreseeing that the war would be long, leaders tried to caution people to avoid impulsive actions, uncontrolled fury or contempt for the enemy. Successful organizers did not rely on written communication, but rather talked personally with each peasant. By 1965, the NLF governed most of the Mekong Delta.

Later, the invasion of a half a million U.S. troops and the continuous saturation bombing put the NLF on the defensive again. While some people became discouraged, the Front maintained its organizational coherence. Women cadre and all poor peasants were especially stubborn in their loyalty. Increased repression from U.S. invaders rekindled people's hatred and resolve to fight. The persistent presence of the NLF organization in the form of dedicated cadre who experienced the same misfortunes as everyone else, but who had a strategy to win, made it possible to focus and reorganize the people's energy.

Speaking Bitterness

In the course of decades of hard struggle, people have learned many new ways to develop their ability to fight actively for themselves. Women gain a new sense of their own power in "speak bitterness" meetings. When the people liberate an area, the most downtrodden have their first experience in directly confronting their oppressors without fear. For example, shortly after the Geneva Accords were signed in 1954, about fifteen thousand peasants gathered in the village of Son Nam, twenty miles south of Hanoi, for a speak bitterness meeting. They flew banners denouncing landlordism and several militia women stood guard as the chairman of the tribunal read out the charges against the landlord named Cac. Cac was taller than most Vietnamese, so they forced him to stand in a hole. That way he couldn't look down on his accusers. Then the witnesses began to "recount their sorrows." One middle-aged woman, whose husband had died from a beating inflicted by Cac, moved closer to Cac as she accused him. She seemed about to tear him to pieces, her face distorted with pain as she testified:

Once when I was out collecting manure, you came and tried to violate me. I threw the manure in your face, but you threatened me with your dagger and you took me. And once when I was coming home, you surprised me at the corner of the rice fields and threatened to kill me with your dagger if I did not submit. [2]

Cac turned his head away from the woman's insistent voice. The chairman commanded Cac to turn around again to face her and she cried in disgust:

Yes, and after you killed my husband, you sent your wife to persuade me to be your concubine. . . . Because of your threats and attempts to violate me, I had to take the children and go and live elsewhere. . . .

A 19-year-old woman testified next. As she began to speak, she was trembling all over, but her voice was hard and clear. She had been sold to Cac by her starving mother when she was eight years old.

You beat me everyday for six years, she said, her accusing finger an inch or two from his nose. . . . *Once early in the morning, when I was cooking food for the pigs, you said I had not learned my lessons and you beat me with the firewood. Then you wrenched off my clothes, took a piece of burning wood from the fire and plunged it into my vagina. . . .*

As Cac tried to deny this accusation, another woman shouted from the crowd:

You took it to plunge into the vagina of my girl.

She got to her feet and pushed her way through the crowd to face the ex-landlord. She was dressed in rags:

Cac! You're a savage. I sold my daughter to you when our family was dying of starvation. You beat her almost to death every day and once you violated me at dagger point . . . nothing but a savage, that's what you are. Now thanks to the Lao Dong Party, I can come here and denounce your wickedness . . . you're finished now.

Meetings like these happened everywhere in the DRV. At first revolutionary cadres organized them, but later, they became so popular that villagers would initiate them on their own. Sometimes the most brutal landlords were sentenced to death. The DRV recorded 500 executions during the land reform period. More often, landlords who refused to reform got sentences of fifteen to twenty years in prison. Speaking bitterness dramatized the possibility and reality of new self-determination for women and men. The denunciation itself marks the beginning of the process to abolish all patriarchal power based on feudal exploitation.

Cadre training schools

In the early days of the revolutionary movement against the French, some male Party members had more than one wife. French repression and illiteracy made it hard to spread the new revolutionary program. Ho Chi Minh found that the most effective way of spreading revolutionary politics was to put the program of the Viet Minh to verse. Singing these verses may have been the first step many women took towards political leadership.

A woman cadre described the gradual process of gaining confidence and political skills in the South today:

When you go into the village the women [cadres] will go up to other women and say, "Come on; we really need you, right now." And they say, "But, oh, I can't do it, I'm so feeble; I just can't do anything. I know I can't." And we say, "Well, yes you can do it. You must do it!" [3]

She described how even grandmothers learned to read and write so they could make their reports to the revolutionary committees.

In 1960, the original Political Program of the NLF included a commitment to apply a policy of actively favoring, fostering and training women cadres. Bui Thi Me is now Vice President of the Union of Women for the Liberation of South Viet Nam as well as Vice Minister of Health of the Provisional Revolutionary Government. She analyzed the origin of women's passivity and talked about how they work to overcome it:

When women stayed at home all the time, they lost touch with society. Their isolation bred insecurity and, after a while, shyness and passivity seemed like women's "natural qualities." In this way, the ideology of feudalism became internalized. We work to overcome this problem by struggling against feudalism. Men are also the victim of feudalism, so they join us in the struggle. . . . We also think it is important to struggle everyday with ourselves to overcome our shyness. I include myself—if I don't struggle with my own shyness, I can't struggle with society. We also use political courses to help overcome shyness. When the shy ones mingle with the women cadre who are confident, little by little, they overcome their passivity. [4]

Every NLF cadre, and every resident in PRG zones, whether male or female, must study the importance of women's equality, the tradition of women's heroism in Vietnamese history, colonial and feudal oppression of women, and women's role in the national liberation struggle. Women involved in these courses have learned how difficult it is to challenge traditional patriarchal notions of manhood:

I have to tell you there are many cadres in the NLF who indeed, in courses, in big meetings, in big forums, when they take the floor, make very beautiful speeches about the equality of women. Beautiful, marvelous speeches. But in reality, at home, he is behaving with his wife like a feudal lord. So his colleagues have to practice criticism to remind him that he should bring together his words and his deeds and also the women in the Women's Union have to wage battle against them. It's not a very easy job. [5]

The Union of Women for the Liberation of South Viet Nam organized a special school for training women in political and military leadership. They named the school after Minh Khai. Throughout the war years, many women traveled long distances to attend three-month sessions at the Minh Khai School, somewhere in liberated territory. District and Provincial meetings of the Women's Union chose the women from their areas who would go to the school. They lived and studied together, and after three months, they would return to their village or battlefield to apply what they had learned.

The curriculum included: the general international situation; the current situation in Viet Nam; strategic stages and tasks of the revolution; how to build the movement among the people—especially women; the particular accomplishments of women, their role and potential; and women's and children's health care—including a first aid course. After each lesson, the women gathered to discuss it. They compared what they had done in their village with what they studied in class, and learned by criticizing their past practice. Sometimes, after a year of applying their lessons, a few cadre returned to the school for more advanced leadership training.

Experienced political leaders take special care in training new cadre. They assume that if a student has reservations when she leaves the class, she will not be effective later on. The leaders encourage all participants to voice questions and criticisms. Debate continues until the doubts are resolved.

After the Paris Peace Agreement, education for women in some areas of the South became easier. Women could gather without fear of enemy reprisals. By March 8, 1973, the Women's Union for the Liberation of South Viet Nam had set up thirty new training courses for one thousand women cadre in Quang Tri alone. [6] During the two-week training period, women read documents by Ho Chi Minh and others about political organizing and women's liberation. They compared what they had read with their own practical experience. Their goal was to learn how to mobilize women to defend their rights and to rebuild their villages.

In the North, similar cadre training schools for women have had the support of the State since 1954. But in 1960, the Second National Congress of the Viet Nam Women's Union called for an acceleration in women's education:

To confidently promote women cadres and develop their abilities in taking part in the management of production and in state management. . . . Our guiding principle for the promotion and fostering of women cadres is to boldly promote women cadres to higher positions, to entrust them with important tasks and to train them patiently. . . . If we are bold enough to give women the responsibility for work at all levels, they will have opportunities for training, to develop their capacities and mature quickly. [7]

Le Thu, Director of the Women's Union Cadre School in Hanoi, explained the importance of cadre training:

It's a very big task to mobilize women—in order to develop a strong women's movement, we must have women cadre because women understand each other more clearly.

By 1973, the Central School for Women in the DRV had trained nearly 3000 women cadres, most of whom returned to work at district organizations of the Women's Union. [8] The length of the courses vary from one week to one year, depending on the type of cadre being trained. Most of the women studying are peasants and workers, although a few come from intellectual backgrounds. Le Thi Xuyen, Vice President of the Viet Nam Women's Union, explained some of the goals of cadre training:

We try to teach them about the enemy—his weak and strong points. If they only learned about his strong points, they would lack confidence. We explain our program and strategy for overcoming the enemy. We try to foresee difficulties in advance, while we stress our strong points. We always teach the general policy of the Party and State and its particular application to women. Training also includes discussions about how to mobilize women, women's problems and rights, and how to help women in their private lives. . . . In the past, when most of the cadre were illiterate or when we were an illegal organization, we could not rely on written materials. Today, it's easier and we combine reading, lectures and discussion. . . .

In the end, the most important thing for a cadre to understand is that her main task is to develop the capacity of the population because cadres cannot do everything themselves . . . [9]

The inner struggle

Ngo Thi Nguyen, a member of the Executive Committee of the Women's Union in Vinh Linh, is a graduate of one of these schools. She is 57 years old and has been active in the Women's Union for 29 years. She is a peasant. Before the August Revolution in 1945, she was completely illiterate. Now, she has a 4th grade education which includes a month-long cadre-training course she took in 1960. Nguyen has five children, all of whom are either in the army or studying. Her husband is retired. She hasn't lived with him for six years because her duties as a Women's Union leader require that she spend virtually all her time away from home. She travels from village to village, staying in three or four villages each month. In each village, she lives in the home of a local family, sharing the work. She tries to learn what the women are doing, what they are feeling proud of, what are their grievances, problems and accomplishments. She tries to explain the current program of the Women's Union and give the local people a sense of the national political situation.

Nguyen explained how, as a cadre, it was her responsibility to take initiative in struggling against contempt for women still common among some men.

It shouldn't be necessary for a wife to have to seek help. It is the responsibility of the Women's Union. For example, there's a man named Hoang Tu who used to curse and sometimes beat his wife. I went to their home and tried to explain to him in a personal talk that his wife is also a human being, that she has the right to be treated equally and that the revolution had been fought for everyone. He said he agreed, but he did not really change his bad behavior. So we invited him to the Women's Union headquarters to give him a collective criticism of his behavior.

Collective pressure convinced him that he must abandon his feudal ways. We also tried to give his wife more confidence to struggle with him. We use the same step-by-step procedure to get men to share in the housework or to allow their wives to go out at night. We used to have a lot of men who resented their wives taking classes at night. The Peasants' Association also takes some responsibility. When the men continue to ignore us, they can be punished by law. [10]

The Vietnamese refer to this continuing struggle against "feudal ideology" as the "Inner Struggle." A representative explained:

The struggle is not a clash between men and women, but between institutions and ideologies, and between the new government and old customs. [11]

In peasant associations, in trade unions, in schools, and in the home, groups of people meet together, evaluating their work and planning future work. After each task is complete, they try to help each other understand their weaknesses and faults, and also their strengths, in order to provide positive alternatives. They call this process *kiem thao*—self-criticism/criticism. Mutual respect and solidarity is the basis for self-criticism/criticism and self-criticism/criticism also strengthens solidarity. They have learned:

It is natural that we have errors and disagreements, but self-criticism/ criticism helps us to keep our unity and to create greater love among us. We never use heavy pressure. If the error is one of principle, we struggle to the end. But if the error is one of personality, we usually let it pass. In any case, no one is ever pressed into the mud. Our struggle is always in the spirit of love. [12]

After an initial personal discussion, the group will meet and will raise the problem. Then the man who has been "behaving like a feudal lord," for example, will try to show he understands the problem by talking about ways to solve it. This process breaks down traditional hierarchical relationships and gives the group collective responsibility for the problem. So no individual woman has to struggle alone for her rights.

Learning by example

The fact that the Vietnamese people were struggling for generations, against the French, U.S. and Saigon troops, has strengthened women's ability to fight back. In the course of protracted struggle, men learn to cook, care for children and wash clothes. Women learn to use automatic weapons and anti-aircraft guns. Women who once hid from the bombs, squeezing their eyes tightly to shut out the horror, now have primary responsibility for downing bomber planes. Luu Quy Ky, Secretary General of the Journalists' Union, explained:

From the beginning the aim was to get people to lift their heads and look at the planes. When your head is down, you think the sky is full of planes. But when you lift your head you see there is one here, one there and you know how many. If you hear the sound of the explosions, you are alive, so you have nothing to worry about. If you don't hear them, you are dead, so you also don't worry. . . .

He also explained how anti-aircraft gunners learned not to fear the supersonic speeds of the planes, since militia women on the ground fire in front of the plane from the opposite direction:

The faster the plane, the quicker the bullet meets it. [13]

The experience of shooting down a B-52 or F-111 helps to overcome the sense of inferiority a woman felt. The new experience of repairing her machine in a factory when it breaks down helps convince a woman that she can be self-sufficient. Cam Thanh, a writer who spent a lot of time at the front, explained:

At first women don't think they can do such things. But the truth is a convincing answer. [14]

The Vietnamese call this process *tu giai phong* or self-liberation. By participating in new activities, they begin to question and reject the old, oppressive ways. Women also have new pride in their traditional roles. For example, when a woman supplies meals to the Liberation Army, she feels a pride that she didn't feel when she served meals to a landlord or a husband she didn't love.

Each woman who learns to fight becomes a model and inspiration for the next. For example, Ut Tich was exceptional because she joined the guerrilla forces when she was only 14:

"Take me with you!" she told the soldiers. Surprised at such a request from a thin little girl, they asked: "Why do you want to come with us?" "It's hard to be a servant." They replied, "But it's also very hard to fight the French." She responded, "But at least you can hit back. As for me, when my mistress beats me, I can only run away." [15]

In time she became a local guerrilla commander, organized a group of women fighters and earned a reputation as an amazing fighter in countless battles. She was the mother of six children and a national hero in Viet Nam. She died in battle in 1970.

Ut Tich fought in South Viet Nam. In Hanoi, there's a team of women tractor drivers who work at the pier unloading ships. Their team's name is "the Ut Tich Team." Thuoc, one of the drivers, was interviewed recently. The interviewer asked her how long it took her to learn to maneuver the tractors which pulled a line of heavily loaded trailers around the wharf. Thuoc responded:

The day I began work on the wharves, I was scared to death: the lanes were narrow, with lots of curves and small bridges, and traffic was so heavy! An accident could happen so easily. When I was at driving school, we drove light tractors over good roads. But now it's another pair of shoes! We women are not very strong. During the years of the American air raids, we often worked at night. The trailers were heavily loaded, the lanes were poorly lit—it was truly hard work. Sometimes the tractors broke down with all kinds of troubles: ignition trouble, engine failure, carburetor out of order; or trailers would brush against each other causing goods to fall all over the place. But we stood fast. Our team bears the name of Sister Ut Tich, hero of the South. . . .

In 1967, an all-woman team was formed. At first, it was not such smooth sailing. Many of us were hampered by a kind of inferiority complex: no one knew about labor management, engine maintenance and especially leadership work. . . . Besides there were all kinds of individual idiosyncracies. But we strove to learn from the example of sister Ut Tich. [16]

Thuoc worked especially hard because she was from a province in the North that was the sister province of Ut Tich's birthplace in the South. Thuoc considered herself the adopted sister of Ut Tich and tried to be worthy of the special relation. She used to come to work an hour early to watch the other drivers and learn from them about engine repair. Later she proposed a way to save tons of fuel by designing a new method of starting the tractors. Now she can drive or repair any vehicle. Her team has overfulfilled its work quotas and received a commendation for "comradely feelings among its members, perfect equipment maintenance and total lack of accidents and waste." As news of their work spreads, young women are encouraged to take new leadership in tasks previously reserved for men.

Heroic fighters and workers have emerged in every Vietnamese village. Local Women's Unions organize movements—called emulation campaigns—that encourage all women to follow the examples of their sisters.

The Three Responsibilities Movement

In the DRV, the Three Responsibilities Movement has been a major national emulation campaign for women. Since 1965, the campaign has taught women about the tasks the revolution needs them to do and has provided the encouragement for them to accomplish these tasks. Every local chapter of the Women's Union—whether based in an agricultural cooperative, factory, school or office—participates in the Three Responsibilities Movement.

During the height of the war, the Three Responsibilities were for production, defense and the family. Since the end of the air war against the North, the Three Responsibilities Movement has new content: (1) to take responsibility for production and political leadership in "carrying out duties to the country;"(2) to ensure effective organization of the family for the growth of future generations; and (3) to struggle for equality between women and men. Local chapters decide the most appropriate ways for members to fulfill these responsibilities. At the end of a six-month period, the collective evaluates their work in fulfilling the Three Responsibilities and awards those women who have done outstanding work. For example, in Ngu Thuy Village, during the war, the Women's Gunner unit won many "Three Responsibilities Awards" for their success in sinking U.S. warships. Today, in a nearby agricultural cooperative, the Three Responsibilities Movement is focusing women's energy on cattle raising. Women may get Three Responsibilities Awards for family work in taking care of orphans or in organizing successful birth control campaigns.

In the South, there was a similar emulation campaign—the "Five Goods Movement." Women received awards for work in (1) defense, (2) production, (3) learning and improving their own capacity, (4) organizing the Women's Union, and (5) the family. During the first six months of 1974, 30% of the women in Quang Tri Province received the "Five Goods Award." Many women received awards for their success in encouraging ARVN soldiers to desert. [17]

Lessons in leadership

Organization is a tool which can help women learn to fight. One of the major tasks of the Viet Nam Women's Union is political and technical education of women. The Women's Union has provided a source of education, support and power for Vietnamese women in one form or another since 1930. Until the country was partitioned, there was one organization. By 1950, it had nearly three million members. After 1954, Diem repressed the Union in the South. It re-formed in 1961 as the Union of Women for the Liberation of South Viet Nam. Today this organization has several million members. The Viet Nam Women's Union in the North is now a separate organization with five million members.

Both unions are organized at every level of society, but, until recently, the Union in the South functioned secretly in cities controlled by Thieu. Women belong to the Union through chapters organized at production and office units, since they believe that the rights of women must be settled where they work. At this local level, there's continuous political education in regular bi-monthly meetings which include the entire membership. In the North, the Union publishes weekly and monthly magazines which cover anything that serves the major tasks of the Union: defending women's rights, defending peace, working for reunification of the country, and building socialism.

The weekly *Phu Nu Viet Nam* (Vietnamese Woman) distributes 120,000 copies—making it the second largest circulating magazine in the country. It is the central organ of the Viet Nam Woman's Union so women regularly discuss magazine articles in their local Women's Unions. They respond enthusiastically to articles publicizing experiences of their sisters which counter traditional prejudices against women. Each month the editorial board receives more than a thousand letters from their readers—not counting letters addressed to "Heart-to-Heart-Talk," the advice column. [18]

It's the policy of the Viet Nam Women's Union to encourage men to share all housework, childcare and marketing. Many meetings have been devoted to discussing the most effective ways to carry on the inner struggle with men. In order to insure that women have the freedom to learn from each other, the Union collectively reprimands uncooperative husbands who want their wives home at night. In the North, every cooperative farm and factory has childcare facilities, so baby-sitting needs don't prevent women from improving their educational level. The Union also enables women of different generations to teach other. Through concerted political education, the Union has brought together daughters and mothers-in-law—overcoming traditions of hostility and jealousy.

Out of this mass participation emerge new leaders. A few women, who later became national leaders, received direct political education from Ho Chi Minh. He was not only the most important leader in the Vietnamese revolution, but also a poet and a model of gentle strength and modesty. Truong Thi My, a member of the Central Committee of the Viet Nam Women's Union and also Vice President of the Viet Nam General Confederation of Trade Unions, attended a one-month training course for cadres in 1941. In those days, Ho Chi Minh, along with all revolutionaries, led a clandestine life. Those going to the course traveled through the jungle on foot for nine days. Truong Thi My remembers:

Although I was used to paddy leeches, it was my first experience with jungle leeches. When we entered a mountain cave to get some sleep, I got quite a shock from what I saw sticking to my legs. . . . [After someone told her how to get rid of the leeches and stop the bleeding] I was no longer afraid of jungle leeches. . . .

Once they arrived, they were greeted by a man who presented himself modestly as Comrade Thu's courier. Comrade Thu was believed to be an alias of Nguyen Ai Quoc, who later called himself Ho Chi Minh.

. . . The next day the old courier came again. He told us, "Come with me to class." We came to the foot of a mountain. . . . The old man walked ahead with nimble gait up the steep and slippery path. I was second. . . . There was another woman in the column: Sister Trung, of Cao Bang. She and I had cut for ourselves strong bamboo walking sticks, and each of us carried a bundle of clothes slung across the shoulder. Our male companions often slipped. But I fell not once! This was due to the fact that I was used to hard work in the fields, and besides was walking barefoot. . . . Our class was held on top of the mountain, where a few big trees gave us shade. . . . Our lecturer was the old courier himself. In his opening lecture, he talked to us about the importance of Marxism-Leninism. . . . As for me, I was deeply impressed by the old man. I thought to myself: "If his courier is so knowledgeable, how learned must be our leader!" One remarkable thing about the old man was that he very seldom used difficult terms, which made his lectures easy to understand. . . .

. . . The class ended. My classmates returned home. I fell ill and had to stay. Once every few days, the old man called upon me to inquire after my health. He was like a grandfather to me. Only later did I learn that our old lecturer was Nguyen Ai Quoc, Uncle Ho, our beloved and venerated leader. Thus he gave us guidance. The time I spent in his class is the most sacred, the most precious period in my entire revolutionary life. [19]

Years of struggle reinforce these lessons. As time goes by, by-standers disappear and more and more women join the revolutionary process. Novels, short stories, poems, songs, plays, newspaper accounts, movies, paintings, sculptures—in the North and South—present examples of women heroes who inspire increased strength on the part of still more women. The overwhelming majority of leading characters in the art and literature of revolutionary Viet Nam are women—mostly heroes who have overcome incredible obstacles to make either productive, political or military contributions to the revolution. Most Vietnamese insist that these characters are not romanticized. They have a saying: *Women are the greatest victims of the war, but they are also its greatest heroes.*

A new generation of young women is growing up, learning from heroes like Ut Tich and Minh Khai. They learn from paintings and woodcuts that show women as sturdy, with strong arms, backs and shoulders—engaged in combat or production. Girls in liberated zones in the South learn to read with stories about sister Phuong who sets booby traps while her mother is away from the village fighting. One of the favorite children's stories, "In Mom's Absence," provides a strong lesson in revolutionary abolition of sex roles:

To Anh, her mother meant the glittering cartridges with which her mother taught her to count. . . . Bé, for her part, did not find her mother's absence at all boring. To climb to the top of the coconut tree was her habit. . . . She climbed it every day, acting as observer informing the rest of the village of the places under enemy aircraft attack. . . . Bé leaned the ruler against the coconut tree, and in so doing, she recalled the picture of her mother leaning her rifle against a pillar in the house [20]

The story portrays a day in the life of these children while their mother is away fighting. Towards the very end, the reader learns that their mother is the famous Ut Tich.

There are no Dick-and-Jane-type readers in the North either. During the B-52 raids of Christmas 1972, a 16-year-old woman named Dang Thi Ha was killed. They discovered her journal in the rubble and the Hanoi daily newspaper printed some poems from it. Here is one which shows the lessons of her early womanhood:

THE LIBERATION GIRL

*From a child, I have been dreaming of becoming a fighter
Against U.S. aggression and a defender of the land.
I'll say farewell to my dear ones and respond*

*To the vibrant call of the Truong Son Range.**
Wrapped in the affection of the whole country,
I'll be tempered in the crucible of war,
Aware of the Truong Son hardships
Aware that it's an immense school of life. [21]

*The Truong Son Range runs from the DRV into South Viet Nam. It contains the "Ho Chi Minh Trail."

Notes

1. Quoted by David Hunt in "Organizing for Revolution in Viet Nam," *Radical America* vol. 8, #1-2, p. 111. The following section called "Beating the Drum" draws heavily on Hunt's discussion, especially pp. 34-38 and 137-138.
2. This and other testimony from the Speak Bitterness session comes from Wilfred Burchett, *North of the 17th Parallel,* pp. 126-134.
3. Quoted in Marsha Steinberg, "Women of the South: An Interview with PRG Woman in Paris," *Second Wave* vol. 2, #2 (1972), p. 10.
4. This and other information about cadre training in the South were discussed in interviews between author and Bui Thi Me, Quang Tri Province, September 21, 1975.
5. From Steinberg interview with PRG woman. p. 11.
6. Thu Huong. "Quang Tri in the First Days of Peace," *Women of Viet Nam* #1-2 (1973), p. 40.
7. "Tasks of the Vietnamese Women in the New Stage," *Proceedings of 2nd National Congress of Viet Nam Women's Union* (Hanoi: 1960), pp. 20-21.
8. "DRV in Brief," *South Viet Nam in Struggle* #205 (July 9, 1973), p. 6.
9. From interview with author, at National Women's Union Headquarters, Hanoi, September 29, 1974.
10. From interview with author, Vinh Linh District, September 22, 1974.
11. Kathleen Gough Aberle. "The Indochinese Conference in Vancouver," p. 15.
12. From interview between author and member of Women's Gunner Unit, Ngu Thuy Village, Quang Binh Province, September 23, 1974.
13. Unpublished transcript by Jill Rodewald of interview between delegates of Indochina Peace Campaign, May 17, 1973.
14. From interview with author at headquarters of the Writers' Association, Hanoi, September 30, 1974.
15. Nguyen Thi. "A Fighting Mother or the Story of Nguyen Thi Ut," *Vietnamese Women* (Vietnamese Studies #10; Hanoi: 1966), pp. 85-86.
16. Minh Ha, "Ut Tich's Adopted Sister," *Women of Viet Nam* #1 (1971), pp. 11-12.
17. From interview by author with Tran Thi Hung, President of Quang Tri Union of Women for the Liberation of South Viet Nam, September 20, 1974.
18. From interview with Nguyen Thanh Huong, member of the Editorial Board of *Phu Nu,* Hanoi, October 1, 1974.
19. Truong Thi My, "The Old Courier," *Women of Viet Nam* #3 (1969), pp. 24-25.
20. Nguyen Thi, "In Mom's Absence," in *The Little Shoeblack of Saigon* (South Viet Nam:Giai Phong Publishing House, 1972), pp. 9-37.
21. Dang Thi Ha, "Poems," *South Viet Nam in Struggle* #185 (February 5, 1973) p. 3.

10.
TO PRODUCE IS TO FIGHT

Let the women of the North shed more sweat so their sisters in the South could shed less blood.

—slogan of the Viet Nam Women's Union

Viet Nam is a nation of peasants. About seventy-five per cent of the 24 million people in the North till the soil. In the South, eighty-five per cent of the people were peasants until forced urbanization uprooted ten million people from the land—nearly half the total population. After Thieu's defeat, thousands of South Vietnamese began to return to the land. But it will take several years before full life blooms again in the South Vietnamese countryside. Since the war, the fields and village affairs have been largely in the hands of women.

Feeding each other

Peasant women have always labored in the fields, but in the past they mostly did backbreaking labor, following the landlords' orders. In the North, where land reform is complete, the basis of their power is collective work and ownership of the land and tools, and the abolition of the landlord system which extracted enormous rents and taxes. Everyone is paid according to the work she or he does for the cooperative.

This land reform is the foundation for the socialist transformation of the DRV. The defining features of a socialist economy are that economic decisions—what to produce, how to produce it, and who to produce it for—are made by the producers themselves. There are no individual owners of the factories, fields, and natural sources of the nation's wealth. Organizations of workers, peasants, and intellectuals plan their own work after many public discussions to figure out what's humanely possible and what will meet the needs of as many people as possible. Under capitalism, on the other hand, factory owners make decisions for workers; agribusiness tells farmworkers what to do; and the publishing industry makes decisions for writers. All decision-makers have one goal in mind—individual profit. Profit-making, the source of gross inequalities, has been eliminated in the DRV.

For example, in the Bui cooperative, Ha Nam Province, every landless peasant received a plot of land and then decided to join together to work it collectively. By breaking out of their isolation, they succeeded in repairing dikes and saving the crops from floods. In Viet Nam, there's a saying that explains the increased well-being and productivity in the Bui cooperative and others like it:

> *In hell, people starve because their hands are chained to six-foot-long chopsticks,*

> *too long to bring rice to their mouths.*
> *Heaven is the same—*
> *Only there, people feed each other.*

The women of the Bui cooperative overcame centuries of sex-typed roles. For the first time, young women guided buffalo and drove plows. They learned to use mechanical pumps and began fish breeding. Women leaders have responsibility for the co-op's seed selection, storehouse, animal breeding, and technical innovation, as well as finances.

The chairperson and eleven of the fifteen members of the co-op's managing committee are women. The Bui coop is typical. Nearly all peasants in North Viet Nam have joined cooperatives. Women do seventy per cent of the agricultural production. Women are the chairpeople of 4300 of the 5000 People's Councils at the village level. [1]

When U.S. planes began to bomb the North, women who worked in the factories evacuated and dispersed. They continued production in caves and remote, camouflaged areas. But since rice fields could not be moved, peasant women dug trenches inside their homes, along the way to the fields and along the edges of the fields where they worked. They took rifles with them to the fields and learned how to defuse the most modern U.S. time and magnetic bombs. In the District of Vinh Linh, just north of the 17th parallel, women stubbornly continued to work, defusing the bombs which fell *every day* for eight years.

In the South, by 1963, the NLF had liberated seventy-five per cent of the land from Diem's control. As soon as they liberated an area, the people began to implement the NLF's program: (1) reducing rents, (2) confiscating the land owned by the imperialists and their agents and redistributing it to landless peasants, (3) abolishing "agrovilles," Diem's concentration camps, (4) guaranteeing fair distribution of land ownership. A cooperative movement began, along similar lines as in the North, but the massive invasion of U.S. troops, beginning in 1965, made agricultural production and cooperativization much more difficult. Each liberated village became a combat village capable of facing enemy attack. In combat villages, everyone joined the local guerrilla units, learned to make rudimentary arms, built lookout posts and fortifications, laid booby traps and then tried to continue production as normally as possible.

As in the North, the majority of peasants have been women. As they worked in the fields—at night if necessary to avoid the bombs—they sang. Their slogan was:

> *Let our songs drown out the explosions of the bombs.* [2]

In spite of the bombing and ground invasion, these peasants have increased their productivity by collectivizing work and eliminating the inefficiency of the feudal estates. While the Thieu regime had to import rice from the U.S., harvests in the PRG or liberated areas continued to feed villagers and members of the PLAF.

Since the Paris Peace Agreement, peasants in the PRG zones have concentrated their efforts in production—especially reclaiming the land. They fill thousands of bomb craters, repair dikes and dams, cut down dead trees, plant in areas made barren by defoliants, and are beginning to find and defuse the millions of land mines and unexploded bombs left by U.S. troops. In the area just below the 17th parallel, the people have harvested their first crop in ten years—the same area that visitors once described as having been bombed so much it looked like the surface of the moon. The relative prosperity of the PRG zone attracted hundreds of thousands of people. Before Thieu fell, these people took tremendous risks to leave Saigon-controlled zones and return to the villages, but they were secure once they arrived. [3]

A labor heroine

Pham Thi Vach is one of the many women honored in the North with the title "labor heroine" for her work in agriculture. She grew up in a very poor family and her father tried to marry her off against her will. She defied her father and sought the aid of a revolutionary cadre in persuading her father to call off the marriage. At 16, after managing to free herself from the marriage, she began doing odd jobs, helping and cooking for the guerrillas who were preparing to fight the French.

Soon she became the first woman guerrilla of Hung Cuong village and launched a campaign for the mass participation of women in the people's militia. She helped her friends overcome their timidity:

> . . . If we don't hit the mark, how ashamed we'll be.

Vach replied:

> Everything men can do, we can do. We work in the fields as they do, don't we? Anyway, let's try! [4]

They learned to shoot.

In 1960, she formed the first brigade of volunteers to build a new dike. Then she began a campaign for her village to join the cooperative movement. Her father was one of the staunchest holdouts. Fearing that her father's suspicions would discourage the other villagers from joining the co-op, she lied to her neighbors, pretending her parents had agreed to join. After forty villagers signed up and it became clear that the co-op would benefit them all, her father finally joined.

Once the co-op was organized, Vach did the work of five. She led the Militia and the Youth Federation and became a member of the co-op's Control Commission. She also did more than her share of work

In Vinh Linh, women work in fields at night and fight during daytime.

in the fields. She designed a rake and made other suggestions that cut working time by two-thirds and increased the output of corn enormously. Her effectiveness as an organizer came from the fact that people readily identified with her. They knew she would always participate in whatever tasks she asked others to do. She would make bold suggestions for innovations. Gradually people's confidence in her grew as more and more of her plans proved successful. Later, the Worker's Party—Lao Dong—admitted her as a member. She cherished this membership as her greatest honor.

"Every meter of cloth is a bullet against the enemy."
—slogan at Nam Dinh Textile Mill

A woman in a textile factory wrote this song. Now the women in her factory's cultural group sing it:

> *The cloth which comes out of my loom tonight*
> *Will be the national red flag*
> *And the scarves of our children*
> *Going to school in the morning.* [5]

She and thousands like her have virtually taken over all responsibility for running the textile factories of North Viet Nam. The women in these factories work hard, long hours. They often walk miles to work. They did not see their children for long periods of time, when the children were evacuated to the countryside to protect them from the bombing.

While their work and sacrifice resemble the work women did in the United States during World War II, the situation is actually very different. National enthusiasm for defeating Hitler blinded women to the fact that industry was making huge war profits from their labor. Women "took over men's jobs" during World War II as temporary understudies. Employers renamed job categories so that women in manufacturing earned sixty-five per cent of what men earned for the same work. Thousands of women left their children in the factory parking lot, locked in parked cars. There were an estimated two million children needing federally sponsored child care; but, at their peak, only one hundred thousand children benefited from federally sponsored programs. The programs ended in 1946. [6]

In the DRV, there is no factory owner who makes a profit from women's labor. As the song says, the cloth they weave is for their country and children. The more they produce, the more cloth will be available for soldiers' uniforms. If there's a surplus their children will get new clothes and they can improve their working conditions. But no individual will get richer. The workers in the factory elect a management committee to run the factory. The management committee doesn't spend time behind desks. They take responsibility for production work too. Most important, these women are not working under an illusion when they feel that the work they do is the work of the whole nation. They understand the importance of their jobs, and the Women's Union urges them to "master one profession and know several." It's unlikely that they'll feel like cogs in an anti-human machine.

In 1954, the Vietnamese took over the Nam Dinh weaving complex, previously owned by the Frenchman Dupre. Women workers became their own managers. Later, when the Nam Dinh textile factory became a favorite target of American bombers, the workers decided to suspend the day shift. Production suffered, because the constant threat of bombing made it hard to sleep for more than a few hours, day or night. A 23-year-old woman named Trinh Thi Sim was in charge of a self-defense unit within the factory. She could quickly distinguish the various types of planes used by the U.S. Air Force, Navy and Army, and explain in detail their functions and weak points. A few ex-servicemen, veterans of Dien Bien Phu, were under her command. They called her "comrade commander." She told an interviewer:

I myself could not imagine how I came to have them under my command. It's simply paradoxical! And yet they strictly carry out my

orders. They are Party members. With their knowledge and experience
they could command much better than I. But I understand the Party
wants to help train me. [7]
Her modesty may have prevented her from seeing that her youth,
energy and the ability of women workers to identify with her were the
qualities the workers felt were needed for leadership.

In Hanoi, women are not only responsible for running another
weaving mill, they are also responsible for building it. In 1960, the
Women's Union initiated a national campaign to raise funds to
construct the mill. Women workers in other factories increased their
productivity, peasants raised hens and planted extra banana trees,
civil servants set aside part of their wages and artists did special performances. Within months, women raised enough capital to complete
the plant. They named it the March 8th Mill after International Women's Day.

Two-thirds of the construction teams in the DRV are women.
Building homes, schools and hospitals has priority. Vietnamese and
foreigners alike marvel at the success of these teams. Within a year
and a half after the bombing stopped, everyone had a home. In the fall
of 1974, as we drove south on Highway One, we followed construction
teams, often riding over roads paved minutes before. During the air
war, women worked day and night to repair roads so supplies to the
front would not be interrupted.

Construction work in Viet Nam is nothing like in the U.S. There
are few machines. Women transport materials in baskets suspended
from carrying poles that rest heavy on their shoulders. I worked for a
brief time with a team of seven women digging a foundation. We
formed a line. The first would heave a few shovelfuls of earth onto a
wicker basket, the next would pick up the basket and pass it to the
next. And so on. After about an hour of work, our human conveyor belt
moved the same amount of earth a steam shovel might have moved in a
minute. The team works every day from 6 a.m. to 5:30 p.m. with about
three hours off at mid-day.

A high cooperative spirit among the women working helps ease
the physical burden of the work itself. We worked well together, taking
turns at the hardest shoveling job. Whenever one woman seemed
tired, the others worked harder so she could rest. They were proud of
the work they were doing. They hoped to complete their task sooner
than planned as their part in the local Three Responsibilities
Movement.

Teachers and doctors

Women have also taken the major responsibility for educating the
population. Phan Minh Hien is a teacher in the liberated zone of South

Viet Nam who met with North American women at the Indochinese Women's Conference in Vancouver. She weighs eighty-six pounds, but walked with a forty-four-pound pack for three months through the jungle from the South to Hanoi where she could get a plane to Canada. As she walked through each new village, she would explain her destination to the people. In each place, villagers gave her scarves, combs, pictures, anything to serve as a gift for their "North American sisters." Once in Vancouver, Hien told us:

While working as a teacher, I receive good care and affection from the villagers. We don't have a salary. When we work in the jungle, we get from twenty to forty pounds of rice or manioc [an edible root] per month. The villagers share everything with us—even medicine tablets when we fall ill. [8]

Hien became an orphan during the war against the French. She went to high school in the jungle in the liberated zones and attended university-level evening classes for two years. She decided to study chemistry so she could help recondition the soil that had been poisoned by the war. Her three children stay with friends and she hasn't seen her husband for four and a half years.

Nguyen Thi Xiem was illiterate until she was 15. She enrolled in school during the one year of peace after the August Revolution, 1945. When the French reoccupied her province, she fled from the city of Hue to the mountains, where she joined the youth organization and continued her studies. She became a teacher and was active in the Women's Union. As a known political activist, she had to go north with her father when troops were regrouped in 1954. Her mother and the other children stayed in the South. She hasn't heard from them since 1957. In 1959, she graduated from the medical college of the University of Hanoi and later studied abroad for two years.

Xiem is an obstetrician and also does research on the treatment of injuries from toxic chemicals, fragmentation bombs, napalm, and the variety of venereal diseases introduced by U.S. troops in South Viet Nam. Many of her patients come from the South to Hanoi for special treatment. Women with uteruses perforated by pellet bombs and women with deformed babies receive expert specialized care at the Institute for the Protection of Mothers and Children in Hanoi. [10] Xiem is one of the nearly one thousand women MD's in the DRV—about half the total number of doctors. [11]

Most of the health workers in both zones of Viet Nam are not doctors. They're "assistant doctors" and other kinds of paraprofessionals trained in emergency surgery techniques, as well as nurses, midwives, pharmacists and traditional medical practitioners. In the North, there's a medical team for every village and in the South, there's one in every liberated village. Most of these teams are staffed by women. Health work is one of the most respected kinds of work because in People's War, every life is sacred.

But whether a woman is a peasant or a doctor, she is proud of her work. In revolutionary societies, like Viet Nam, labor, especially manual labor, has a high value, and people often view daily work as heroic activity. Women who shoulder the main burden of production in Viet Nam do not see their responsibility as an unpleasant one. They work collectively and feel part of a national campaign whose goals are their goals. Everyone seems to trust and understand the logic of the needs of the revolution.

Most of the same women who have worked in production throughout Viet Nam also form the ranks of the "Long-Haired Army."

Notes

1. Information on the Bui co-op is from Mai Anh, "Up from the Mud," in *Vietnamese Women* (Vietnamese Studies #10; Hanoi: 1966), pp. 153-192. For an excellent account of peasant life in the DRV, check Gerard Chaliand's *The Peasants of North Viet Nam* (London: Pelican, 1969).
2. Pham Cuong, "In the Liberated Areas," in *South Viet Nam: From NLF to PRG* (Vietnamese Studies #23; Hanoi: 1969), p. 112. Other details about the NLF's agrarian reform program also come from this article.
3. Chris Jenkins, "Life with the PRG," *Indochina Chronicle* #32 (April 17, 1974), pp. 3-4.
4. "Pham Thi Vach," in *Vietnamese Women*, p. 273.
5. "Let Our Songs Drown the Bomb Explosions," *The Vietnamese Trade Unions* #2 (1969), p. 12.
6. Information about women in the U.S. from William Henry Chafe's book *The American Woman: Her Changing Social, Economic and Political Roles, 1920-1970* (New York: Oxford Univ. Press, 1972), pp. 158-170. If you want a lot of hard facts about women in the U.S. during World War II, check chapters 6-8.
7. Vu Can. "With the Nam Dinh Weavers," in *Vietnamese Women*, pp. 238-239.
8. Quoted by Kathleen Gough Aberle, "Indochinese Conference in Vancouver," *Bulletin of Concerned Asian Scholars*, vol. 3, #3-4 (Summer-Fall 1971), p. 6.
9. Chanh's story is not fiction, but was made into a moving biographical short story by Mona Brand called "Return to Life" published in *Daughters of Viet Nam* (Hanoi: Foreign Languages Publishing House, 1958), pp. 13-42.
10. Dr. Xiem told her story to the Indochinese Women's Conference in Vancouver.
11. These figures are estimated from statistics that are a bit dated given by Chaliand, pp. 150-151, and *Women of Viet Nam* #3-4 (1971), pp. 8-9.

11.
THE
LONGHAIRED
ARMY

"Come along with us, demand the right to live,
With us defend our young lives and happiness!"
The whole enemy unit moved and stirred,
Then stepped aside,
Then followed the demonstrators.

—from a poem by Giang Nam called
"The Long-Haired Army"

The work of persuading people to join the struggle, organizing protest demonstrations, planning rallies to raise people's spirits, and persuading soldiers in the Saigon army to desert—all this is called "political struggle." They call the movement which has carried on this political struggle the "Long-Haired Army" because women take responsibility for most of its activity.

In People's War, political struggle has always had priority. The first unit of the Vietnamese People's Army, formed in December 1944, was called the "Armed Propaganda Brigade for the Liberation of Viet Nam." President Ho Chi Minh said:

The unit shows by its name that greater importance should be attached to the political than to the military side. [1]

Later, General Giap explained why political struggle is so important in the context of a national liberation war. First, he wrote,

. . . Only by proceeding from solid political organization was it possible to build up solid para-military organizations and to advance towards the creation of small guerrilla groups closely linked with the revolutionary masses and thereby capable of operating and developing.

Secondly,

. . . political struggle plays a very fundamental role because it is in the political field that lies our fundamental superiority and the enemy's fundamental weakness. [2]

Even Henry Kissinger has grudgingly made the same analysis of the sources of NLF strength:

One ironic aspect of the war in Viet Nam is that, while we profess an idealistic philosophy, our failures have been due to an excessive reliance on material factors. . . . The communists . . . owe many of their successes to their ability to answer the question of the nature and foundations of political authority. [3]

In practice, liberation forces don't engage in a military activity until they lay a strong political foundation for it. For example, no matter how strategic a contested area might be militarily, the PLAF would not initiate a battle there unless it was clear that the people in that area had been involved in a political struggle and would welcome the liberation forces. Women play the decisive role in this work.

Political activity was particularly important in areas where military action was difficult—in cities or near U.S. military bases. Open political activity, using all the legal possibilities, served to defend people's rights, undermined the authority of the Thieu Regime, and educated people. At the same time, underground activities eroded the enemy's rear, immobilizing large numbers of U.S. and ARVN troops. The liberation forces themselves say that lightning attacks on the cities—like the Tet Offensive of 1968—would have been impossible without careful political preparation beforehand and without the active participation of large numbers of the city population itself. The escalation of political mobilizations in the fall of 1974, calling for Thieu's resignation, was important groundwork for the final military campaigns of 1975. Again, women played a decisive and leading role in this work.

Minh Khai

Minh Khai set an early example for political militants. She began participating in revolutionary actions when she was only 16 years old. That was in 1926. We already mentioned that she had to leave home because her parents harassed her too much for her late night activities. Her name in those days was Nguyen Thi Vinh, and she was a favorite student of Tran Phu, who became Secretary General of the Indochinese Communist Party in 1930. She changed her name many times to avoid detection by the French. Her best-known name, Minh Khai, means "bright pioneer." She too was one of the founders of the ICP and the Women's Union.

She traveled to China in 1930 with Ho Chi Minh and other Vietnamese revolutionaries who were trying to coordinate Asian campaigns against all colonialists. The English in China arrested her on account of her anti-colonial activities. After three years, she was released and went to study in the Soviet Union. She represented the ICP at the Congress of the Third International in 1935—a meeting of representatives of revolutionary organizations from many nations.

There, she read a sharply worded speech praising women's contribution to the revolution and also criticizing revolutionary organizations for not placing enough importance on women's emancipation:

The women heroes of China, the women workers of Japan and India, the women workers and peasants of Indochina are becoming a real force in the revolutionary ranks of the Eastern colonies. . . . Dear Comrades, I would like to say that work among women is not given proper attention not only in our own country but also in many other Communist Parties. We may see how few women have expressed their view on the important problems discussed in this Congress. . . . What does this show? It proves that the work among women workers, peasants, unemployed and housewives in the struggle for a United Front has not been carried out correctly. As delegates of the Indochinese Communist Party, we will do our best to apply a new spirit so as to correct and develop our work. . . .

When Minh Khai returned to Saigon, she worked non-stop organizing underground trade unions. She became one of the most popular workers' representatives. The requirements of her political work made it impossible for her to live with her husband and child. A friend raised her daughter.

Finally, the French arrested her in 1940. They also caught her husband, whom she hadn't seen for two years. The French authorities brought the two together, hoping they would divulge each other's identity by recognizing each other. Minh Khai repressed her feelings, appeared indifferent and claimed she had never met their prisoner—her husband—before.

The French believed Minh Khai was responsible for an important insurrection in Nam Ky. In 1941, after months of torture, they brought her to trial and sentenced her to death. She remained defiant and dignified throughout the proceedings, even though they shaved her head and her body was wracked with pain from the tortures. Before the French executed her, she made a pillowcase from her prison clothes and arranged to have it sent to her mother whom she hadn't seen in twelve years. When her sister broke down in court, Minh Khai comforted her, "Don't cry dear. I have fulfilled my task. Don't forget my words!" She left these words inscribed with her own blood on the wall of her prison cell:

> *A rosy-cheeked woman, here I am fighting side by side*
> *with you men!*
> *On my shoulders, weighs the hatred that is common to us.*
> *The prison is my school, its mates my friends,*
> *The sword is my child, the gun my husband.* [4]

The words "rosy-cheeked," in traditional Vietnamese literature, describe the ideal, frail, upper-class woman who is more an ornament than a person. Minh Khai reinforced the irony of her words on the day of her execution. She refused a blindfold and shouted, "Long live the Vietnamese Revolution!" just before they shot her. Today, in Viet Nam, women's work teams, fighting brigades and schools are often named after Minh Khai.

In the tradition of Minh Khai, women organized clandestine trade unions under the noses of Thieu's police. All trade unions, along with any public gatherings of non-family groups, were illegal in Saigon. In 1970, more than seven hundred thousand workers joined a general strike demanding both higher wages and peace. In another strike, the seven hundred workers of the "Con O" battery factory in Saigon, most of them women, struck for more than three months. The women provided an inspiring example for all workers in Saigon as they held out in the face of brutal beatings, arrests and threats of starvation. While they were occupying their factory, other workers came to visit them with food and relief money. After Mrs. Truong Ba Hue, the general secretary of the union, was brutally stripped and beaten, eighteen other unions in Saigon launched a work stoppage to protest the brutality at Con O. Even some "deputies" in the Saigon parliament declared their support for the strikers and the Women's Committee to Defend the Right to Live pledged their full solidarity. In January 1972, they finally won the wage increases they demanded and the reinstatement of seventeen women who had been fired arbitrarily. [5]

A year later at another factory, the Eternis Company, the workers risked imprisonment to protest the abuses of the company's manager. He consistently harassed the women employees, making sexual advances and insulting them. The workers also insisted that the Saigon regime take measures to protect women's dignity—a demand that could only embarrass the Thieu regime. [6]

Spreading the movement like a drop of oil

Both under French colonial rule and under the disguised colonial rule of the U.S., there was no free press, no possibility for mass meetings, no possibility for any public political activity. Bui Thi Me, now Vice Minister of Health of the PRG and Vice President of the Union of Women for the Liberation of South Viet Nam, is a veteran of the Long-Haired Army. She explained how they incorporated women into the movement in the days when possession of a leaflet would doom a sister to arrest and torture:

We extended our organization like a drop of oil. Little by little. One of us would speak to three others. Each of the three would speak to three more. Before we spoke to anyone, we would study her history, beliefs and feelings to prevent infiltration. In People's War it is the people who must make the propaganda. [7]

Revolutionary activists, leadership cadre, gained the trust of the rest of the people by practicing the "Three Togethers"—living with the people, working with the people and eating with the people. Tuyen, a Women's Union cadre, explained how she learned the "Three Togethers." In 1948 she left home at age 16, to work in the liberated areas. Her mother had been a shopkeeper in a village near Saigon. Tuyen expected everything in the liberated areas to be perfect . . . according to the revolutionary theory she had learned. During the first few months she lived, worked and ate with the people in the countryside, but she often got impatient and angry with people who did not live up to her ideals. She did not trust them and probably they resented her contempt. During the weekly meetings she had with other cadres, they tried to summarize what they had accomplished and decide their next tasks. Tuyen's comrades often criticized her methods of work as "bourgeois idealism." Tuyen recalled:

I had a hot temper. They tried to explain to me that no one was perfect. That the revolution would take a while. They were very friendly and gentle. Not heavy-handed. They made clear that they respected me and urged me to be gentle in my criticism of others the way they had been with me.

Another experienced activist explained, through example, why it was so essential that leaders not be separate from the rest of the people. Hoang Thi Me is in her late sixties, and had been a leader in the women's movement against French colonialism. Their goals at that time were to fight against high taxes and rents and for women's equality by demanding that women be allowed to own land:

We worked with women in the fields. As we planted, we talked about the issues. The women wanted to be active and were very militant because we were struggling for women's rights. They wanted land. They were angry about being arrested because they couldn't pay taxes. We would talk to three or four people and they would talk to others. In this way, we would make propaganda a long time in advance for demonstrations. But we wouldn't pass the word about the actual time and place of the demonstration until the day before, so the police would not find out. We would pass the word quickly as we met friends on the way home from the fields or market. . . .

The Women's Union often played a key role in struggles like this one. Over the years, they have developed a step-by-step process that organizes women's energy and increases their unity. Le Thi Xuyen, Vice President of the Viet Nam Women's Union, described the five steps—steps which are often taken simultaneously:

1. Study the situation and problems to learn as much as possible about the women involved.

2. Make propaganda that explains to women the cause of their problems, gives them confidence in their power when they are united,

and a vision of their potential good life. If they are confused about who their worst enemy is ask them "who is most powerful." If they lack confidence, explain how women in socialist countries have made progress and describe victories of workers and peasants from our own and other peoples' history. These explanations are also part of a step-by-step progress. "We do not try to do everything at once."

3. Organize concrete struggles that focus on gaining a crucial demand. This, in itself, is a step-by-step process that begins with people's consciousness of their own interests but raises a consciousness that demands a larger political solution.

4. Choose new cadres from among those who are most active and militant in the struggle and give them further political education.

5. Involve more women in the organization and in the struggle. Xuyen added:

We learn with experience. Although we share a common enemy, we learn to talk differently to women coming from different social strata: peasants, workers, students.

Demonstrations of power

Women led the mass political ferment that ushered in the August Revolution in 1945. Before full-scale armed insurrection began against the French, women organized various challenges to French and Japanese authority. On May 1, 1945, in Hung Yen Province, women formed a protest march a kilometer long. Throughout the country, women joined in meetings and displays of strength, seizing grain stocks stored

Hanoi,
1938

by the fascists. Nguyen Thi Hong, one of the organizers of the assaults on the granaries in Hung Yen Province, recalled:

The attack on the granary was a real military operation. We had to assemble, organize and guide units of protestors from all parts of the province. We had to split them into teams, entrust each of them with a separate task: lay hold of granaries, disperse paddy and carry it to the rear, protect demonstrators, map out a plan for the march, choose the retreat route and beat off the enemy soldiers called in to repress us. [8]

Later they coordinated demonstrations with military activity and helped divert troops away from guerrilla placements. For example, while local guerrillas were in the process of taking over a Saigon Army garrison, thousands of women who were the mothers and wives of men who had been forced to serve in the Saigon Army demonstrated outside the local governor's office. They demanded that "their boys," who had been "conscripted" at the point of a bayonet, be given higher pay and less dangerous jobs.

Le Thi Thien's description of how demonstrators prevented the takeover of villages by stopping troop movements provides a dramatic example of the military skill of these women organizers.

We in Ben Tre decided to calculate the exact space of the streets and squares of all district centers and the provincial capital to know how many people we needed to fill up the whole space. Then we could organize the necessary number from the countryside. This had to be done carefully too, so the exact numbers would arrive from different directions to be in town at 5:00 a.m. Every square yard of space was occupied by our "human sea" so the target town would be paralyzed by dawn. In this way it was impossible to repress us, because the troops and the police couldn't move; nothing could move except us. We organized demonstrations of up to 20,000 people, almost all women.

If the authorities were able to call out troops and they threatened to open fire, we had special spokeswomen with high political conscious-ness. . . . [They would say] "Sons, you could all be my children. My two lads are in your Army. They look just like you. If you shoot at us it will be just like shooting at your own mother or wife. Why have we come here? To stop people from getting killed. Maybe your mother is in a village being bombarded or your wife being raped by Diem's troops at this very moment." [9]

Actions like these require high morale, ongoing organization, and leadership capable of prompt effective reaction to enemy counter-attacks. Behind each demonstration, many women are working to supply the demonstrators with provisions, to take responsibility for family care at their homes, and to keep reserve forces ready in case reinforcements are needed.Sometimes demonstrators occupied areas for weeks. Each village kept a force for political struggle in full readiness. [10]

In other demonstrations, women mobilized under the pretext of "demanding protection from the Saigon regime" against its own crimes. Demonstrators brought piles of branches and livestock killed by chemical defoliants. They threw the mess in front of the troops demanding an end to the destruction. These demands embarrassed Saigon officials and also won new sympathy for the liberation forces from among low-ranking civil servants, troops and even policemen of the Saigon regime. Some of these demonstrations have involved hundreds of thousands of women in simultaneous actions in thirty or forty provincial and district towns at a time.

One demonstration in 1960 has become famous all over Viet Nam and continues to inspire heroism. Thousands of women marched on the provincial capital of My Tho to protest an operation in which six villages had been burned by Diem's men. When they arrived at Bird's Cross Road, a solid block of Diem's troops met the women. They shot a pregnant woman who was carrying the first banner. As she fell, she cried,

Compatriots Advance!

A second woman grabbed the banner and was also shot dead, then a third. The marching women halted only long enough to pick up the bodies which they carried at the head of the demonstration.

A fourth woman seized the banner and the troops, stupefied by such courage and already swamped by the marching, furious crowd, gave way. The angry crowd continued on to the provincial governor's office, where they displayed the bodies of the three dead women and demanded compensation for the burned villages and for the families of the new martyrs. The governor had to grant their demands. [11]

Persuading the enemy

Women also played a key role in undermining the fighting morale of the Saigon troops and encouraging them to desert. Apart from a small number of top officials, the PRG considered men in the Saigon army to be "retrievable." Most ARVN soldiers were forcibly conscripted and resented their officers and U.S. "advisors" who treated them with contempt and brutality. Often demonstrations—expected to be "pro-Vietcong"—surprised Saigon troops by displaying banners demanding "Higher Salaries for the Troops." Once when a district chief asked demonstrators for proof that the salaries were too low, the women replied:

Everyone knows that during raids on villages, the soldiers steal chickens, rice and even cooked fish. This shows that they don't have enough to eat, so we're asking a salary increase for them." [12]

Many Saigon soldiers must have appreciated the women's sense of humor.

Besides demonstrations, women would persuade troops to desert more directly. Every night in some part of South Viet Nam, wherever there were Saigon army posts, there might be women with megaphones, walking cautiously around the posts, among the trees and tall grasses. They started the evening program by chanting a poem evoking memories of home and village life. And then:

Chanh, Chanh, it's your cousin Thi Lan, why do you shoot? I'm only a village girl. I have no guns. . . . Chanh, why don't you give up this dishonorable life, leave the bad road you are on and go back to your village. Land has been set aside for you in your village. Be on the side of the people. Why should you get yourself killed for the Yankees? [13]

As women performed this important political work or staged ambushes against U.S. troops stationed near their homes, their children also participated. Young people carried messages, kept watch and served the liberation forces in countless ingenious ways. Jane Barton, who worked in Viet Nam and speaks Vietnamese, reported that children were fond of teaching GI's how to "count" in Vietnamese. They made the GI's repeat five words which the GI's though were "one, two, three, four, five." Instead, the children were really having the soldiers recite the Vietnamese words for "Down with the American Imperialists!":

Dả Dảo Dế Quốc Mỹ

In 1963, forty-five thousand soliders in the pay of the Saigon regime deserted. Within the next ten years, the number multiplied by nearly ten. Between 1973 and 1974, in Hai Thuong village, Quang Tri Province, for example, women were proud that they encouraged more than 300 ARVN soldiers to desert. When the soldiers returned to the village, they each received a small plot of land, building materials and seed to start a new life.

Bui Thi Me explained that the PRG and the Union of Women for the Liberation of South Viet Nam were taking special steps to encourage reconciliation rather than revenge. During the period after January 1973, they gave hero awards to women who encouraged ARVN soldiers to desert, rather than to those who killed enemy soldiers.

If we took revenge, we would be falling into the trap of "Vietnamization"—allowing the U.S. government to set one Vietnamese against the other. No Vietnamese is our enemy. Only the U.S. government. Thieu is not Vietnamese. American blood flows in his veins. Even with big traitors, we try to make them agree with the policy of reconciliation. If they are too stubborn, we punish them, but only as a last resort. [14]

PRG leaders have devoted a lot of political education to the need for national reconciliation. The success of this education is impressive. The women at Hai Thuong village, for example, had reason to want revenge. Nine hundred out of the thousand adult women in that village had been tortured by U.S. or Saigon soldiers. But they welcomed ex-Saigon soldiers as misguided brothers. They understood that revenge was not necessary for victory and that peaceful reconstruction required national reconciliation and concord. Within months after the total victory of the PRG, all of Thieu's million-man army were enjoying the benefits of this policy of reconciliation.

Denunciation markets

The political struggle never really stopped. The women took advantage of every opportunity, even chance meetings, to undermine the morale of Saigon soldiers. Women often turned markets into political forums. For example, in one village, the women secretly organized lots of people to become "traders" and to come to sell their possessions before the Saigon troops plundered them. The routine marketplace became what they called a "denunciation market" when buyers heard:

If I don't sell these chickens, they'll be taken away by the Republican soldiers. . . . Look at these tiny bamboo shoots. If I don't sell them, those ruffians will come and uproot them anyway.

the anger became contagious and denunciations escalated. Known police informers would disappear during these times, fearing mass indignation. [15]

Women have taken major responsibility for more conventional forms of propaganda as well. A young woman student explained how they smuggled an entire printing press out of Saigon, passing through many checkpoints:

We took the whole thing apart. The type was taken out on the backs of scores of "market women"—actually, they were us students—in baskets topped with unsold fruits and vegetables. The rollers were a bit of a problem, but we greased them well and attached them to the bottoms of sampans. . . . Our problem before was to print in Saigon and smuggle copies out to the countryside. Now it is the opposite; we print outside and smuggle copies into the city. [16]

From the North, Thu Huon broadcasted three hours daily on Radio Hanoi. She is one of the several women announcers whom GI's nicknamed "Hanoi Hannah." She's thirty years old, has two children and rides a bicycle to work. She told a reporter:

I take great interest in speaking to these men who are fighting my people. They did not ask to come here. They were sent to fight an aggressive war against a people who are struggling for liberty and independence. [17]

Another "Hanoi Hannah" was a famous nightclub singer before independence. She joined a group who traveled through the liberated areas in the early 1950s, entertaining the anti-French resistance forces. She joined because she could no longer tolerate the arrogance of the French soldiers who frequented her nightclub. They behaved as if they owned all of Viet Nam—including her. She lived and worked in the liberated areas under extremely difficult conditions but repeatedly refused offers to return to a life of luxury where she would have to sing for the French.

Her songs, like the songs of the mobile units of Song and Dance Troupes today, aim to entertain and encourage the fighters. These troupes reflect and stimulate the pride Vietnamese feel for their cultural traditions and express the NLF commitment to defend the Vietnamese people against cultural assault by degrading entertainment imported from the U.S. Traditional and modern songs reflect the continuity in Viet Nam's history of struggle against foreign domination. These entertainers performed in combat zones, sometimes in caves and underground shelters. They often picked up arms and joined the combat forces.

Jane Fonda asked members of the National Liberation Song and Dance Ensemble, most of whom are women, if they ever had any trouble with sexual advances from male soldiers. Although the interpreter was an expert, the performers did not understand the question. They simply could not conceive of their "fellow comrades" engaging in any form of sexual aggression against them. Sexual aggression was rare among most Vietnamese until the U.S. created a demoralized and corrupt Saigon army.

Madame Binh

The woman who is Vice President of the Union of Women for the Liberation of South Viet Nam is also the Foreign Minister of the Provisional Revolutionary Government. Her name is Nguyen Thi Binh. She has represented the Vietnamese people all over the world, traveled to Cuba and many countries in Africa and Asia. She was the chief negotiator in Paris for the PRG and is a member of the Presidium of the Afro-Asian Solidarity Organization.

Madame Binh does not think her life has been special. She says, "It is how Vietnamese patriots live." She is the granddaughter of Phan Chu Trinh, a famous reformer and patriot who was one of the early campaigners against French colonialism. When she was 18, the war against the French began and her father, a minor civil servant with a radical reputation, had to flee Saigon. Her mother had died earlier. As the oldest of six children, Madame Binh became a tutor to support her sisters and brothers. She also took courses to qualify her for a regular teaching position. This is how she described her education:

I learned French and French history. Not our history. We were despised by the colonialists. I was often indignant, humiliated. I saw how poor my people were. I wanted to be a doctor then, to help my people. I saw how they went to doctors and were asked first how much money they had. [18]

While a student, she joined the political struggle and took part in a huge demonstration in 1950 in Saigon when U.S. ships docked in the harbor. This demonstration was the first to recognize U.S. responsibility and support for French colonial policies and was a significant show of force against both. Once Binh became known as an activist in patriotic women's and students' organizations, she was arrested and spent four years in a French jail. After she was freed from prison in 1954, she married a man she identified as "someone I had known for a long time." Until recently, she had to keep her husband's identity a secret to insure his safety and political effectiveness against the Thieu regime. In 1954, she and her husband were together for only a few months before he had to escape to the countryside. She stayed in the cities and organized peaceful demonstrations against Diem's dictatorship. But finally, in 1957, she had to flee to the countryside to avoid arrest. She remembers those times as hard years:

We organized village by village. Those who knew how to fight taught others. It was the third time we fought. One day we will have a beautiful life, if not for ourselves, then for our children.

Binh has two children: one born in 1961 and the other in 1967. In 1970, she said,

I can count the days—not weeks, not months—in all these years that I have seen my husband. My children count the time they have seen me or their father in days. People say we are accustomed to this life. But we have the same desires and wants as everyone else. The same. It is difficult to live as we do.

Madame Binh, a leader of the Long-Haired Army and a world-famous diplomat, sent a message to women in the United States on the occasion of International Women's Day, March 8, 1972. She sent affectionate greetings to her American sisters and welcomed their participation in the common political struggle:

July 1971:
Nguyen Thi Binh

San Francisco, Sept. 2, 1971: women's march against Presidio Army Base

... *In the past year, your continuous and really creative activities have filled us with much enthusiasm about our American sisters' strengthening their solidarity and playing an ever more positive and important role in the American people's common struggle for an end to the aggressive war in Viet Nam and for social progress in the United States.*

The South Vietnamese women have been encouraged by the news of their American sisters' actions [rallies, etc.] ... serving as a severe warning to the Nixon administration's reactionary home and foreign policy.

I am convinced that the American women, with their feminine inborn sensitiveness, sympathize with the South Vietnamese people's— particularly with the South Vietnamese women's and children's—woes and sufferings multiplied by years and years of war, and consequently understand fully the ardent and profound aspirations of our people.

All of us, women of Viet Nam and America alike, long for a rapid
end to the war. . . . We all want to establish between us, between our
children, between the people of the two countries, new friendly rela-
tions based on fair equality. . . .

We hope that, given our common ardent aspirations for peace, the
American women and people will enhance solidarity with the Vietnam-
ese women and people, make strenuous efforts to press the Nixon ad-
ministration to listen to the voices of reason—the voices of peace.

Peace and justice will triumph!

All my sincere wishes for your success in this spring drive!

[signed] Nguyen Thi Binh, Vice President of Women's Union
for Liberation of South Viet Nam [19]

Final battles of the Long-Haired Army

The PRG did not start a new war. The liberation forces pledged to keep the peace and defeat Thieu in the political battlefield—fighting militarily only in self-defense. Women who became seasoned political organizers took on more and more leadership roles as the political power of the PRG grew. On March 8, 1973, thousands of women in Quang Tri got together for the first time in public celebration of International Women's Day. They pledged to struggle for the enforcement of the Paris Peace Agreement, especially the release of the political prisoners still held by Thieu.

By October 1973, it was clear that the U.S. and Thieu would not respond to political pressure alone. They continued violating the Peace Agreement—including the bombing of PRG zones. On October 15, 1973, the PRG issued a call to all liberation forces and to the entire population of South Viet Nam to join in the struggle:

for the maintenance of peace and the materialization of national con-
cord by meting out due punishment to the U.S. and Saigon for their
acts of sabotage against the Paris Agreement. . . .

On another front, inside Saigon and other cities then controlled by Thieu, women of the Third Force continued the struggle. These women were not part of the PRG and followed their own strategies in pressing for the withdrawal of American troops and for freedom in Viet Nam. Perhaps one of the earliest representatives of this political perspective was Nhat Chi Mai, a teacher who worked part-time in the Buddhist School of Social Work in Saigon. On May 16, 1967, she told newsmen to come to the Tu Nghiem Pagoda. When they arrived, they found her seated in traditional ceremonial fashion. Beside her were pictures of the Virgin Mary and the Buddhist Goddess of Mercy, Kwan Yin.

162

I wish to use my body as a torch
to dissipate the darkness
to awaken love among the people
and bring peace to Viet Nam. [20]

She poured gasoline all over her body, lit the match and as fire consumed her body, she prayed for peace. Nhat Chi Mai called herself "She Who Burns Herself for Peace." She acted alone. In the following years, many Buddhist women organized and worked, in the spirit of Nhat Chi Mai, for peace and independence.

In the fall of 1974, thousands of people in the cities under Thieu's control risked their lives to demonstrate for Thieu's resignation. The Buddhist Order of Mendicant Nuns—the *Khat Si* Nuns—became leaders of the militant struggles in the streets and spearheaded the People's Front Against Famine. Huynh Lien, one of the nuns who sat down in the streets to block Saigon military transport and fought with police, told a reporter:

Our first goal is to implement the Paris Accords. Our second goal is to give rice to all poor and hungry people. . . . A lot of women whose husbands are dead and who have a lot of children, maybe eight or nine, come here asking for rice. . . . We don't organize our demonstrations at all. We just go out into the streets and the people follow us. Yes, of course, I am afraid of the police. They beat us very much. But we forget the pain because the common people suffer so much. . . . We'll continue until we are dead. [21]

Madame Ngo Ba Thanh, a founder of the Women's Committee to Defend the Right to Live, emerged from Thieu's prisons as one of the central leaders of the Third Force campaign. She led the Peoples' Movement to Implement the Paris Agreement which joined with the Buddhist and Catholic groups and organized the unprecedented movement in the fall of 1974. Until that upsurge of political activity against Thieu, the PRG continued to attempt to negotiate with him to implement the Peace Agreement.

However on October 8, 1974, the PRG issued a new policy statement which cut off negotiations with Thieu. The statement endorsed the demands of the political movement calling for Thieu's overthrow and the installation of a new government which would implement the Paris Peace Agreement. The PRG also reiterated its demand for an end to all U.S. intervention in the internal affairs of South Viet Nam. Finally, the statement committed the PRG to negotiate with any government that replaced Thieu's—as long as it seriously implemented the Paris Agreement.

After October 8, the pace of political activity escalated. Thieu re-shuffled his cabinet and made some pretense at reform. In the spring of 1975, as his army disintegrated, Thieu lost his few remaining al-lies. He was forced to resign on April 21. Poor and working women, militant supporters of the PRG for many years, had built a strong po-litical foundation for the popular insurrections that swept every South Vietnamese city. These insurrections were essential to the success of the Ho Chi Minh Campaign which ended on April 30—the day the PRG became the government for all of South Viet Nam. People in Viet Nam celebrated. Madame Binh sent the following cable to the celebration in New York City:

After 30 years of relentless efforts, countless hardships and sacri-fices, the struggle of the South Vietnamese people for independence and freedom has reached complete victory. Real peace is back in Viet Nam. Viet Nam again belongs to the Vietnamese.

In this glorious moment of our age-old history, we convey greetings of peace and friendship to the American people. In particu-lar, our warm feelings and profound gratitude to those Americans who for years worked untiringly to end the unjust, criminal war and, most recently, to cut aid to the warlike fascist Nguyen Van Thieu junta. The people of South Viet Nam are healing the wounds of war and building a new life in the spirit of national reconciliation and concord. We hope you urge the U.S. government to show a responsible attitude towards the great losses caused to the land and people of Viet Nam, thus helping us to rapidly normalize life and reconstruct our country.

May friendship between the peoples of Viet Nam and the American people develop unceasingly. [22]

Now members of the Long-Haired Army are reorganizing for the new tasks of the post-independence period. At a celebration of Buddha's Birthday, May 25, 1975, Madame Ngo Ba Thanh announced that the Women's Committee to Defend the Right to Live was going to merge with the Union of Women for the Liberation of South Viet Nam. In her speech to the organization she said,

Now our country is completely liberated. Women are in a position of being equal citizens in an independent and free country. . . . As for women, there is no question of the struggle to defend the right to live. Women come together with the entire people to become masters of the country. Therefore the Women's Movement to Defend the Right to Live has no reason to exist. The members of that organization now have the duty to join the Women's Union to make a strong, unified organization of women . . . [23]

The new unified women's movement in South Viet Nam intends to dedicate itself to healing the wounds of war, reconstruction, and working towards the peaceful reunification of Viet Nam.

Notes

1. Ho Chi Minh, "Instruction to Establish the Viet Nam Propaganda Unit for National Liberation," in *Ho Chi Minh on Revolution,* edited by Bernard Fall (New York: Signet, 1968), p. 138.
2. Quoted by Vu Can in "The NLF and the Second Resistance in South Viet Nam," in *South Viet Nam: From NLF to PRG* (Vietnamese Studies #23; Hanoi: 1969), p. 40.
3. Quoted by Tran Van Dinh, "Viet Nam People's Army," *Indochina Chronicle* #31, (February 28, 1974), p. 3.
4. Speech by Minh Khai at 7th Congress of the Communist International is reprinted in *Viet Nam Courier,* #35 (April 1975) p. 14. Other information about Minh Khai from: Ma Thi Tu, "The Vietnamese Woman, Yesterday and Today," in *Vietnamese Women* (Vietnamese Studies #10; Hanoi: 1966), p. 33.
5. "An Example of Courageous Struggle," *The Vietnamese Trade Unions* #89 (January-March 1972), pp. 27-29.
6. "In the Cities," *South Viet Nam in Struggle* #199 (May 21, 1973), p. 3.
7. All quotations in this section are from interviews conducted by author in September and October, 1974 in Viet Nam.
8. "Vietnamese Women and the August Revolution," *Viet Nam Courier* #346 (November 8, 1971), p. 3.
9. Wilfred Burchett, *Inside Story of Guerrilla War* (New York: International Publishers, 1965), pp. 63-64.
10 Vu Can, p. 43.
11. Burchett, *Inside Story of Guerrilla War,* pp. 65-66.
12. Xuan Vu, "Flames in the Night," in *Vietnamese Women,* p. 74.
13. Burchett, *Inside Story of Guerrilla War,* p. 207.
14. From interview between author and Bui Thi Me in Hai Thuong Village, September 21, 1974.
15. Hien Trang, "Things That Happened at X Market," *Women of Viet Nam* #1 (1971), p. 28.
16. Burchett, *Inside Story of Guerrilla War,* p. 207.
17. Quoted in the *San Francisco Chronicle,* January 5, 1969.
18. Martha Gelhorn's interview with Nguyen Thi Binh originally appeared in the *London Times* and was reprinted in *Liberation News Service* #308 (January 9, 1971), pp. 11-12. This quote and the others in the following paragraphs are from this interview.
19. This letter has appeared in many publications. It can be found in an excellent anthology of writings by women taking part in struggles all around the world called *Women,* available from P.O. Box 187, Dayton View Station, Dayton, Ohio 45406 (page 53 is Madame Binh's message).
20. Don Luce, John Schafer and Jacquelyn Chagnon, *We Promise One Another: Poems from an Asian War* (Washington, D.C.: Indochina Mobile Education Project, 1971), p. 111.
21. "Courageous Voices Speak from Saigon," *Indochina Focal Point,* (Nov. 22-Dec. 13, 1974) p. 3.
22. Text of the cable appeared in *The Guardian* (May 21, 1975) p. 3.
23. Giai Phong Press Agency release, May 29, 1975.

12.
WOMEN WITH WEAPONS

If I am here in High Command, it is because the people taught me. But I am no different than thousands and thousands of other women. I am merely one of them. And how many combatants have fallen, women and men, who could have filled my post!

—Nguyen Thi Dinh, Deputy Commander in Chief of PLAF, and President of Union of Women for the Liberation of South Viet Nam

Reports in the U.S. press about "Vietcong troops" inevitably assume that the troops are men. But millions of Vietnamese women have taken up arms to defend their country. For example, during the Tet Offensive of 1968, the NLF staged a military and political coup by taking over the U.S. Embassy in Saigon. Newspapers all around the world printed pictures of the NLF flag flying from the roof of the fortress-like building. But none mentioned that a women's commando group was the force which occupied five of the seven floors of the Embassy, killed two hundred U.S. personnel, and forced Ambassador Bunker to flee in a helicopter.

The team was named after Le Thi Rieng. She had been a Vice President of the Union of Women for the Liberation of South Viet Nam and a member of the Central Committee of the NLF. In 1967, Saigon authorities captured her. For a year, they tortured her. They finally executed her in the early morning of February 1st, 1968, within hours of the embassy takeover, as U.S. and Saigon officials were still reeling from the large-scale offensive. Le Thi Rieng is one of the many heroes who live in the names of women's fighting brigades and work teams. With the understanding that their production served to strengthen the anti-U.S. war effort, women in one Northern province worked 44,392 extra work days to avenge her murder. [1]

First against the French

In December 1944, thirty-four soldiers calling themselves the "Armed Propaganda Brigade for the Liberation of Viet Nam" took the oath with General Giap to fight for an end to French colonialism. Within a few years they grew to be the Viet Nam People's Army. There were three women in that original group. In the face of French intransigence, Ho Chi Minh issued an appeal to the entire Vietnamese people to wage resistance war in December 1946:

Men and women, old and young, regardless of creeds, political parties or nationalities, all the Vietnamese must stand up to fight the French colonialists to save the nation. Those who have rifles will use their rifles; those who have swords will use their swords; those who have no swords will use spades, hoes or sticks..... [2]

Women responded enthusiastically to Ho Chi Minh's appeal. Ha Que, who is now the President of the Viet Nam Women's Union, formed the first women's guerrilla unit. Nguyen Thi Ngai commanded a military action which seized power in Sadec, south of Saigon. Women all over Viet Nam maintained the tradition of the Trung sisters by taking up arms against the French invaders.

Vo Thi Sau was one of the one million women who fought with arms against the French. She came from a very poor workers' family and joined a secret guerrilla unit when she was only 14. She did spy work and once managed to kill thirteen French soldiers with a well-placed grenade. Several months later, she tried to assassinate a notorious French agent, but was caught. First they tortured her, then they tried to bribe her to give information about her comrades. She remained defiant. She became the youngest woman ever to face a firing squad in Viet Nam when the French shot her without a trial. Thousands of women vowed to avenge the death of Vo Thi Sau and aided in the final defeat of the French at Dien Bien Phu in 1954.

Between 1954 and 1960, the anti-French resistance fighters (Viet Minh) obeyed the Geneva Accords. In the North, the people, with Ho Chi Minh's leadership, began to build socialism. In the South, dictator Diem began rounding up and executing whomever he could find from the Viet Minh and many of their supporters. Opponents of Diem continued to abide by the peace agreements, demanding their enforcement with demonstrations and peaceful political activity. Diem, with the decisive encouragement of the U.S. government, responded with systematic terror campaigns. By 1959, it became clear that Diem would never fulfill his treaty obligations, and the South Vietnamese people began to rebel militarily against his terrorist regime.

In January 1960, Madame Dinh led an uprising in Ben Tre Province. For the first time, an insurrection triumphed in an entire province and forced the withdrawal of thirteen thousand Diemist troops. The strength of the Ben Tre insurrection was based on a skillful combination of armed and political struggle that was to become the model strategy for liberation forces throughout the South. The insurgent forces, involving large numbers of peasants, stormed Diem's militia posts, ousted Diem's village administrations, and replaced them with People's Committees for Self-Management.

The first regional military detachment took an oath in the presence of the people. They set up self-defense units in all the hamlets—peaceful villages which quickly became combat positions. Their defense against a massive counterattack by Diem's troops was successful. A

General Dinh visits all-woman guerrilla unit in Mekong Delta.

huge demonstration by women, occupying Mo Cay town in Ben Tre Province for a week, forced the government administrator to order the withdrawal of the troops.

Ben Tre gave the signal for a general uprising. Armed insurrection spread throughout the South. On December 20, 1960, Madame Dinh joined other political leaders to officially form a new political organization to unify and lead the struggle for national liberation—the National Liberation Front of South Viet Nam. [3] The People's Liberation Armed Forces (PLAF) became the regular army fighting under the leadership of the NLF. Madame Dinh received the rank of General and became the Deputy Commander of the PLAF—the commander is Tran Nam Trung, the Vice President of the Central Committee of the NLF.

The PLAF operates according to revolutionary principles. Commanders and rank and file are generally from the same class origins, mainly peasant. Before an operation, commanders and rank and file discuss the plans on an absolutely equal footing. But during the operation itself, discipline is total. After the action, everyone participates in critical summing-up sessions on an equal basis. Visitors to PLAF bases have been impressed by their unity and respect for each other:

One rarely hears a command, doubtless partly because of the long years living "integrated with the enemy," but also because discipline and confidence in the leaders is such that a commander does not have to shout in order to impress. The quietness with which everything is handled in NLF units is a characteristic that has impressed all who have visited them. [4]

170

Women are full-time members and often leaders of the PLAF. Forty per cent of the regimental commanders of the PLAF are women. The PLAF are the troops who deal with the enemy's mobile reserves, initiate offensive operations and attack major enemy concentrations. All PLAF members are volunteers. They receive no salary and when they're not in combat, they help in harvesting, building homes and schools, and administering free medical care and medical training.

There are also regional guerrilla forces, full-time fighters who operate only in the region where they live. They engage the enemy forces stationed in the same area, break up enemy raids, lay ambushes, encircle bases, and attack posts in their regions. Then there are local self-defense guerrillas, or militia women, who are not full-time soldiers, but fight when their area is attacked, pin down local enemy forces, and keep their local posts permanently encircled. A higher percentage of women are in the local militia and regional guerrilla units than in the PLAF. The local militia kept villages fortified with trenches, traps, and spikes. These defenses have been decisive in wearing down the morale of Saigon and U.S. troops. [5]

In the North

Nearly all North Vietnamese women are part of the militia and form the core of self-defense teams in factories and fields, schools and villages. The "Three Responsibilities Movement" established defense as a primary task of women. They became experts with anti-aircraft weapons and took credit for downing hundreds of U.S. aircraft. Women's gunner units protected scores of fishing hamlets by sinking U.S. warships which shelled them. In preparation for repelling an invasion, often threatened by U.S. ground troops, all women in the North received military training—including training in hand-to-hand combat.

But few women are members of the regular Viet Nam People's Army (VPA)—the mobile, full-time soldiers who usually travel far from home. It was not general policy to send women to the front. But few North Vietnamese would suggest that women are incapable of becoming full-time members of the VPA. I asked a Vietnamese friend if the VPA discriminated against women and if women had a lower status than men in society because they rarely went to the front. Her answer was proud:

Every country must limit its full-time army because the army cannot be economically self-sufficient. Some people must stay home to take care of production and the children. Besides, the militia is very important. We could not win the war without village defense. The entire country recognizes the contribution of women in fulfilling the "Three Responsibili-

ties"—production, defense, and the family—not just defense. In any case, we do whatever the revolution requires without calculating personal gain.

General Giap, the Minister of Defense of the DRV, has also underlined the importance of the militia:

Local people's war, self-defense militia and regional forces are the firmest and broadest basis of the whole armed struggle and all the people's armed forces. [6]

Most of the women who were members of the VPA served in highly skilled, often dangerous jobs as bomb defusers, medics and liaison workers. These specialties are highly respected, but partially segregated along sex lines. Many women served as support troops and supply carriers. They became the heroes of movies and songs which praised their "feet of brass and shoulders of iron." Members of these units were mostly young women without children.

Women with children, including grandmothers, won recognition for their contribution to the military effort in other ways. When I traveled in Quang Binh Province, just north of the 17th parallel, people invariably referred to Mother Suot, an older woman, whenever they spoke of their province's military achievements. For years, she had defied blizzards of bombs and shells to ferry troops and ammunition across the river near her home. She became a martyr at sixty, when a bomb finally hit her ferry. More often women her age were active in the Association of Mothers of Fighters—a mass organization of women over fifty. Their main tasks were to encourage the fighters and help disabled soldiers and the families of those who died in battle.

This sexual division of labor expresses the conviction of the Vietnamese people that raising children is primarily women's responsibility. Many household chores like childcare are collectivized and, when men are home from the front, they are expected to share in these jobs. But Vietnamese women don't feel that their emancipation depends on the total elimination of division of labor based on sex because motherhood enhances their dignity.

The image of woman in North Viet Nam is multi-dimensional. She is a respected mother and she is a fighter. One of the most-used postage stamps in the DRV has a picture of a small woman—but not weak—holding a bayonet, leading a downed U.S. pilot, his head bowed in shame. The picture originally comes from a news photo of a militia woman in action in the area of Ha Tinh. The national poet of the DRV, To Huu, wrote this poem about her:

> *The small guerrilla holds her gun at the ready,*
> *The burly American bends his head low,*
> *After all, a stout heart is better than a big belly.*
> — *One need have no beard to become a hero.*

Magazines and newspapers of the North, especially those for women, carry endless stories of the combat activities of their sisters in the South, as well as publicity of militia work in the North. This military activity and education gives women new confidence in their ability to take on new tasks and emancipate themselves. One woman who worked as a bomb defuser in the most heavily bombed province, just north of the 17th parallel, summarized the experience of most women in Viet Nam:

> *We women must try to perform things normally considered beyond our capability.* [7]

Heroes without beards

In the South as well, women fighters are not only young and single. Many are mothers. They follow the example of Ut Tich—the woman we first mentioned in chapter nine who joined the guerrillas when she was only 14. She began her military life as a scout and courier. Like most liaison women, she learned to carry messages in her outside pockets rather than close to her body, because French troops were fond of unbuttoning women's shirts and running their hands over the breasts of young women.

In the early sixties, the NLF had few weapons. Ut Tich, like liberation soldiers everywhere, had to use cunning to get the weapons needed for future battles. Ut worked with a group of women guerrillas who invited the men of a Saigon Army post to a banquet. Only one man stayed behind to guard the post. Ut easily tricked him into turning over his rifle to her, kept him at a distance, and quickly handed out the arsenal of the post to guerrillas waiting outside.

She became an expert at ambush and taking over Saigon's military barracks. She continued commanding a guerrilla unit as her family grew. She had confidence that her neighbors and the village school would take good care of her six children while she was away at battle. In 1965, in one amazing battle, she shot down a helicopter and killed thirty-five Saigon soldiers. The NLF is proud that she commanded a guerrilla unit—especially because she was the mother of six. When Ut Tich left her village to attend the Congress for Heroes and Elite Fighters of the Liberation Armed Forces, one of her daughters, who by then was a regional guerrilla herself, and another who was a platoon leader, joined in the farewell party. Ut Tich died in battle in 1970.

Ta Thi Kieu is another woman hero of the People's Liberation Armed Forces. As early as 1965, she had led more than 100 political struggles and 33 armed combats, and destroyed 471 strategic hamlets. Now she trains other women as fighters. She originally came from a very poor family and was practically illiterate when she began to work for the PLAF at the age of 20. The NLF's publishing house, Giai Phong, has printed an entire book in English about her life. The book emphasizes the tremendous odds she had to overcome as a woman in order to gain respect as a fighter. The night before she attacked a Saigon Army garrison for the first time, she told herself:

I must succeed to show the men they shouldn't make mock of women. [8]

Some of the men in her unit hadn't wanted women to participate in the action because they feared the women wouldn't be strong enough to carry away the wounded. In the end, Ta Thi Kieu and another woman took the garrison alone. The men had mistimed their actions. When the two women entered the fort, Kieu boldly announced, "The liberation forces are here!" The Saigon troops took her word for it and surrendered.

A woman member of the Jarai national minority, Rachem H' Ban, became famous for the leadership she took in preventing Diem's troops from taking over her area. She told how when Diem began a terror campaign against her people,

Life became impossible. From other villages came news of our tribes-people being killed, women raped, houses burned, pigs and buffalo stolen. We decided that to live we must fight back. [9]

Two days after a village meeting, eleven of Diem's soldiers came to the village and arrested all the young men. They confiscated knives and crossbows after searching every house. The people fought back, even without weapons. The troops surrounded the arrested men and the rest of the villagers surrounded the troops.

The chief of Diem's troops shot one of the arrested men in the leg. Everyone became furious at the sight of a brother's blood. Rachem called out instructions in the Jarai language and the women quickly armed themselves with pieces of firewood from under the huts and hurled themselves at the soldiers. Rachem and two others went for the unit chief, knocked his gun out of his hand and strangled him. Five other soldiers had already been clubbed to death, while the rest fled. The tribespeople now had weapons. Rachem was only 17 years old at the time, but she became a leader of the NLF district committee. Within nine years she was, at age 26, listed along with members of the Central Committee of the NLF in a directory of "Personalities of the South Viet Nam Liberation Movement."

Of course, most of the women who have fought in the South remain anonymous. Madame Dinh recently summarized some of the highlights of women's participation in armed struggle in South Viet Nam:

... *With their bows and arrows, booby traps, spiked pits, homemade guns, muskets, mines and grenades, our women killed the enemy in many places and at many times. . . . In 1965, when the United States sent troops into the South on a massive scale, the movement to have women join the armed forces increased. . . .*

For instance, the women guerrillas of Cu Chi district . . . destroyed 99 vehicles in the first six months of 1966. The Quang Nam women guerrillas swam the Bau Nuoc Lon River to attack U.S. troops. After killing 21 of them, they swam back to their areas and resumed farming as if nothing had happened. Mrs. Ngo Thi May alone killed 25 American soldiers and won the "anti-U.S. Elite Fighter" title three times. . . .

In the first three months of 1968, some 10,000 women joined the armed forces in central Trung Bo. In Huang Nam and Phu Yen, more than 500 women carried out dangerous missions as members of guerrilla units. In Nam Bo, 40 per cent of the women joined guerrilla formations . . . The guerrilla women of Tri Thien, Cho Lai, Lam Dong, Bach

Hanoi, May Day, 1973: militia units of national minority women

Ai, Ben Tre, etc. also fought very heroically and wiped out more than
1,000 enemy troops. . . .

Many secret women's self-defense organizations were founded in
cities. . . . The Hue women's self-defense unit, composed of 11 young
women, defeated a U.S. Marine Battalion during the Tet Offensive.
The Le Thi Rieng women's self-defense unit fought on the Saigon
streets, wiped out 100 security agents . . . [10]

The Tet Offensive of 1968 became the decisive turning point in the
war to repel the American troops from Vietnamese soil. The U.S.
military command hastily issued orders bringing GI's in from the rural
areas to try to maintain control over the cities. After 1968, U.S. troops
would never again be able to hold any territory in the countryside.
Politically, the NLF demonstrated that it had widespread support—
even in the cities. Shortly after the offensive, the Alliance of National,
Democratic and Peace Forces (ANDPF) was founded, which reflected
the increased participation of the urban middle classes in the war
against U.S. aggression. A year later, the ANDPF and the NLF held a
Congress of Representatives of the South Vietnamese People which
established the Provisional Revolutionary Government of South Viet
Nam.

Immediately after Thieu staged his own one-man "presidential
election," in 1971, students set fire to the U.S. library in Saigon.
Leaflets signed by the "Movement to Drive Out the American Aggressors," told people that a young woman named Vo Thi Bach Tuyet was
President of the Movement and led the action. In the coming weeks,
the same group launched a systematic campaign to "make life dangerous for GI's on the Saigon streets." Hundreds of jeeps and other U.S.
vehicles went up in flames.

Also in the cities, women who were members of the PLAF served
as secretaries and servants to top officers of Thieu's Army. They relayed
valuable information to the Liberation Army and also had the
opportunity to plant explosives in the meeting rooms of the top brass in
Saigon. General Dinh of the PLAF pointed out how their upper-class
life style made Saigon's officers vulnerable:

They know we do this, but they have to hire servants.

Peasant women, who served GI's, doing laundry, shining their
boots, selling them fruit or soft drinks, often worked with the PLAF.
During the daytime, they routinely gained entrance to U.S. bases and
measured the exact locations of targets they planned to shell the
coming night. The following day, they returned to the base to check out
the results of the previous night's mortar attacks. When they had
found that they had missed their target, they would repace the dis-

176

Vinh Phu Province, DRV: militia woman captures B-52 pilot Edgar Johnson

tances—all the while smiling meekly to the GI's they passed. The second night, they would shell the base again according to the new measurements. Even General Dinh entered a U.S. base disguised as a peasant woman.

General Dinh

Like Ta Thi Kieu and many other fighters, General Dinh also came from a poor family and was illiterate until her revolutionary comrades taught her to read. She joined the anti-French resistance in 1937, when she was 17. Three years later, the French arrested both Dinh and her husband. He died of torture, but she escaped in 1943. She was an effective agitator, in spite of the fact that she had to live in hiding. She was the leader of the first armed uprising against the French in her province of Ben Tre in 1945. With the success of the August Revolution in that year, she led the triumphal march of thousands of insurrectionists towards the provincial capital.

General Dinh first met Ho Chi Minh in 1946, when a delegation from the South went to Hanoi to get arms for the struggle against the French. She wrote in her memoirs:

On my arrival in the capital, I was overwhelmed by emotion. I was barely 26, a country girl. I had never left my native province of Ben Tre. Now that thanks to the revolution I had a chance to visit the national capital, everything seemed strange to me. But the warm hospitality we received from our kin in the North made me feel immediately at home and filled me with happiness. . . . After we were seated, the President began asking questions about the South. . . . During the subsequent meal, he talked to each of us individually. To me he said,

"Stay here for some time for study before returning south to carry on the resistance." Then he gave me some advice which I have kept engraved in my mind: "A revolutionary must study all her lifetime; she must study theory; she must learn from the masses and from practice. Otherwise, she would be like someone traveling at night without light, without a walking stick. Soon she would trip and fall. Don't you think so?"...

A few days later we called again to congratulate him on his birthday, May 19.... [After explaining that there would be no special meal or entertainment because of the suffering of the people still fighting the French] he said, "Our entire people are of one mind in struggling against the French aggressors. We are bound to win . . . then we'll celebrate victory together." The President wept. We too wept. [11]

By 1947, General Dinh took charge of bringing supplies to the southern part of Viet Nam from the North where liberation forces were stronger. In those times, she lived from one high-risk mission to another. The war had its ebb and flow and whenever the French recaptured her province, Dinh was forced to hide in tunnels underground. When they captured her, the villagers acted quickly and rescued her.

After the signing of the Geneva Accords in 1954, she was one of the only revolutionary leaders who stayed in the South. Diem assumed she went North, so she remained free by changing her name and home frequently. By 1957, Diem found out that she was still in the South and offered a huge reward for her capture. They posted her picture everywhere, but the peasants protected her whether she disguised herself as a market woman or someone's sick daughter. When Diem's soldiers searched her hide-out, the family protecting her would cover her head and she would moan loudly. Once, however, she disguised herself as a wealthy lady and traveled securely with an ARVN escort.

178

Madame Dinh became Deputy Commander in Chief of the PLAF in 1961, after she led the Ben Tre insurrection of 1960—the insurrection that served as a model for a national liberation strategy. The 1964 congress of the NLF elected her to the Presidium—the leading body of the Central Committee of the NLF.A year later. the first Congress of the Union of Women for the Liberation of South Viet Nam elected her President.Her background as an illiterate peasant, her bonds of love with the people, her experience in political and military struggle, and her wisdom and courage—all combine to make her a leading strategist of People's War for the South Vietnamese people. But people who have met Nguyen Thi Dinh are overwhelmed by her modesty. Her appearance is the same as any other peasant woman. Her bearing is dignified but humble, even though she is the leader of the army that defeated the most sophisticated technology of murder that the U.S. government could devise.

Many Westerners assume that when a woman takes a role that is traditionally performed by men, she has to harden herself. But we have seen how People's War is different from aggressive war. In People's War, strength comes from the political support of the population, from careful planning, from political unity and mutual respect among the fighters—not callous indifference to suffering or brute force. People's War is women's war and Madame Dinh has lost none of her sensitivity as a woman.

Two Cuban visitors to the liberated zones describe an encounter with Madame Dinh. They were watching a performance of a memorial to Nguyen Van Troi—a South Vietnamese martyr who had been executed the year before in Saigon for attempting to assassinate LBJ's Secretary of Defense Robert MacNamara. It was true guerrilla theater, deep in the Vietnamese jungle. Van Troi's widow struggled to hold back her tears, but Madame Dinh wept openly. Then, an enemy bombardment interrupted the performance and Madame Dinh quickly dried her eyes and resumed her responsibility as military commander—issuing instructions for dispersal. [12]

Decisive victory

In the Spring of 1975, Thieu's army collapsed. On April 26, 1975, the People's Liberation Armed Forces launched the Ho Chi Minh Campaign—a military campaign, including massive insurrections by civilians, that would bring peace to Viet Nam. The goal of the campaign was to climax the spring offensive with a decisive blow against Saigon, the last foothold of the U.S.-sponsored regime. The historic Ho Chi Minh Campaign ended in complete victory on April 30, 1975. A sea of PRG flags welcomed a column of Liberation Army tanks into Saigon.

A young, well-armed woman hailed and halted the first tank. Nguyen Trung Kien, eighteen years old, is a commando fighter in Saigon. She climbed aboard the tank to guide it by the shortest route to the Presidential Palace. Minutes later, 11:30 am, Saigon time, members of the PLAF raised the PRG flag over the Presidential Palace in Saigon. Inside, the following historic scene occured:

Thieu's replacement, President **Duong Van "Big" Minh**, rose and greeted the first PRG troops to enter the palace. He said:

The revolution has come. You have come. We have been waiting for you this morning to hand over power.

The PLAF officer replied in a gentle, but firm voice:

The revolution has seized complete power. The former administration has been overthrown. No one can hand over what they have lost. You must surrender immediately. [13]

The PLAF, PRG and the people had fought many years for this victory. They were prepared for peace.

The immediate organizing of the city was completely carried out by local people, both students and older people. They had planned in advance for the collection of arms, ending the looting, feeding the homeless ARVN soldiers, cleaning the streets, protecting the gas stations that were left and calming the people. . . . One friend, Dung, tells a story of going out with her 16-year-old sister right after the surrender and taking down the RVN [Saigon] flag and hanging up the PRG flag at the local administrative office. Fleeing ARVN soldiers saw them there, and began piling their guns at the two sisters' feet, to get rid of them. Dung saw this was a good thing, and she and her sister each picked up a rifle so as to look official [neither one knows how to shoot]. Then dozens more soldiers piled their guns there, and Dung waited for some other people to help her take the guns to a building and lock them up. [14]

General Dinh explained to some Cuban friends how local women's militia units and members of the Women's Union took over official posts of the Thieu regime in many cities before the PLAF arrived. She herself had led a group of women in taking over the villa that once housed two U.S. Army colonels and a Navy commander. The women arrived at the villa on April 29th. The U.S. officers fled in the middle of a meal. General Dinh smiled as she recalled: *They were very frightened and left without taking a single needle.* [15]

Like a puppet with no more strings, the whole Saigon apparatus collapsed within hours. The next day, May Day, there was no official parade, but a spontaneous popular demonstration of joy and relief. The whole city population was in the streets. Saigon was not conquered. It was liberated. A formal national celebration began on May 15. In Saigon, two million people packed into the central square in front of the ex-Presidential Palace, waving flags of the PRG and DRV. The celebration included a military parade where women's army and militia divisions marched—proud of the enormous contribution they had made to the decisive victory.

Notes

1. Minh Ha, "The Indissoluble Bonds between North and South," *Women of Viet Nam* #3-4 (1971), p. 25.
2. Ho Chi Minh, "Appeal to the Entire People to Wage the Resistance War (December 20, 1946)," in *Ho Chi Minh on Revolution,* edited by Bernard Fall (New York: Signet, 1968), p. 162.
3. For further details on Ben Tre and early days of NLF check Vu Can, "The NLF and the Second Resistance in South Viet Nam," in *South Viet Nam: From NLF to PRG* (Vietnamese Studies #23; Hanoi: 1969), pp. 23-26.
4. For more details on the organization and strategy of the PLAF see Wilfred Burchett, *Viet Nam Will Win* (New York: Guardian Books, 1970).
5. David Hunt, "Organizing for Revolution in Viet Nam," *Radical America,* vol. 8, #1-2 (1974), p. 143.
6. Vo Nguyen Giap. *Peoples War Against U.S. Aeronaval War* (Hanoi: Foreign Languages Publishing House: 1975) p. 146.
7. Duy Thuy, "Opening the Road to the Front: The Story of Ho Thi Canh," *Women of Viet Nam* #3-4 (1971), p. 37.
8. Phan Thi Nhu Bang, *Ta Thi Kieu* (South Viet Nam: Liberation Editions, 1966), p. 43.
9. Burchett, *Inside Story of Guerrilla War,* (New York: International Publishers, 1965), p. 163.
10. "Women in the PLAF," *Tricontinental News Service,* vol. 2 #5 (March 13, 1974) pp. 18-19.
11. Nguyen Thi Dinh, "President Ho Chi Minh and the South" (from her memoirs) *Women of Viet Nam* #3 (1969), pp. 26-27.
12. Marta Rojas and Raul Valdes Vivo, *South Viet Nam* (Havana: Book Institute, 1967), part 2, pp. 112-115. Other, previously unpublished information about General Dinh from unpublished interview between Dinh and Jane Fonda, reported April 19, 1974.
13. Victory scenes described in *New York Times,* May 3, 1975 and *South Viet Nam in Struggle* #300 (May 12, 1975) and #301-302 (May 19, 1975).
14. Letter from Claudia Krich quoted in *Indochina Chronicle* #42, (July-August 1975), pp. 13-14.
15. Associated Press release, May 23, 1975.

13.
LIBERATED WOMEN IN LIBERATED AREAS

The [Vietnamese] word I learned for woman really meant "young lady" and that is a far cry from the words Front women use to refer to themselves, such as "liberated woman," "strong woman," "woman who is equal and free."
 —*Jane Barton, in a letter from Quaker Rehabilitation Center, Quang Ngai Province, where she worked for two years*

Since April 30, 1975, all of South Viet Nam is liberated—governed by the PRG. Some areas of South Viet Nam have been liberated since the early sixties. On May 1, 1972, Quang Tri became the first liberated province of South Viet Nam. In other areas the people's takeover of power is more recent. The depth of the change is uneven. Problems vary. The accomplishments of an area that has been liberated for a long time become the vision and promise for newly liberated territory.

In the village of Hai Thuong, Quang Tri Province, for example, women have long experience as guerrillas and also in governing their village as members of the People's Revolutionary Committee. On the other hand, in newly liberated Hue, young women at a girls' school were having their first experience marching. They still wore their traditional long silk dresses and high heeled shoes as they trained for the newly formed students' militia. Their new leader, eighteen-year-old Le Thi Kim, was only recently released from her isolation cell at Con Son Prison. [1]

Saigon and other large cities in South Viet Nam also present the new revolutionary government with problems that are inconceivable in the liberated countryside. The U.S. built an artificial consumer society in Saigon, resting on a foundation of dependence and corruption, rather than on industrial production. Saigon became a gruesome reflection of the worst of U.S. culture—a haven for pimps, dope pushers, Honda-riding cowboys, black marketeers and prostitutes.

Now the PRG is devoting its resources to providing millions of homeless, unemployed people with rice, shelter and jobs. The U.S. government tried to define democracy for the Vietnamese people as the freedom to wear miniskirts and buy hondas. Revolutionary cadre have begun to challenge this warped concept of democracy with the new reality of independent South Viet Nam—where the people's dignity rests on being *collective masters of their own country*.

Residents in the various precincts of Saigon are electing their own local government—People's Revolutionary Committees. These committees have been sending out the word that people are welcomed back to their native lands in the countryside. The PRG is providing free transportation, land and farming tools, plus 50 kilos of rice to anyone returning to their villages. Thousands of people who were forced to go to Saigon to escape U.S. bombing are going home to the land now. The local People's Revolutionary Committees are also encouraging former prostitutes to join the re-education programs to enable them to start a new life. Villas of departed U.S. officials are becoming training institutes for homeless children who used to have to beg and sleep in the streets. Others become centers to care for the sick and mutilated.

A visitor to a newly liberated area in November 1973 described a scene that would become typical of other areas:

There's a kind of pioneer atmosphere in the PRG areas. In Don Ha City there is the excitement and enthusiasm of a frontier town as well as the hardships. We visited an adult education class and then wandered through the crowded but unlighted streets of the city one evening. The ice cream shop that I remembered from visits four years ago [when Saigon controlled the city] is still there. Le Phuong, Director of Cultural Affairs, told me as we walked through the market place the next morning: "We don't speak so much about what the B-52 bombers destroyed. We are most proud of what we have saved and what we have made use of." [2]

But life in the liberated areas has been physically difficult for everyone. Until the signing of the Paris Peace Agreement, January 27, 1973, liberated zones were also free fire zones—subject to constant saturation bombing. In areas where the bombing was the heaviest, life continued in underground shelters. But rheumatism, TB and skin disease spread among people deprived of sunlight and oxygen. Tens of thousands of students kept up their studies in 4,000 classrooms beneath the earth's surface. All hospitals were built underground. In defiance of the U.S. war machine, people in liberated zones affirmed life. A young mother who gave birth to a baby in a camouflaged tent during a B-52 bombing raid on Quang Tri named her child "B-Nam Hai" (B-52). A year later, in 1973, the strong child greeted foreign visitors. [3]

In the months following the signing of the Paris Peace Agreements, defying Thieu's attempts at assassination and bombing, thousands returned each week to their homes in the liberated areas. [4] There they began the arduous task of rebuilding their lives and homes. They used the steel plates abandoned at U.S. bases for the doors of their new houses; they wove handbags out of the yellow and red electrical wire taken from minefields; they planted flowers in mortar casings; they made scarves and raincoats from abandoned nylon parachutes; they packed rice in leftover U.S. sandbags. [5]

The Provisional Revolutionary Government

The PRG defended itself against Thieu's military violations of the Paris Peace Agreement. At the same time, it consolidated its power—

both by building a firm economic base and by encouraging more and more people to participate in the political process. One PRG official explained:

The consolidation of mass organizations such as the Peasants' Union, the Women's Union, the Ho Chi Minh People's Revolutionary Youth Union, etc. constitutes one of the guarantees for the consolidation of the liberated zone and of revolutionary power. [6]

Revolutionary power in South Viet Nam has meant new power for women. The same war that brought unspeakable hardship to women in the South, also brought the national liberation struggle. It has been through this struggle that women have taken such giant strides towards their emancipation. The battle has been right at their doorsteps.

But war conditions alone won't emancipate women, as any one of Saigon's ex-prostitutes will testify. Women's emancipation also requires the solid commitment of the political leaders of the struggle. The National Liberation Front, in its founding manifesto, called on all the South Vietnamese people to unite and fight for a ten point program. Part of that program specifically aims to "guarantee equality between men and women."

NLF leadership was not lax in implementing this program. They conducted an active campaign against men treating women as sex objects. Even in the early days, before the NLF had a strong base, they refused to compromise on the issue. A defector explained:

I belonged to the basic social class [peasant]. I performed my tasks well. I did well in the training courses, but I was accused of having bad behavior because of my lewdness and my illicit love affairs, and for this reason, I wasn't admitted in the Party early even though I became a Labor Youth member in 1962. [7]

In 1967, the NLF elaborated its initial program and implemented the following concrete policies with regard to women:

—*To pay utmost attention to raising the political, cultural and vocational standard of women in view of their merits in the struggle against U.S. aggression, for national salvation. To develop the Vietnamese women's tradition of heroism, dauntlessness, fidelity and ability to shoulder responsibilities.*
—*Women are equal to men in the political, cultural and social fields.*
—*Women who do the same job, receive the same salaries and allowances and enjoy the same rights as men.*
—*Women workers and civil servants enjoy two months maternity leave with full pay before and after childbirth.*
—*To promulgate progressive marriage and family regulations.*

—To apply a policy of actively favoring, fostering and training women cadres.
—To protect the rights of mothers and children. To develop the network of maternity homes, creches and infant classes.
—To eliminate all social evils brought about by the U.S. imperialists and their lackeys, which are harmful to women's health and dignity. [8]

These provisions were part of a larger political program that the NLF issued to unite all South Vietnamese people to fight for "an independent, democratic, peaceful, neutral, prosperous and reunified Viet Nam." This program defined the political campaign launched by the NLF in preparation for the Tet Offensive in 1968. Many people in the cities joined in the Offensive on the basis of this program. Once they liberated their villages, they elected local People's Revolutionary Committees to begin to implement the program to improve people's lives. The program was also popular with nationalist businessmen and intellectuals who wanted a free economy and national culture. In April 1968, representatives of the urban middle classes formed the Viet Nam Alliance of National, Democratic and Peace Forces. (VANDPF)

In May of 1969, delegates from the NLF and VANDPF agreed that because of the successes in the national liberation struggle, it was time to establish a provisional revolutionary government for South Viet Nam. They convened the South Viet Nam Congress of People's Representatives in a liberated area near Saigon on June 6, 1969. The three-day meeting included delegates representing various political parties, national minorities, religious communities, trade unions, women's unions, units of the PLAF, and the People's Revolutionary Committees of the areas already liberated.

Women's power in the PRG

—Madame Nguyen Thi Binh: Foreign Minister
—Madame Nguyen Thi Dinh: Commander of the PLAF
—Dr. Duong Quynh Hoa: Minister of Public Health
—Bui Thi Me: Vice Minister of Public Health
—Nguyen Dinh Chi: Member of the Advisory Council of PRG

All these women are important leaders of the PRG. There are more women in top-level leadership positions in the PRG than in any other country in the world. While they still hold a minority of these positions—about one-fourth—they represent the growing power of women in South Viet Nam.

Women's political power is stronger at the local level than at the national level. As of early 1973, People's Revolutionary Committees, the grass-roots governing bodies of the PRG, were elected and functioned in 44 provinces, 6 cities, 184 districts and towns, and more than 2000 villages. Women often form the majority on the village-level committees and in 1970 more than thirty per cent of the representatives on the district and provincial committees were women. Also, more than thirty per cent of the NLF cadre are women. One is Tran Thi Hung, Vice Chairperson of the People's Revolutionary Committee of Quang Tri Province. She is also the President of the Women's Union in that province, a veteran of the anti-French resistance and a grandmother. [9]

The Union of Women for the Liberation of South Viet Nam protects and expands the advancements of women. It was founded on March 8, 1961—International Women's Day. On the tenth anniversary of the Union's founding, General Dinh, its President, wrote:

Our movement symbolizes the strength of the women's movement against imperialism in the present period. . . . [We] pledge to stand shoulder to shoulder with our sisters of the North, united closely with

Quang Tri Province, PRG, 1972: Ex-ARVN soldiers turn their weapons over to People's Revolutionary Committee.

the women of Cambodia, Laos and the whole world to fight to the end for national independence, democracy, social progress and for the happiness of women and children. [10]

The Union is better established in some areas than in others. As early as 1964, it was meeting biweekly in the village of Ben Suc. Today the Union has several million members. Since April 30, 1975, they can meet publicly and have the additional power which comes from the support of the PRG. Over 50,000 women in Danang participated in a rally in April, to celebrate the liberation of the city and the founding of the city's Women's Union on a public basis. Similar rallies occurred in other provincial capitals shortly after liberation. [11]

While the Union took major responsibilities in the national liberation struggle, it also set up Committees for the Protection of Mothers and Children, trained medical workers, and organized schools and day care centers. The Union reinforced the effects of these services by taking leadership in the struggle "against patriarchal feudal beliefs." Now that peace is achieved, the Union will be able to focus more energy on serving the particular needs of women. On June 13, 1975, for example, Liberation Press Agency in Saigon reported that the Women's Union in Saigon had opened its first day care center in that city. Bui Thi Me, Vice Minister of Health of the PRG, attended the opening celebration. The fact that all of the top women officials in the PRG are also leaders of the Women's Union adds strength to the programs of the Union.

Economic reforms for independence

Land reform sponsored by the PRG has provided the economic basis for equality between the sexes in the countryside. Every peasant in the liberated areas has a plot of land that can support her or his subsistence. Tenant farming is abolished and those who harvest a surplus often voluntarily donate their crops to those in need. It is no longer necessary for a woman to become a concubine in order to survive. There is no longer any economic pressure forcing families to arrange unhappy marriages for their daughters.

By the end of 1972, more than four million acres had been redistributed to the people in liberated areas. Most of this land had been newly cleared or confiscated from absentee landlords and reactionary landlords who collaborated with the U.S. and then fled when the PRG took power. This process accelerated after April 30, 1975. For example, once ex-President Thieu fled Viet Nam, the forty-four acres he owned were redistributed to fifty local peasants. [12] Much new land is being reclaimed by hundreds of thousands of ex-Saigon Army men returning to the countryside.

First rice harvest since liberation in Quang Tri Province

Peasant women, who were forced to become prostitutes when they were driven from the countryside by U.S. bombing, are also returning home. One is Tuyet Anh, whom GI's called "Linda." A German reporter who knew her recalled that when Saigon was first liberated, she was terrified and wanted to leave Viet Nam. A week later, after getting to know some women guerrillas, she changed her mind and told the reporter excitedly, "They say I can go back to my village." She had changed her clothes and looked like a peasant again. [13]

PRG policy protects the ownership of the land by those who work the land. As of August, 1975, the "national democratic" stage of the South Vietnamese revolution continued. That is to say, there is no attempt to nationalize or socialize the enterprises owned by people friendly to the revolution. Those large landowners who cooperate with the PRG in reducing rents and aiding the revolution are allowed to keep their land in areas where the peasants already have what they need. Liberation forces have helped peasants clear new land so that the amount of arable land had increased three times by 1973. They have also set up more than 50,000 mutual aid teams, so that no one has to work alone. In those areas which have been liberated for many years, most of the peasant households have joined cooperatives. {14}

Cooperative work makes the job of reclaiming land easier. In 1973, Quang Tri harvested its first crop in six years. The leadership that women gained in production during the heaviest years of the war continues. Le Diem, editor of *Liberated Quang Tri*, the daily newspaper, told a delegation of Cuban visitors, headed by Fidel Castro:

Now we are working under the slogan of maintaining the spirit of combat in production so that we can develop this province rapidly and surely. [15]

In the cities, especially where thousands of people faced famine under the old Saigon regime, the PRG is promoting the revival of native industries. In May, 1975, the people of Danang repaired hundreds of boats destroyed by the Thieu regime. The new government supplied boatowners with fishing nets and gasoline. Within a month, the industry supplied enough fish to feed the people in the Danang area as well as to supply dried processed fish to other regions. [16]

In the newly liberated cities, factory life is also on a different footing. Women now get equal pay for equal work. Those factories which were owned by the U.S. and its Vietnamese collaborators who fled Saigon, are now managed by committees of workers. All workers, regardless of who their supervisors are, now enjoy the rights guaranteed by the PRG workers' program: a decent minimum wage; abolition of corporal punishment and arbitrary firing; the right to take part in management and freedom to join trade unions. Workers in many factories are increasing production to aid in strengthening the economy of their country. For example, even before the PRG flag flew over the Presidential Palace, the directors of the Sicovina Textile Mill fled and women who worked there raised the PRG flag on the roof of the mill. Nguyen Thi Chau, Vice President of the mill's once-illegal trade union, reported:

The first thing we did was gather all the workers, technicians and engineers. On May 2, more than 700 women reported for work and now their total has swelled to 1000.

Another worker explained why they have doubled production:

Since liberation, we no longer feel afraid—no scoldings, no bullying, that's why I'm working with great enthusiasm. [17]

Yet, an enormous task of economic rebuilding lies ahead. Ten million peasants were forced off their land during the war, including one million who served in Thieu's army. The first step in eliminating unemployment—which ranges in the millions—is to revitalize South Viet Nam's countryside. The old Saigon economy was so distorted that the Thieu regime even depended on the U.S. for imported rice. On July 27, 1975, a Reuters dispatch reported that Huynh Tan Phat, Prime Minister of the PRG, announced that his country would become self-supporting in rice this year and would regain its exporter status in 1976.

A former Foreign Ministry official of the Saigon regime unwittingly pointed to the prospect of economic independence for all South Vietnamese women. He told a reporter:

The (PLAF) soldiers were very deferential to me and my wife, but were conspiring with our maid to leave her employment. They tell her that a maid's work is demeaning. They think that in their society, everyone can be free! [18]

Education and culture

In spite of the tremendous energy they had to spend on military defense, women made great progress in education in the liberated zones. It's difficult to present current statistics because the pace of change is so rapid, especially since peace has been achieved. By early 1972, there were more than 7100 schools, serving more than one million students from pre-school through high school. By early 1973, 1500 new schools opened, serving 35,000 more students. By early 1974, 10,000 new classes opened for several hundred thousand primary school students. In Quang Tri and Thua Thien, each village in the province has a primary school and each province has two training schools for elementary school teachers. The pace of growth of continuing education, especially for adult women, is similar. New schools are made from crates that used to hold U.S. munitions and chalk comes from the white clay discovered at the depths of bomb craters. [19]

In contrast, 50 per cent of the city people and 75 per cent of the rural people living in areas controlled by the Thieu regime were illiterate. Between 1972 and 1973, 20 per cent of the students had to drop out because they could no longer afford tuition and the rising cost of living. [20] There is no tuition in PRG schools.

I visited the Trieu Phong District School in Quang Tri Province in the fall of 1974. The students at the school were adults—nearly all women. Many wore white mourning bands around their hair. They were peasants. Many had been guerrillas. As we walked the path from one classroom to another they pointed out the ruins of a home where a family of nine was killed in one bombing raid. When the bombing stopped in January 1973, not one school was left standing in Quang Tri Province. They were proud of their school, which they had built themselves with materials supplied by the PRG.

In the year since their school opened, hundreds of women learned to read and write. In one classroom, twenty-three women and two men, all of whom had been illiterate the year before, were studying mathematics at a fourth-grade level. Most of the students were in their twenties and thirties. There are special classes for women over fifty. The same school has classes to train "an army of teachers." In six weeks, those who already have a primary school education are learning to teach others. In 1973, about eighty-five per cent of the people in Quang Tri were illiterate. Now they have virtually eliminated illiteracy.

PRG students learn to share their knowledge—not to compete. Anyone who has more than a year of schooling is considered responsible for passing that knowledge on to at least two more people. They use every available opportunity. One group of illiterate peasants, some of whom were grandparents, learned the alphabet during their lunchbreaks. Each day, their young teacher refused to allow them to return to their fields until they learned their quota of new letters. [21]

There's no difference between the education received by boys and that received by girls in the liberated areas. They're equally represented and go to the same school. While in old Saigon, girls learned to beg and sell pornographic postcards to GI's, in liberated zones, young girls and boys learn to write by copying stories like this one:

Little Buoi has a very important task of carrying messages for the National Liberation Front. Little Buoi was never late in taking messages to their destinations, and she has never let the enemies find out what she is doing. Nor has she let a letter or message fall into the hands of the enemy.

They learn math like this:

The enemy entered the village and arrested 12 youths. The people of the village demonstrated against this arrest and forced the release of 8 youths. How many more youths' releases do they still need to demonstrate for? [22]

Young children, girls and boys alike, have learned amazing resourcefulness and bravery in their classrooms. Sometimes classes met in underground tunnels, sometimes on boats—where the children even had to camouflage their writing tablets. They learn through the examples set by many heroic women—like the eleven women of Hue who held off a Marine battallion during the Tet Offensive. They learn that the possibility for change is endless after seeing their mothers and grandmothers, who have been illiterate for centuries, learn to read and write and run village affairs.

Young children go to school in shifts. Older ones take care of their younger sisters and brothers while their mothers attend classes

Everyone, even the young children, works at reclaiming the land when class is not in session. After the people have cleared all the mines, harvested their crops, built new hospitals and homes—when the worst wounds of war are healed—they build day care centers.

In one district of Saigon, the PRG organized thirty new literacy classes within one month of liberation. Education specialists from the DRV and the PRG held a working conference and announced to the French Press Agency on June 25, 1975, that they would abolish illiteracy in all of South Viet Nam by the end of 1976.

The people in liberated villages participate in a thriving cultural life as poets, writers, painters, dancers and musicians. Every village has a song and dance troupe. Their performances are so popular that often thousands of people attend their shows—including many who sneaked away from Thieu-controlled areas just to see the show. In early 1967, a Japanese reporter visiting the liberated areas noticed that, after rifles, the most widely distributed modern conveniences were transistor radios. Programs featured news, songs and stories which encouraged the liberation struggle. [23]

Today, in Saigon, people no longer have to listen to Liberation Radio in secret. In addition to news and important information, the radio broadcasts music and poetry readings. Theaters have reopened and the cost of a ticket is half what it used to be. On May 19, 1975, millions of people all over South Viet Nam attended performances and ceremonies celebrating Ho Chi Minh's eighty-fifth birthday.

Family

Marriage and family life form the nucleus of Vietnamese society. But it is clear that the nature of these institutions is inevitably changing as a result of the necessities of war. In traditional Viet Nam, a woman's duty to her father was the overriding imperative. The NLF did not confront this issue of filial piety head-on. Rather, they showed new recruits that if they put their obligation to fight first, in the long run, they would also be serving their fathers' best interests. Daughters who decided to join the NLF against their fathers' wishes had to stand firm against heavy paternal pressure. For example, one father complained:

You're my girl. Because you have left this house day and night and abandoned your home chores, one half of our land has not been completely cultivated and weeds have grown up everywhere. Where can we get food to eat? Many persons can work for the revolution, but I can find nobody like you! People who make the revolution do not receive any salaries. . . . I can't stop you from working for the revolution, but you should at least take pity on me and not compel me to cook your daily meals. Unfortunately, if you're killed in a bombing or shelling I will have to bury you. This truly is an unhappy lot. According to the heavenly law, as our ancestors said, children should bury their parents.

If you continue to go out day and night to make contacts . . . and attend meetings with those cadres, you might be led into a loose life. You might lose your virginity and get pregnant. In that case, I think it would be better for me to kill myself than endure the shame. . . . If you take your family so lightly and only think of your organization, do whatever you want. But don't tell your cadres to come here to warn or try to motivate me! [24]

The woman who had to counter these harangues received a lot of support from her comrades. She also gained new strength and political understanding of her role as an independent woman.

These changes are encouraged by stories broadcast on liberated radio. The following story, initially written for radio, was printed in *South Viet Nam in Struggle,* the official newspaper of the NLF. Pham Hoa, a member of PLAF, returned home unexpectedly after three years' absence. When he walked into his house, he noticed a knapsack on the bed and an American-made belt with two grenades fastened to it. No one was home. He asked himself:

Has my wife become a guerrilla? Her timidity was well-known throughout the village. Nobody was as white-livered as she. She would shut her eyes at the sight of anyone cutting the throat of a chicken . . . she feared water rats and snakes. What pained me most was her fear of the enemy . . . even when they were a half a day's walk away, she would fly into her secret underground shelter. What has made my wife change so thoroughly?

That night the reunited couple lay in bed together without speaking. Gunfire interrupted their embrace. Nam sat up immediately—but not out of fear. She explained to her husband what was happening, told him to get some rest, grabbed her rifle and left. He followed her out the door and met with an older woman who scolded him,

Don't take her away from us.

He replied, *I wouldn't dare.*

The old woman went on,

All right! You're a reasonable young man. She's an elite fighter, don't you know that? You should not underrate her!

The husband joined his wife in her trench. He remembered,

Without the comfort of a room . . . but standing in a trench of muddy water behind two sub-machine guns, we spent the happiest moments together since our wedding day. [25]

Cora Weiss sheds light on how typical this couple is. When she visited PRG territory in the fall of 1973, she noted:

I did not meet one women in the South who lives with her family. Everyone's skills require that they work where they are needed. [26]

Cora Weiss' traveling companion specified one such change in family life:

A birth control program has recently been started. The subject was taboo two or three years ago we were told. Now it is part of every village's health program. The director of the Women's Union in Tuyen Quang told us that it is more popular with women than with men. "Usually women like to have some birth control after the fourth or fifth child. But very few men like to participate. In our whole province, only two men have agreed to vasectomies." [27]

PRG medical centers provide birth control advice and devices free upon request.

Whether married or not, women who joined the NLF often received help from their political co-workers in solving their personal problems. For example, in one instance, Tuyet, an NLF woman, felt confused and preoccupied since she had fallen in love with a man already committed to a relationship with another woman. After much discussion, the two women in her political collective persuaded Tuyet to control her emotions. She gave up all attempts to establish a relationship with the man involved. They all agreed that the emotions of the man's first lover had to be respected and that women's solidarity should have priority. The North American woman who reported this incident was most impressed by the way the group's support prevented Tuyet from feeling depressed or resentful. [28]

It is too soon to generalize about the effects of peace on family life. It will take many months before everyone returns to their homes and social relations reestablish the rhythm of peacetime. However, in a frank conversation with two Vietnamese friends, they gave me a glimpse of one change they thought would be typical. They were both older men who were veterans of the anti-French resistance. Many of their contemporaries and friends were Southern married men who had gone North in 1954. Their wives had remained in the South because they were not Viet Minh cadre at the time and because they expected that the men would return in two years. Instead, twenty years passed and while the men were in the North, the women joined the NLF and fought actively against the U.S. invasion. My two friends understood that because of their war activity, most of the women now outranked their husbands. One admitted that his friends were worried:

The men think it's natural for women to have high political rank, but inside the family, it's something else. When my friends return home, there will be struggles and the husbands will learn that the days of male "home rule" are over.

Health

Women have made important strides in health care. No PRG doctor makes a profit from people's sickness. The PRG takes responsibility for ensuring women's health by emphasizing disease prevention and by combining the most effective traditional and modern health practices. Every village has trained medical workers—even those in remote mountain regions. By 1974, seventy per cent of the liberated districts had doctors. Each province has an organized Medical Service, which trains medical workers in complementary education classes. A majority of the health workers are women. [29]

The PRG trains them to meet the emotional as well as the physical needs of their patients. Jane Barton, who worked in a Quaker hospital near PRG territory, reported that PRG nurses would routinely stay up all night comforting patients, read to them, visit their families, and try to provide as much emotional support as possible. Barton also reported that PRG doctors who travel with mobile medical teams try to take equal responsibility for menial tasks along with the other members of the team. In a deliberate effort to break down professional hierarchies, doctors would often prepare meals for the other medical workers.

At the new hospital in Quang Tri, medical workers told me:

The war against the French and the U.S. has trained our doctors to be close to the people. Their ideological convictions make it possible for them to suffer hardship. There is no trace of Paris left in our doctors— they are just like peasants.

The hospital itself was a complex of long, thin, low mud-and-thatch buildings constructed by the local population in less than a month. Before the cease-fire, there could be no central hospital at all, only mobile medical teams. The doctor told us that in those days, eighty per cent of the women they examined had cervical inflammations caused by living in tunnels, often partially filled with stagnant water. She was glad to be able to report that they had eliminated most of these infections.

This hospital still treats hundreds of people who accidentally trigger mines left by the U.S. invaders. Other problems most often treated at Quang Tri hospital are malaria, gastro-intestinal disease and anemia. When I asked about nervous diseases, the doctor responded, "Liberation from the grip of the enemy frees the mind." All the medical care at the hospital is free. In the fall of 1974, people living in areas still controlled by Thieu took great risks in defying Thieu's tabu on travel to the "Viet Cong Hospital." I saw a nun, dressed in full habit, waiting patiently on a bench along with others needing dental treatment. The dentist was a young woman trained in Hanoi.

Mobile health teams concentrate on prenatal care and epidemic prevention. In remote regions, they must teach the people elementary hygiene and fight superstitions such as the belief that a pregnant woman should drink the urine of a male infant to gain strength. These measures make it possible for women to bear children without fear of dying in childbirth. They will make it possible for a new generation to grow up strong, defying the effects of toxic chemicals and venereal disease left by U.S. forces.

In Saigon, PRG doctors are making an enormous effort to eliminate VD, which reached astronomical proportions before the war ended. The Viet Nam News Agency announced that health teams inoculated four times more people against cholera and typhoid in June 1975 than the Thieu regime had done in all of 1974. They must also do battle against drug addiction. According to estimates by the Thieu government itself, there were 130,000 drug addicts in Saigon—seventy per cent under twenty years old. In 1970, only two per cent of the students in Saigon boarding schools were addicts. By 1973, seventy per cent of all boarding school students used hard drugs. [30] There were never any reported cases of drug addiction in the liberated zones. The PRG launched an all-out battle against addiction in the newly-liberated cities on June 1, 1975, International Children's Day.

The greatest health problem the people in the countryside face is the presence of millions of unexploded land mines and bombs hidden in the fields. The peasants have tried every method of detection including burning the fields, but mines still make farming an extremely hazardous occupation. After visiting the northern region of the PRG in April 1974, Jane Fonda reported:

Just to clear the area around the quarters we stayed in, approximately the size of a square city block, 400 mines had to be detonated. We were

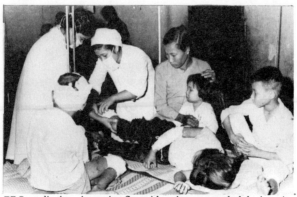

PRG medical workers give first aid to those wounded during air raid on Loc Ninh by Thieu's bombers, Nov. 7, 1973.

*told that in the year following the signing of the Peace Agreement, 300
people and 1000 buffalo have been killed in Quang Tri by the
mines.* [31]

In addition, jagged pieces of shrapnel remain which can easily infect
farmers and barefoot children with tetanus. The U.S. violates the
Peace Agreement by refusing to sweep these mines and military
debris. The U.S. government can never repay the Vietnamese people
for their suffering; but it must take responsibility for healing these war
wounds as required by Article 21 of the Paris Peace Agreement.
Meanwhile, the PRG's policy that good health is everyone's right is
implemented as fully as possible.

Just the beginning

PRG women are certainly much closer to the goal of equality
between the sexes than women in most countries. These women themselves also recognize that the struggle against sexism must continue.
Perhaps the most formidable problem. after material reconstruction, is
challenging the effects of U.S. cultural imperialism among both the
women and men who were so jaded by life in old Saigon.

Even among long-time residents in the liberated zones, the "inner
struggle" continues. Women still have primary responsibility for children and the home, even though men will take over these jobs if the
women are busy fighting or at a meeting. Some men remain hostile to
women's liberation. This man's criticism of NLF women inadvertently
acknowledges the progress they have made:

*. . . To encourage women, the Front's policy is to give "equal rights to
both men and women." Many women are now assuming important
functions in various agencies of the Front. Personally I have no idea
about the ordinary women, but the women cadres whom I met on my
various missions and those who worked in the Province Medical Station
seemed to have lost all the charm of the fair sex. In my opinion, women
cadres have actually become masculine and ridiculous. They all liked to
argue and use grandiloquent "revolutionary" words such as "we must
consolidate our spirit to overcome all kinds of hardships—we must
strengthen our ideology and fight for final victory etc. . . ." I never
liked women cadres, so I had no girlfriend among them.* [32]

General Dinh represents the liberated women of South Viet Nam.
She is loved and respected as a military leader and also as a warm,
motherly woman. She once gave birth to a son, but never raised him
herself—rather she chose to devote all her energy to the resistance.
Today, the South Vietnamese sometimes speak of her as if she were the
mother of the entire People's Liberation Armed Forces. These lines

from a poem by a famous Vietnamese male poet, Luu Trong Lu, express the tension between the reality of women's liberation and the persistence of traditional sex roles. They also show that women's strength is the overriding aspect in this continuing contradiction.

NGUYEN THI DINH

In the assault you command a hundred squads.
Night returns, you sit mending fighters' clothes.
Woman general of the South,
*   descended from Trac and Nhi**
You've shaken the brass and steel of the White House.

* Trac and Nhi refer to the Trung sisters who fought the Chinese in 48 A.D.

The Vietnamese are proud of their traditional culture and the continuity between past and present. In the course of making the revolution, they work to maintain the positive elements of Vietnamese tradition, while, at the same time, struggling against oppressive "feudal hangovers." The struggle has many dimensions and is bursting with possibilities for women—especially now that all the resources once devoted to defense can be used for creating a new life.

Notes

1. Marta Rojas, "Arrival in Hue," *Granma*, (June 1, 1975) p. 12.
2. From unpublished letter by Don Luce about his travels to Viet Nam, Nov. 1973.
3. Statistics about life underground from *Granma*, October 28, and Miguel Rivero, "Glimpses of the Liberated Zones of South Viet Nam," *Direct from Cuba* #81 (August 15, 1973).
4. For information about the relation between liberated zones and contested zones before complete independence see Katsuichi Honda, "The National Liberation Front" (Tokyo: Committee for English Publication, 1968) p. 11
5. Virtually every visitor to PRG territory has commented on the people's ingenuity in putting U.S. waste to good use. See, for example, United Press release, "War's Wasteland in South Viet Nam," *San Francisco Chronicle,* November 26, 1973, p. 10.
6. Tam Duong, "Initial Success in Building the Free Zone," *South Viet Nam in Struggle* #229 (January 1, 1974), p. 5.
7. Quoted by David Hunt, "Organizing for Revolution in Viet Nam," *Radical America,* vol. 8, #1-2 (1974), p. 141.
8. Quoted in full from section 9 of Program. *South Viet Nam in Struggle* #50 (December 20, 1969), p. 5.
9. Statistics from "Four Questions on the PRG," *Viet Nam News and Reports* #18-19 (June 1973), p. 5. Also Nguyen Thi Dinh, "Ten Years of Victorious Struggle of the Women of South Viet Nam," *Women of Viet Nam* #1 (1971), pp. 5-6. Information on Tran Thi Hung in article by Cora Weiss, "Profiles in Liberation: Women of Viet Nam," *American Report,* vol. 4, #5 (December 10, 1973), p. 11.

10. Nguyen Thi Dinh, "Ten Years" (see fn.9), pp. 7-8.

11. "In the Liberated Zones" *South Viet Nam in Struggle* #297 (April 21, 1975) p. 2 and "In Newly Liberated Areas," *South Viet Nam in Struggle* #300 (May 21, 1975) p. 8.

12. *San Francisco Chronicle* (June 26, 1975) p. 16.

13. *Indochina Chronicle* #42 (July-August 1975) p. 25.

14. Information for this paragraph from the following: "Four Questions on the PRG" (see fn. 9); Pham Cuong, "In the Liberated Zones," in *South Viet Nam: From NLF to PRG* (Vietnamese Studies #23; Hanoi, 1969), pp. 124-125; Chris Jenkins, "The Provisional Revolutionary Government," *Indochina Chronicle* #32 (April 17, 1974); "Program of Action," *South Viet Nam in Struggle* #50 (December 20, 1969), p. 5.

15. Quoted in *Granma* (English edition), October 28, 1973, p. 11.

16. Agence France Press Agency release, June 19, 1975.

17. "In the Newly Liberated Areas," *South Viet Nam in Struggle* #300 (May 21, 1975) p. 8 and "The New Masters of the Weaving Industry," *South Viet Nam in Struggle* #305 (June 16, 1975) p. 4.

18. Peter Arnett reported this in *Los Angeles Times* May 27, 1975.

19. Details here come from "Four Questions on the PRG" (see fn. 9); Tam Duong (fn. 6); and Rivero (fn. 3).

20. Ngoc Bao, "A Rotten Regime," *South Viet Nam in Struggle* #227-228 (December 20, 1973), p. 7.

21. Reported in personal conversations with Jane Barton, who worked in South Viet Nam for two years.

22. First text is from Katsuichi Honda, *A Voice from the Village* (Tokyo: Committee for English Publication, 1967) p. 10 and second text is from John Spraegens, *Education in Viet Nam* (Japan: Looking Back Publications, 1971) p. 49.

23. Honda, *National Liberation Front*, pp. 42-43.

24. Quoted by David Hunt, "Organization for Revolution in Viet Nam, pp. 143-145.

25. *South Viet Nam in Struggle* #163 (September 4, 1972), p. 5.

26. Cora Weiss (see fn. 9), p. 10.

27. Personal communication from Don Luce, November 1973.

28. Reported in personal conversation with Jane Barton

29. "The PRG and the Liberated Zones of South Viet Nam," *Viet Nam Courier #26* (July 1974) pp. 6-7 and also author's interviews at Quang Tri Hospital, September 20, 1974.

30. Ngoc Bao, "A Rotten Regime" *South Viet Nam in Struggle* #227-228 (December 20, 1973) p. 7 and Nguyen Anh Tran, "Danger of Heroin in South Viet Nam" *Viet Nam Courier #320* (January 1974) p. 24.

31. Jane Fonda, "Daily Horrors of U.S. Mines" *Indochina Focal Point* (June 1-15, 1973) p. 3.

32. David Hunt, "Organizing for Revolution in Viet Nam," pp. 145-146.

14.
EMANCIPATED WOMEN IN A SOCIALIST SOCIETY

When one speaks of a peasant, it is important to bear in mind that now-adays she is usually a woman of many roles. She is a producer, a house-wife, a technician and a combatant.
                    —Bui Thi Tinh, spokesperson at cooperative farm in the DRV

From the days when the Vietnamese revolutionary movement was in its infancy, with a handful of members—hungry and hunted by the French—it has consistently committed itself to women's liberation. The Indochinese Communist Party pledged to struggle for equality between women and men in its founding program in 1930. Some of the people who formulated this program had recognized the importance of women's liberation years before; but the ICP was the first organized, national group to take political responsibility for getting rid of women's oppression.

A year after their founding meeting, ICP leaders got together again and agreed that "women are the most oppressed element of the society" and that women's freedom requires a revolution. [1] Their analysis maintained that women's emancipation and national liberation were inseparable. Nguyen Thi Kim Anh, a revolutionary theorist, wrote a book in 1938 which explained how feudalism and colonialism were responsible for women's grievances. She criticized arranged marriages, polygamy, and double standards, showing their feudal origins. She tried to interpret Marx, Wollestonecraft and other Western theorists and apply them to Vietnamese reality. Her book elaborated the official ICP policy on women. [2]

In 1945, people who had begun their lives as revolutionaries in the 1920's gained control over the full resources of the state in order to implement revolutionary policy. The early ICP program became the law of the Democratic Republic of Viet Nam in 1946. Article 21 of the Constitution of the DRV states:

In the Democratic Republic of Viet Nam, the woman is the equal of man in rights, from the political, economic, cultural, social and family points of view.

For equal work, she is entitled to equal pay. The State guarantees to women workers and functionaries the right to paid maternity leave before and after childbirth.

The State protects the rights of mothers and children, and sees to the development of maternity clinics, creches and kindergartens.

The State protects marriage and the family. [3]

The Vietnamese understand that centuries of sexism won't disappear with the signing of a law. Nguyen Thi Thap, ex-President of the Viet Nam Women's Union, member of the Central Committee of the Lao Dong Party and Vice President of the Standing Committee of the

National Assembly, is the highest ranking woman in the DRV. She worked in the Saigon underground for thirty-five years against the French. She explained:

When we say the interests of women are bound to the class and national interests, obviously, this does not mean that when the revolution is successful, and the working class seizes power and destroys the rights of private property in production, then the problem of women's liberation will be immediately resolved.

In reality, after the revolution has been successful, women—especially women strongly influenced by feudalism—still have to struggle for true equality with men by raising their political level and knowledge, and taking part in production, the management of society and in the activities of every social sphere. [4]

Theory and practice

Ho Chi Minh often reaffirmed the Party's commitment to women's emancipation, not only in public declarations, but also in action. In a typical visit to a training session for District-level Party members, the first question he asked was:

How many comrades are attending this class?
The reply: *Two hundred and eighty-eight, Uncle. Among these 131 are district cadres.*
Ho: *How many of them are women?*
The reply: *Sixteen, Uncle.*
The President looked displeased and insisted:

This is a shortcoming. The comrades in charge haven't paid enough attention to the training of women cadres. This applies to our Party as a whole. Many people still don't estimate the worth of women correctly, or are shackled by prejudices. They are wrong. At the present, many women are participating in leadership work at the grass-root level and they are doing their jobs very well . . . they are not only zealous, but also competent . . . they are less likely to commit embezzlement and waste or to indulge in drinking and show arrogance than the men. Isn't that true? Speak up if you don't think what I'm saying is correct.

Ho didn't let the matter rest after everyone nodded in agreement:

So I hope that you'll set right your biases vis-a-vis women. As for the women, especially those who are district cadres, they must fight hard for their rights. Otherwise, those of the men who are prejudiced against women won't mend their ways. [5]

In many districts, before women were allowed to take leadership positions, the men bolted, rejecting the possibility of women having executive power. The Party Secretary then suggested that they should make a survey of women's work in the various communes in the District. The survey discovered: (1) women performed more workdays than men; (2) women knew as much about the situation in the fields as men; (3) women were more hard-working and industrious than men; (4) women had fewer opportunities to learn and received no support or help in their work from men.

At the next meeting after the survey, the committee decided unanimously to appoint women cadres. But at the commune level, some of the men still resisted. There were more mass meetings and surveys. All Party cells, in the cooperatives and communes, were required to hold self-criticism meetings in which male chauvinists acknowledged their mistakes and responsibility for failing to promote the women's movement and women cadres. [6]

A movement of their own

In the course of leading the Resistance against the French and building socialism, the Party succeeded in introducing the concept of women's liberation into most people's lives. Women identify their struggles with the struggles of the Party and the people as a whole. Nevertheless, Le Duan, one of the top leaders of the DRV, echoed Ho Chi Minh when he told a national conference of women activists in a 1959 major policy speech:

... women should not merely take part in a general movement but also build a revolutionary movement of their own. [Emphasis in Vietnamese edition.] [7]

Le Thi Xuyen, a Vice President of the Viet Nam Women's Union, recalls the early enthusiasm that made the Union powerful:

A dream, formerly unrealizable, was now coming true. With the revolution, we women lived, in fact, a new life. We had an organization of our own. ... Taking part in that first meeting [in 1946, after Independence] were delegates of working women, country women, intellectuals and other social strata, religious and social assistance organizations, the People's Militia from Hanoi and other provinces. They debated their immediate tasks in their particular social conditions. Never did we feel closer to one another. Never had our collective strength been so great. [8]

This Viet Nam Women's Union is the direct descendant of the Union founded in 1930—before the country was partitioned—for women all over Viet Nam. Membership in the Union is open to all women over 16 years old, to special-interest groups and to women's sections

Hanoi, March 1974: Sign reads "Fourth National Congress of Vietnamese Women." The Presidents of the Women's Unions in North and South hold banner.

within trade unions. The Union represents women to the government and the government depends on the counsel and advice of the Union to defend women's rights; to design new laws and implement all laws to protect women. A number of the leaders of the Women's Union are leaders of the government of the DRV as well. The Union works on a daily basis to strengthen various services that meet the needs of women: adult education, child care, canteens, community service teams, and health education and maintenance.

The Viet Nam Women's Union recently held its first National Congress in twelve years. In the months of preparation for the Congress, discussions and elections of delegates stimulated and reawakened a strong consciousness of the particular needs of women. A total of five million women participated in provincial, district, town and workplace meetings. Every local group made reports that were combined into district reports. District-level groups elected representatives to the first round of Congresses at the province level. At each Provincial Congress, delegates discussed the drafts of reports for the National Congress, evaluating the growth and accomplishments of the women's movement, and making recommendations for future work. They also discussed the report and recommendations submitted by the National Central Executive Committee, and sometimes made suggestions for changes. For example, the first-round Provincial Congress in Quang Binh suggested that the National Report put more emphasis on the role women had played in shooting down U.S. bomber planes.

These meetings elected 540 of the 600 delegates who attended the National Congress. The delegates included:

— 185 agricultural and industrial workers
— 132 scientific and technical workers
— 86 industrial and agricultural managers
— 82 administrative committee members, and
— 22 women who are members of the National Assembly.

Also:

— 20 of the delegates were veterans of the women's movement for more than forty consecutive years.
— 315 participated in the anti-French and anti-U.S. resistance, leaving nearly half who have joined the movement in the last few years.
— 52 per cent of the delegates were high school graduates.

General Dinh led a delegation of women from the PRG at the Congress and represented the close ties between women in the South and the North. She said, "We have come to Hanoi, the heart of the whole country."

The Congress, ending March 8, 1974, incorporated younger women into leadership positions and elaborated the scope and responsibilities of the Union. Le Duan probably set the tone of the Congress in his address to the opening session of the meeting. He said,

We cannot be complacent about the results obtained [towards women's liberation]. Among the people and even among cadres, there still exist the remains of backward feudal thoughts of respect for men and contempt for women, and tendencies to disregard and not protect women's legitimate interests, and not to free women from family ties, and even cruel and inhumanitarian acts of violence against women. In the face of this situation, we must struggle harder in many fields to fully achieve equality between men and women so as to be able to completely liberate women. [9]

When I was traveling in Viet Nam, seven months later, Le Duan's speech was still a major topic of study and discussion. Le Thi Xuyen, a Vice President of the Women's Union, summarized the major themes of the speech:

We must work to create the conditions for women to be collective master in three fields: the nation, society and the self. This means taking leadership in political, economic, cultural, legal and social life. To be collective master of oneself means to have full control over your body, the right and possibility to decide when and if you will have children and what kind of career to pursue. We must expand the ways to take collective responsibility for childcare and household tasks. We must increase the political consciousness of women as well as our scientific and technical knowledge.

The Central Executive Committee presented a Report to the Congress which articulated many ways of achieving these goals. [10] Then the National Congress passed resolutions outlining the tasks for the women's movement "in the new revolutionary stage." At the time I was traveling in Viet Nam, Women's Unions in the provinces were having their second round of province-level Congresses to discuss the ways they would implement the national resolutions.

In Quang Binh, for example, 300 women were about to attend the Congress. They represented the 150,000 members in that province. They planned to spend a day hearing reports and speeches by delegates and representatives of the Party and government. Then the next day, delegates would discuss reports and the recommended resolutions in small groups. On the final day, they would elect a new Provincial Executive Committee, vote on the resolutions and celebrate their achievements.

Governing

The political strength of women in the DRV has shown a pattern of dramatic growth. In 1946, the first year women ever voted in Viet Nam, women held only 10 out of the 403 seats in the National Assembly—the highest legislative body in the DRV. In the second Assembly, women held 53 seats. By the third, they held 66 seats. By the Fourth National Assembly, in 1970, there were 125 women among the 420 members. Some are peasants; some are militia women who shot down U.S. planes; some are heads of production teams, builders of food processing plants, and some are specialized animal breeders. The oldest is 60. The youngest is a 21-year-old worker in the Nam Dinh Textile Mill and is also an anti-aircraft gunner. Several of the women in the National Assembly have been national political leaders for a long time. [11]

The People's Provincial Councils are just below the National Assembly in the government structure. Councils are elected once every three years by secret ballot. Everyone over 18 votes. Forty-two per cent of the members of the People's Provincial Councils are women. Women's membership in the District-level Councils rose from 26 per cent to 43 per cent between 1965 and 1969. At the local village level, women are the chairpersons in 4300 out of a total of 5000 People's Councils. The Councils implement State laws at their respective levels. They have responsibility for planning economic and public works, con-

Dang Minh Thuan, district mayor in Hanoi, visits anti-aircraft gunners at factory in her district.

struction, and cultural activities. They examine and approve local budgets, maintain public order and security, protect rights of citizens, and safeguard rights of ethnic minorities in their respective areas.

The People's Councils have the power to elect and recall the administrative committees and chiefs of justice in their areas. The fact that women do seventy per cent of the nation's agricultural work is reflected in the government of the countryside. More than two-thirds of the members of village administrative committees are women. These committees carry out the policies of the People's Councils, make day-to-day management decisions, rule on divorce cases and also enforce the marriage law that ensures women's rights.

In the DRV, the governing political party is the Lao Dong Party—or Workers' Party. Other political parties exist legally as long as they're not actively hostile to socialism. The overwhelming majority of people believe that the Lao Dong Party best represents the interests of workers and peasants. The Lao Dong Party is a direct descendant of the Indochinese Communist Party which formed in 1930, unifying three pre-existing communist groups that were active in the twenties. The ICP organized and led the Vietnamese people in defeating French colonialism, but it was never very large. In 1945, for instance, it had five thousand members all over Viet Nam—including those in jail. [12] In 1951, in the North, the ICP became the Lao Dong Party. In the South, the organization with a similar political ideology and commitment took the name People's Revolutionary Party.

The Lao Dong Party has grown enormously since the establishment of the Democratic Republic of Viet Nam. In 1959, it had more than four hundred thousand members, and in 1970-71, one hundred thousand new members joined. By 1975, the Party had about one million members. But most of the national leadership of the Party comes from the generation of Ho Chi Minh—those active since the thirties—when few women took part in political affairs. Women in the DRV have had to struggle for respect as political leaders. A woman who was mayor of one of the four districts of Hanoi explained:

Prejudice against women still remains in some people; not all thoughts of inequality have been wiped out. Some are doubtful about women's capacity, especially about women's capacity to govern. So we try our best to fulfill our tasks and defend the honor of women. [13]

In 1965, the percentage of women in the Lao Dong Party was only 5.4. In 1967, Party Resolution number 152 urged that women cadre be trained and promoted to leadership. Within five years 30 per cent of the Party members were women. [14] The Party is committed to continue incorporating more women until there's full political equality between women and men.

Women's emancipation in work

When the Vietnamese recovered control over their economy from the French, they began to eliminate private profit-making as the driving force of the economy. Nguyen Thi Thap, ex-President of the Women's Union, explained the significance of these changes. She showed how getting more jobs for women doesn't necessarily ensure their well-being or equality. More jobs can mean more oppression because the employer exploits his workers by keeping the profit from their labor for himself. As long as a man is an employer who owns and controls the factories, fields and shops, he will always be richer and more powerful than his workers. Thap insisted:

There can never be equality between the exploiter and the exploited. When the oppressing class still dominates, the true equal rights of women cannot exist. [15]

In 1945, the Vietnamese began to take the first steps towards building a socialist economy by distributing land once owned by French landlords, reducing rents, abolishing high taxes and erasing peasants' debts. These moves began to destroy the institutional foundations of women's oppression—the institutions which were also responsible for the starvation of two million people.

In 1945, sixty-two per cent of the peasants in all of Viet Nam had no land and worked as sharecroppers. Land reform in the countryside eliminated the huge concentrations of wealth that forced women into concubinage and slavery. Today, everyone shares the land and the harvests according to how much work they do. Nearly all peasants belong to cooperatives where they own the land and tools in common. People work according to their ability and get paid according to the amount of "work points" they've earned. Work points represent the amount, quality and social importance of a worker's labor. This socialist economy calculates work points equally and separately for men and women—whether married or single.

At the 1974 Congress of the Viet Nam Women's Union, the Director of the Xuan Phuong cooperative reported how she fought the tendency for some workers to accumulate more work points than others. All co-op members have responsibility for the rice fields. Most of the women members did not know other trades, while the men who had additional skills, like brick-making or carpentry, could earn relatively more work points. The Director, Mrs. Vu Thi Cuc, also head of the village chapter of the Women's Union, brought the problem to the local Party cell and to the managing board of the co-op. After they studied and discussed the problem, they decided to train the women in new skills like carpet- and mat-making. With these additional trades, the women earned more and, at the same time, made a larger contribution to the prosperity of the co-op as a whole. [16]

In sharp contrast to the U.S., where we have huge differences between the earning power of workers and executives, in the DRV, the highest-paid worker—the President of the Republic—earns only about 3½ times as much as the average peasant or worker. The wages of the President and the university professor are nearly equal. [17] In the DRV, after nearly a generation of building socialism, nearly all the capitalists have become workers or have left the country. No one is wealthy, and no one is haunted by paralyzing poverty.

The occupational structure has changed drastically since 1945. The 30,000 women who served the French as prostitutes received training for productive work and those who wanted to got help from the government in relocating in a new part of the country. In 1960, 20 per cent of the workers and state employees in cities and towns were women. By 1972, the percentage rose to 42. Today, women make up more than half the workers in light industry and a quarter of the workers in heavy industry. The number of women in the professions has grown enormously. In 1945, you could count on two hands the number of women MD's and engineers in all of Viet Nam. Now there

are more than 5,000 women holding these jobs in the DRV. In 1945, there were three or four women chemists in all of Viet Nam. Now there are 3,000 in the DRV. In 1945 there were no women teaching at the university or college level. Now there are more than 2,000. In Saigon, on the other hand, as late as 1960, only ten women had graduated from the School of Medicine, Pharmacy and Dentistry.

Openings in the legal profession not only provide women with jobs, but also help to broaden women's political power and protect their gains. Bui Thi Cam, now a member of the Permanent Committee for the Preparation of Laws in the National Assembly, was the first woman lawyer in all of Viet Nam. Now there are enough women lawyers so that judges in all marriage cases are women. They protect women in enforcing the laws against polygamy and other feudal marriage practices. The Women's Union recruits women like Nong Thi Trung, once an illiterate highlander, to receive training for work in law and other professions. Trung is now the Chief Judge in her province. There are also two women judges in the Supreme Court of the DRV. [18]

On March 8, 1967, the government issued a directive to strengthen the trend towards women's emancipation in work. To ensure that women would rise in management of industrial units and agricultural cooperatives, the new law stipulates that when women make up 40 per cent of the labor force of a factory or co-op, a woman must serve on the management committee. When the labor force is 50 per cent women, the assistant manager must be a woman. When the number is 70 per cent, the manager must be a woman. By providing for their training, the directive also encourages women to advance to more skilled positions and to participate more in the work of state offices and enterprises. The Women's Union helps to implement this directive.

Nguyen Thi Hoi, a 28-year-old peasant woman and militia member, talked about how the directive is working out:

After the co-op was set up, I became Deputy Chief of a production group. I do the same jobs as other cooperators: ploughing, harrowing, pricking out, harvesting. . . . In August 1967, I became a Party member. I give orders to men and women, and they do as I ask because it was they who elected me to lead them. [19]

At the March 8 Weaving Mill, named in honor of International Women's Day, there are ongoing training courses which enable women to become heads of production teams and supervisors. So far, 200 women have replaced men at these jobs. A survey at the Fourth Congress of the Viet Nam Women's Union shows that between 1965 and 1972, the number of women who are directors or deputy directors of factories has increased from 58 to 130; the number of women directors of public institutes has increased from 21 to 65; and the number of women directors of central level government bureaus has increased from 125 to 1837 in those seven years.

Other women study at the Lao Dong Party's theoretical school, trade union schools and supplementary education classes to raise their general educational level. The directive of 1967 says that when choosing a woman for special training, those with special priority are: labor and combat heroes, those who had particularly miserable lives before the revolution, those who have family members who died for the nation, those originally from South Viet Nam and those from national minorities.

The DRV is the only revolutionary society to join a few small women's groups in the West in recognizing that housework is productive labor that should be compensated, even though in the DRV nearly all women work outside the home. Article 29 of the 1960 Marriage Law declared that in the event of divorce, common property would be divided according to the amount of work each partner put into the family's earnings. For the purpose of these calculations, housework is considered equivalent to productive work outside the home.

The abolition of polygamy

Along with political power and economic independence, women have also gained the right to free choice in marriage and the abolition of polygamy—the most oppressive family institution. In provinces where feudalism had been the strongest, the great majority of men had more than one wife. The 1946 Constitution and later decrees laid the foundation for outlawing polygamy and forced marriage. Between 1951 and 1958, the ratio of childhood marriages fell from 25 to 8 per cent while the ratio of free choice marriages rose from 27 to 63 per cent. But the Law on Marriage and the Family, which explicitly makes polygamy illegal, wasn't passed until 1960. In North Viet Nam, a law is passed only when it reflects the attitudes of the people. For fifteen years, cadre from the Women's Union and the Lao Dong Party worked to educate the population to overcome centuries of tradition that favored polygamy. Ho Chi Minh joined the campaign for the new marriage law. He urged·

Failing to free women means failing to liberate half of humanity. Failing to free women means that the building of socialism is only half completed. . . . The law on marriage aims at freeing women, that is, liberating half of society. As women are emancipated, we must eradicate feudal and bourgeois ideology in men. [20]

The Women's Union provided the ideas for the Law; the Ministry of Justice provided the language. The Law not only bans polygamy, it also outlaws forced marriages, child marriages, bride prices, dowries and wife beating. The law requires democracy within the family, allowing neither spouse to have more power than the other. In contrast, in many states in the U.S. today, it is legally assumed that the husband has the power to force his wife to obey him. Therefore a judge may rule that a woman is innocent if she commits a crime in the presence of her husband. [21] In France, until 1966, a woman needed her husband's permission before she could legally get a job. Under the old Saigon regime's Law No. I/50 "On the Family" the husband was legally the head of the family and divorce was forbidden unless there was a "special authorization" by the Head of State.

The law in the DRV, on the other hand, guarantees the right of each partner to freely choose an occupation, and the right of daughters and sons to equal treatment within the family. Children whose parents are not married have the same rights as children whose parents are married. Both women and men have equal rights to divorce—except a man is not allowed to divorce a pregnant woman until a year after she has given birth (unless the woman demands it).

The government and the Women's Union have worked hard to enforce this law. Shortly after the law was enacted, a directive of the Party Central Committee stated:

To insure a correct application of the law on marriage and the family, permanent and long-term propaganda and educational work is necessary among cadres, Party members and people.

Vo Thi The, now a member of the Central Executive Committee of the Women's Union, told me how she led a group of cadre from the Women's Union in a campaign that took the law to the rural strongholds of patriarchy:

We found that young women were married to boys eight or nine years old. The women would work in the fields and the boys would go to school. They had no sexual relations. The boys were too young to understand anything . . . We would organize study meetings to discuss the new law—separate meetings for the youth and the parents. At first, the young brides didn't dare take the initiative in getting the Law enforced. But we used these meetings to stimulate their consciousness. After the meetings, they would come up to us privately and cry and recount the details of their hard lives . . . There were so many who were miserable: victims of forced marriage and polygamy.

Sometimes we would have a fierce struggle with the boys' parents who had already given gifts and paid for their sons' brides. We would explain why they should let the girls be free—how their marriage was a form of servitude—that it was unjust. We explained how we fought the revolution for everyone . . . Those who continued to flaunt the new law

*were fined . . . but there weren't many. . . . Now we have virtually
abolished polygamy and forced marriage.*

At the same time, newspapers frequently carried stories like Bich
Hoa's. Her husband wanted a second wife because after several years
of trying, she had not given birth to a male heir. Rather than lose him
altogether, Bich was prepared to go along with her husband's demand
that she propose to a second wife for him. The Women's Union heard
about the dilemma and sent a cadre to talk to the husband, to Bich
Hoa, and to the prospective second wife. After some struggle, they
convinced the husband that his "feudal ways of thinking" were unacceptable and he abandoned his plan to marry a second wife. [22]
Efforts like these differ sharply from the practice in old Saigon. Under
Thieu's regime, polygamy was officially illegal, but some important
government officials flaunted three or four wives.

Divorce court in Hanoi

In the Law on Marriage and the Family the principle of free choice
in marriage includes freedom of divorce. Vo Thi The explained to me:

*The law encourages matrimonial happiness, solidarity and unity within
the family. . . . But divorce is no longer a humiliation for women. It's a
kind of liberation from the yoke of an oppressive man. The Law and the
Court always defend the interests of women and children. The aim of
divorce is to defend the rights of women against feudal male supre-
macy—no matter who initiates the divorce.*

One of the women judges in the People's Supreme Court, Le Phuong
Hang, explained that they always grant quick divorces to victims of
forced marriages. But in other cases they try to encourage reconciliation. The Court assigns neighbors or co-workers from the trade union
or Women's Union to serve as a reconciliation group.

*To try to reconcile is not to gloss over the faults, it is rather to make a
persevering criticism of the defects and errors and to stress and encourage what is good and inculcate in both parties a correct conception
of marriage and the family.*

If the conflict sharpens, then they grant divorce, dividing the property
according to who earned it. If the needy party asks, the Court will ask
the other party to pay alimony according to her or his means. They
entrust the children to whichever spouse is in a better position to care
for them. [23]

A divorce trial in North Viet Nam is a dramatic struggle against
what the Vietnamese call "feudal hangovers" and to expand women's
equality within the family and society. As I sat in on one trial in Hanoi,

I was struck by the strength of the Women's Union and the advantages women gain from having a legal system committed to women's liberation. In the court itself, there were three judges—two of whom were women. The investigator who researched the case for the judges was also a woman. The defense attorney for the wife was a woman. All the women were members of the Women's Union. There is no charge for divorce proceedings or for attorneys. Nevertheless, the husband did not request the services of an attorney.

The issue of contention was classic. The wife, Nguyet, wanted a divorce because her husband, Hung, had been harassing her for a long time. A lower court had granted the divorce, but Hung was appealing it.

The husband and wife each spoke for themselves, giving their version of the story, responding to each other's testimony:

Hung: . . . *Neighbors tell me she continues to relate to other men. But I am a good husband and want to keep the marriage. . . .*

Nguyet: *Now, after living together, I have found that matrimonial happiness is impossible. We have conflict about everything: what food to buy, clothes, everything. . . . He even beat me and gambled. . . . All his words about my flirtations are lies . . .*

Defense Attorney: *Nguyet, why does your husband accuse you of child neglect?*

Nguyet: *I went to evening classes for vocational education. He was very jealous. He has insulted me and spread rumors about me to my friends. He says I was with other men. . . . I insist on an investigation. Go to my school. It's called "Tay Son" and check to see if I was there. . . . It's my right to have friends and go to classes. . . . He said he would take care of our daughter while I was in class, but then he left her alone. Sometimes he would agree with my complaints and criticisms of him, but he always behaves differently and never puts promises into practice.*

Investigator: *Mr. Hung, how do you respond to what your wife says?*

Hung: *She was too young when we got married—seventeen years old. . . . She's fickle. I've been more steady. Because of her relations with other students, she has lost interest in me. . . . They have made her extravagant . . .*

Investigator: *Your wife wants a divorce because she has no love for you. How do you respond?*

Hung: *Our parents agreed to our marriage. It is her fault that there is no happiness in our family. . . . I never forced marriage. . . .*

Investigator: *But how can you live together if she doesn't want to? What is your real motive for saying you want reconciliation?*

Hung: *I think it is possible.*

218

Judge: *And what about the child?*

Hung: *I insist on having my child with me. My mother and sister will help.*

Defense Attorney: *You want reconciliation and the child. Is it true? Do you want reconciliation because you love your wife or because you want to maintain your child?*

Hung: *For the sake of the child, I want reconciliation. . . .*

Investigator: *Nguyet, how do you respond to the neighbors' reports of your flirtations?*

Nguyet: *. . . They are mistaken. I have many men friends, but they are not my lovers. . . . also, my husband's family made life so miserable for me, that I liked to be away with friends.*

Investigator: *There may have been some flirtation. But we have abolished feudalism and it is fine for you to have male friends.*

After nearly an hour of testimony, the defense attorney spoke on behalf of Nguyet:

Don't consider me subjective because I am a woman also. I'm defending her because of the principles involved, not because of her sex. . . . Nguyet certainly has faults. . . . But there is a strong ideological conflict in this relationship. . . . Once he even got his brother to hold her down while he cut her hair as revenge for her spending time with her own friends. That was feudalism. . . . and that is why she has no feeling left for him. . . . According to Article 34 of the Marriage Law, a husband and wife must have mutual respect. He has constantly violated this article. We must consider this case on the basis of her happiness and the principle of mutual support and respect. . . . We think the child should stay with the mother as she requests.

Investigator: *We defeated the French, liberated the North and restored peace. But remnants of feudalism remain, especially in matters concerning marriage and the family. . . . We do our best to put the new law into practice in our lives. In this case, we object to the early age of Nguyet's marriage. She wanted to annul the marriage, but gave into her parents' pressure to stay married. After some time, the contradictions between the couple increased to the point where we witness this bitter session today. People, even young people, must make their own decisions and not be bent by family pressure. . . .*

The judges left the court and deliberated for less than five minutes. They ruled in favor of the wife on every issue. One of them addressed the husband:

. . . We must drive away all ideology left from feudalism. You cannot force your wife to live with you if she does not want to. She also has the right to her own friends. Lack of love is the basic

grounds for divorce. . . . In the future, Mr. Hung, you may have another wife and you must learn to treat women properly. The Marriage Law says that there must be democracy within the family. The family is part of society and for the sake of society there must be mutual respect and support . . . also according to the law, both parties must share in the housework. . . . The wife has insisted on divorce. The couple has many contradictions in daily life. That is why we allow divorce. . . . The child should stay with Nguyet because Nguyet has a better job and can take care of her better. . . .

Both Hung and Nguyet left the court without looking at each other again. After the proceedings, I asked the judges why they allowed the husband to spend so much time repeating his case and why they thought his accusations against his wife were relevant. They explained that it was important for both parties to say everything that was on their minds in order to avoid post-trial bitterness. They didn't want the husband to go away grumbling that his side of the story was not heard. It was also important for him to say all he wanted so that the truth of the situation would come out. Finally, the judges viewed the trial as only one step in a long process of education that would continue after the trial. Most of the spectators in the courtroom were friends and co-workers of the couple. It was their responsibility to continue Hung's education—to teach him how to change his feudal, authoritarian ways. Hearing his full testimony was necessary for that task.

Continuity and revolution in the family

In 1930, some ICP leaders, anxious to build a society free from all "mystical ties," pushed for the adoption of the slogan of *Tam Vo* or "The Three No's": No religion, no family, no fatherland. The slogan never became popular with the Vietnamese people. The ICP soon dropped it because it neither reflected the aspirations of the people nor did it help to further the struggle against French colonialism and feudalism. [24] Family relations have always been the center of the lives of people in Viet Nam. A leader of the Women's Union used these words to describe people's feelings about the family:

To the Vietnamese people, the relation in the family has always been sacred and very close. [25]

Proverbs and folksongs, still repeated after centuries by most Vietnamese people, express the permanence and importance—both positive and negative—of the family. The proverb goes:

Man has parents and grandparents,
just as a tree has its trunk and
a river has its source.

The folksong goes:

> ... *An unmarried woman cannot help but run around*
> *worried and insecure.*
> *Sisters, it is miserable not to have a husband.* [26]

Ho Chi Minh gave a talk to leaders at a meeting debating the Draft Law on Marriage and the Family in 1959—a year before the law was passed. His talk shows how the political leadership of the DRV tries to combine Vietnamese family traditions with new notions about equality within the family—and even new implications for a revolutionary re-definition of family life:

> *There are people who think that as a bachelor I may not have a perfect knowledge of this question. Though I have no family of my own, yet I have a very big family—the working class throughout the world and the Vietnamese people. From that broad family I can judge and imagine the small one. . . . It is correct to take a keen interest in the family: many families constitute the society. A good society makes a good family and vice versa. The core of society is the family. It is precisely to build up socialism that due attention must be paid to this core.*
> *"Living in concord, husband and wife may empty the East Sea,"*
> *the proverb runs. To enjoy concord in matrimonial life, marriage must be based on genuine love. . . . The Law on Marriage aims at emancipating women, that is, at freeing half of society. The emancipation of women must be carried out simultaneously with the extirpation of feudal and bourgeois thinking in men. . . .* [27]

Here he assumes that families which keep the woman subordinate to the man are the norm only in feudal and capitalist societies. The patriarchal family was the cornerstone of feudalism in Viet Nam. Under capitalism, employers profit from keeping women trapped in a cycle of marital dependency—leaving husbands with more power and forcing wives to work for little or no pay. Under socialism, the goal is to eliminate all social inequalities. Socialist conditions make it possible for women and men to come together as companions—each maintaining their independence, strength and commitment to building a revolutionary society. General Giap remembered that Ho Chi Minh often repeated:

> *The Party is the family of communist militants.* [28]

He meant that the ICP showed great concern for the living and working conditions of all its members.

In practice, while the importance of family life has remained the same, the nature of family life has changed. A popular song in the DRV begins to explain these changes. It describes the initial surprise and then pride of a husband who returns from the front to find his wife is chairperson of the village administrative committee. The foundations for equality within the family are strong in the DRV: economic equality or probability that the woman may earn more, political equality, and social recognition of women's strength and importance in the society at large.

The media repeatedly encourage family separations and the "Three Postponements" that are necessary to serve the war effort. The "Three Postponements" suggest that if a couple falls in love, they should postpone engagement; if they're engaged, they should postpone marriage; and if they're married, they should postpone having children. The ideal is for lovers to be celibate and faithful. The way this ideal differs from tradition is that there is no double standard—men and women are equally committed to practicing the ideal. Women and men, when they are separated, wear aluminum "fidelity rings" made from downed U.S. bomber planes.

An editor of the Women's Union weekly magazine, *Phu Nu*, told me that it is their editorial policy to encourage women's independence.

In "A Heart to Heart Talk"—one of our most popular columns—we urge young women to postpone romance. When a woman is in her twenties, we urge her to concentrate on learning a profession—that is the most important thing. She needs knowledge to be "master of her self, the society and the nation," as Le Duan says. . . . Even if a woman is thirty and she writes for advice because she has no fiance, we urge her not to feel pressured. She'll have plenty of time to choose a good one.

All of the single women I met in Viet Nam were sure they would marry some day. But few seemed preoccupied with romance and none seemed anxious to marry soon. Married women were not preoccupied with their husbands. Tuyen was accustomed to being separated from her husband for long periods of time. But she could not conceive of being unmarried:

It's only natural to marry. If a woman doesn't meet someone she loves soon—it will be later. Everyone here works for a common cause, so it's easy to fall in love. . . . I got married in the liberated zones in a collective ceremony with three other couples. It was September 2, Independence Day, in 1953. After the leader of our group pronounced us married and congratulated us, he reminded us to maintain our dedication to the revolution. Three days later our political responsibilities sent my husband and me in different directions.

But certain differences between the responsibilities of husbands and wives remain which may make it more difficult for women to maintain their independence and eliminate men's privilege. It is Women's Union policy that men should share housework and child care but the policy is not consistently urged in all North Vietnamese media. Le Duan reaffirmed in a recent speech that:

In bringing up a child, the role of father is less important than that of the mother. [29]

Therefore, men go to the front to fight. In some articles, traditional images of women as housewives remain. For example, in an article emphasizing the military importance and heroism of fifteen women who do the dangerous work of defusing bombs, the author applauded one woman who "picks up and saves every bit of wire, nut and bolt she comes across, like a good housewife." [30] It is essential for everyone, not just housewives, to practice thriftiness in pre-industrial societies.

Centuries of polygamy, arranged marriages, Confucianism and Buddhism have had a profound effect on images of women and the meaning of sexuality in Viet Nam. For example, when parents arranged nearly all marriages, men did not have to "win a wife" to enhance their egos. Pressure to treat women as sex objects was alleviated by the fact that parents' wishes prevailed over sons' desires. Today, as in the past, peasant families living in one-room huts cannot mystify sexual relations. Physical intimacy has a different connotation in Viet Nam than in the United States. Western visitors invariably remark

about women holding hands, hugging and fondling each other in public with no self-consciousness. On the other hand, there seems to be no public concern for sexual relations or sexiness.

The Vietnamese experience with ''sexual freedom'' Western style has meant the degradation of women and men that they used to witness in Saigon brothels and bars. But in revolutionary Viet Nam— North and South—there seems to be no public discussion of sexuality or women's alternatives to monogamous heterosexuality—having more than one lover, bisexuality or lesbianism.

In the U.S., groups within the women's movement have insisted that these options be available. These women have begun to analyze the relationship between capitalism, the patriarchal family and sexual repression. Requirements that women be virgins before marriage and that women's sexuality serve men, are part of the system of inequality where women are the property of men. This analysis begins from women's experience living in the West and struggling against an advanced capitalist system. But the goal of abolishing sexual repression should not be rigidly applied as the criterion for evaluating the progress of Vietnamese women towards liberation.

New images of love

Women in the DRV are not treated as sex objects. A well-known male poet explained,

Earlier we wrote poetry about loving beautiful girls who lived in well-tended rooms. In 1953, for the first time, I wrote about an old woman. [31]

The media contain nothing that might suggest that women's problems come from being ''ugly, smelly, pimply or sexually inadequate.'' There's no trace of the notion that women should spend their time making themselves physically attractive. Every U.S. woman who has visited Hanoi has agreed:

The streets feel totally safe at any hour. Although people stared at me because I was a Westerner, none of their stares had any sexual or aggressive content. [32]

I remained a bit skeptical until after my own visit to Viet Nam, when our group of six women walked through a crowd of more than two hundred male soldiers without a hint of harassment.

Most of the women dress alike. Every day they wear loose black pants, a white or sometimes print blouse, and sandals. Most women wear their hair long, pinned back with a metal clasp. Almost none wear make-up and few wear jewelry—except wedding rings. While some people cling to the standards of beauty which love the small frail woman, most women aspire to be strong and robust—able to handle an anti-aircraft gun. The ideal woman in traditional Viet Nam was one who excelled in the "Four Virtues"—each corresponding to one of the four aspects of women's personality:

> *In work, learn to provide a variety of dishes,*
> *and master the art of sewing and embroidering.*
> *In appearance, keep a dignified look,*
> *neither too striking nor too lax.*
> *In speech, employ polite language.*
> *In conduct, be honest and loyal.*

The Viet Nam Women's Union has revolutionized the "four virtues." The new ideals are: (1) to love the nation and people; (2) to build socialism; (3) to prevent disease and maintain a healthy environment; (4) to find new ways of living that reorganize family affairs to combine work, study and cultural improvement.

Women in Viet Nam have always expressed affection towards each other freely and openly. But polygamy and economic insecurity kept some women divided and especially fostered hostility between mothers- and daughters-in-law. A new solidarity among women has grown, created by those who joined together to fight. This solidarity thrives in the DRV where they have abolished the institutional sources of competition among women.

The solidarity among women in Viet Nam is visible and beautiful. I do not recall sitting among a group of women anywhere in Viet Nam where they did not have their arms around each other, sometimes kissing, sometimes caressing, expressing their sisterly/comradely love. While on the road with four Vietnamese women for ten days, I never saw any sign of jealousy, competitiveness or hostility among them. Kindness among them seemed natural, but it was never taken for granted.

The strength of the solidarity among Vietnamese women became especially clear to me when two sisters I was travelling with disagreed between themselves. They argued about the best age to teach a young woman about her body and reproduction. One felt it was a "feudal hangover" not to teach a girl everything about sex before she began menstruating. The possibility of a "child" being thoroughly informed about sex before she was 17 or 18 was very disturbing to the other. The debate was heated. Both women had daughters. It was not an abstract issue for them. Both were adamant, but after some hours, when it was obvious they would not convince each other, they shelved the discussion. Neither had questioned the morality or integrity of her adversary. Their mutual respect stayed strong and, in the days that followed, I noticed no trace of grudge or hostility.

Solidarity and love among these people comes from mutual respect, concern, and the experience that they must identify with each other and sacrifice for each other in order to survive. Nguyen Dinh Thi, writer and political leader in the Army, explained more about egotism and people's respect and love for each other:

Many people who had learned to read and write as adults and who were not well acquainted with foreign words thought when they heard the term "individualist" that it meant "cannibal." They associated the unintelligible concept of individualism with something dangerous, with the cannibalistic. They themselves had never had time to feel unique or singular. They shared work together, lived together, and since time immemorial had made common cause against natural catastrophe and enemy attack. A joy, a sorrow, a difficulty had seldom been experienced alone. . . .

Descriptions of loneliness, of having no way out, of not belonging, of personal disappointment, these matters are not relevant. The question is, rather, "How can so and so be helped in his difficult situation?" . . . That there is no feeling of weariness, that never is there a sign of discouragement, this is because there are so many carrying the same load. Confidence is the response to the enemy's nihilism. We talk about building up, not about laying waste. . . .

As far as my work is concerned, I cannot say that it measures up to the character of a woman I met recently in a village. She had lost two children in the great famine during the Japanese occupation. When the revolution came, she let out only one sigh. Her other children fought against France; another son was killed. She has children in the North and the South. Now her first grandchild is at the front. She has raised children and grandchildren. She is too old now to work in the rice fields, yet she still works at home, cooks, takes care of the smallest children. She has never stopped working. These are our readers. What can we give them? They are the ones who are giving us strength. [33]

Socializing housework and childcare

As society takes more responsibility for housework and childcare, the basis for equality within the family becomes firmer. The process of socializing housework is well-developed in the DRV. Every co-op has a communal dining hall, though any family can voluntarily decide whether they want to eat there or at home. Most industrial units have communal dining facilities. In the cities, the Women's Union sponsors community service teams that deliver food—both prepared and unpre-

pared—to workers' homes. The Women's Union tries to distribute household tasks on a rational basis by organizing teams of workers, unable to perform heavy work, to do sewing and laundry. They free women who work in other areas from the double burden of work at home and in the factory.

At the 1960 Congress of the Women's Union, they resolved:

. . . to gradually organize housework so as to help women concentrate all their time, energy and mind in production and in social activities, so that they may have time for study and proper rest. That is our standpoint on the complete liberation of women of the working class. [34]

This Congress launched an intense campaign to induce more women to use collective housework facilities and "not to be enslaved by petty housework which is tiresome and unproductive." The 1974 Congress resolved to extend community service teams to each block in the city.

More important, childcare, which is considered productive, becomes a collective responsibility:

In transforming and building new relations in marriages and in the family, we must be resolute in wiping out all remnants of old ideas and habits, in order to build families of a new type: democratic, harmonious and in which there is mutual respect, mutual help in work, study and progress, and an equal share in family responsibility including the bringing up of children. [35]

The Women's Union encourages family councils to discuss how household tasks will be shared among mothers, fathers and children. At the 1960 Congress, the Women's Union affirmed that childcare sponsored by communities working collectively and by the State "must fully satisfy the requirements of mothers." Le Duan told the latest Congress of the Viet Nam Women's Union:

In the old society, giving birth to children and rearing them were considered the private tasks of each mother and each family. Therefore, among the oppressed and exploited classes, the mother had to suffer a lot as a servant and in giving birth to and rearing and educating her children. Such a situation no longer exists under our regime. [36]

Child care arrangements and schools vary according to the ages of the children and whether they live in the cities or countryside. During the heavy bombing of the cities, all children—except for those still nursing—were evacuated to the countryside. On the opening day of a new school, children went off to school armed with shovels to help dig the shelters. These children wore thick straw coats and hats to protect them from pellet bombs. Every school area was criss-crossed with trenches and shelters.

The State takes responsibility for training and paying teachers through its Committees for the Protection of Mothers and Children Cooperatives share in the support of the teaching staff and school according to their ability to pay. Pre-school child care is divided between centers that care for children between 2 months and 3 years and those that care for children between 3 and 6 years. Most of the centers for the youngest children have about twenty children each.

A French journalist visited a typical center. He reported that there were two women especially trained in hygiene care for the children. The center is never closed—except for the purpose of cleaning two days a month. Children stay in the center from about 6 a.m. to about 5:30 p.m. They spend most of their time playing, eating and sleeping, but also learn a few simple exercises. One of the teachers shows the older children how to sing and dance. A doctor visits the center once a month for a thorough check-up of each child and pays brief daily calls to make sure everything is OK. The children are well-fed. The cooperative has donated an area of water for fish breeding to the child care center and every mother is expected to spend one day a month working at the pond. There are usually about seven such child care centers for each co-op. [37]

Other child care centers have the resources for keeping children all the time, except for weekends. At the one I visited, there were seventeen children in the class—all between the ages of 3 and 5. One little girl was eager to have us hear the poem she just learned:

> *I want to be a bee,*
> *not to be a butterfly,*
> *so that I can sting*
> *the American aggressors.*

In the cities, there are centers meeting the same needs attached to different factories. At the March 8 Weaving Mill, for example, there is child care for 500 children. These children are cared for in small groups during their mothers' entire work shift plus an additional four hours to give the mother time to relax or study. [38] In industrial centers, the labor unions, as well as the Women's Union, have responsibility for making sure child care is adequate.

The Fourth Congress of the Viet Nam Women's Union received a report of the progress in day care. Table 2 summarizes the reports.

TABLE 2

Year	Rural sector		Factories and offices	
	No. of day care centers	No. of children	No. of day care centers	No. of children
1961	15,567	87,052	1,975	36,000
1965	20,841	178,094	2,333	46,031
1972	23,847	320,114	6,960	101,667

Children over 6 spend their afternoons in Young Pioneer Centers or helping with agricultural work. Child care facilities have expanded rapidly. In 1965, fifty-two per cent of the children in the countryside between the ages of 2 and 7 were in child care centers. By 1969, ninety-six per cent were in child care centers. [39] Children between the ages of 7 and 10 attend primary school; ages 11 through 14 attend secondary school; ages 15 through 17 may attend high school; and after 17, many attend a cooperative or trade school or the University.

Those children not in day care centers—few in the countryside but nearly fifty per cent in the cities—are cared for by older people: grandparents, uncles and aunts. Since children were evacuated for long periods of time and most people in the DRV are peasants, the countryside got priority when scarce child care resources were divided.

The Vietnamese press often has reported stories about women initially ignoring the opportunity to send their children to child care centers. Their traditional conceptions of motherhood made them anxious that their children would not get the proper care at the centers, or they felt that they could depend on grandparents to do the job better. These reports usually show that the Women's Union leaders or Party members would have to struggle with these women—showing the advantages of collective child care. Eventually, most Vietnamese women have become enthusiastic supporters of the program. Today, nearly two million children are in various kinds of child care programs in the DRV.

Education for emancipation

When a reporter visited an agricultural cooperative, a 60-year-old co-op member emerged from the crowd and spontaneously recited this verse:

Yes, I used to be a poor illiterate woman,
Living a dog's life in the darkest of times.
But now, thanks to the Party, I've known a new life.
I can read and write and am no longer blind. [40]

During French colonial days, 95 per cent of the Vietnamese people were illiterate. In the whole of Viet Nam, there were only 407,000 children in school—of whom only 17 per cent were female. Only three women were known to be in universities. Today, in the DRV, there are 4.8 million children in school—about half of them are female. Another million adults participate in compensatory education courses. During the 1972-1973 school year, 43.5 per cent of university students were women. Table 3 summarizes the gains in women's education in the DRV. [41]

TABLE 3

Type of education	No. of women in all Viet Nam 1946	No. of women in DRV 1971
Students in primary and secondary school	138,366	2,178,283
Students in technical schools, colleges and universities	3	47,620
Teachers in general education	1,468	66,269
Women teaching in technical schools, colleges and universities	0	1,900
Women administrating and directing general education	3	4,067

The pace of education expansion for women continues to accelerate. By 1958, illiteracy was eliminated in the DRV. A woman chemistry professor, the daughter of a wealthy Southern family, explained that when she chose to study chemistry, she was the only woman from Viet Nam at the Sorbonne. When she began teaching chemistry years later at Hanoi University, there was one woman in her class. Now, half of the seats in her classes are filled by women. [42] There's a kind of affirmative action policy that favors women and national minorities for university admission. A report of the Fourth Congress of the Viet Nam Women's Union showed that between 1965 and 1972, the number of women graduates from universities and colleges grew from 2,117 to 16,947. In the same seven years, about 75,000 women graduated from technical school. About twenty three per cent of all teachers in the university and professional/technical schools are women. The percentage of women students in higher education varies from forty to sixty, depending on the field.

This educational avalanche—especially during wartime—has put a tremendous strain on educational resources. Schools are open eighteen hours a day with three shifts per day. Each teacher has responsibility for two shifts. Under the French and Thieu regimes, only the rich elite could afford schooling. Today in the DRV, people in schools come from all social classes, but some are given extra advantages in testing for college and university admission. Students from poor peasant or working-class families or from families who lost members during the war receive special points added to their grades on admission exams. [43]

Everyone learns math, chemistry, physics, literature, history, cooking, painting, carpentry. There's no special tracking for boys and girls. Boys and girls learn to sew in the first grade and all children in the fifth and sixth grades learn cooking. There may, however, be some inconsistency in the application of this policy because at least one magazine article on a boarding school was illustrated with photos of boys doing woodwork and girls doing needlework. [44] But educational films usually emphasize themes promoting women's strength and liberation. For example, one movie for children, "Meo Vang," portrays the problems of a female cat who spends her time frivolously primping, but learns she must work seriously if she is to survive. A popular film shown to older students, "The 17th Parallel," tells the story of a South Vietnamese couple who are separated by the war. The husband goes North while the wife stays in the South and becomes a military hero.

The Ministry of Education has made a concerted effort to "Vietnamize" education, eliminating French texts and colonial and feudal approaches to education.

Ho Chi Minh's five principles of education:

- *Love the country and your compatriots. Hate the aggressor.*
- *Constantly improve work and study.*
- *Strengthen unity and observe discipline.*
- *Practice hygiene.*
- *Be modest, frank and courageous.*

All schools try to practice the motto:

> *Combine instruction with work—theory with practice.* [45]

Younger children, as well as older ones, spend a lot of time in productive work. They participate in campaigns to glean rice, keep paths clean and other needed tasks. Under the slogan "A kilo of pests equals a Yankee's head," thousands of children worked to remove a kilo of insects each from food plants.

An official at the Ministry of Education explained why students continue doing manual work, even while they are in the university:

Our education is not a privilege for the rich. Our students don't study irrelevant things, but rather develop needed skills in science, technology, art and literature. Each student spends one month a year constructing schools, another month working in a factory or agricultural co-op, and a third month doing practical work in her specialized field. In their last years of study, they spend all their time away from the classroom in the field. When students live and work among the people, they understand the needs of the people, learn from the people, and improve their political consciousness.

232

He also talked about the relations between students and teachers:

They are relations among comrades. They work together in the class-room or in the factory. It is the teacher's responsibility to give the students knowledge and help in their collective life. Once a month students meet to evaluate the teacher's work and help her improve. We don't have a problem with authoritarianism because when it appears, we criticize it at once. Teachers are integrated with the community at every level.

Health

In the DRV all health care is free and the revolution has given special priority to women's health. While expert surgeons in Saigon got rich by performing cosmetic surgery, health workers in the North have eliminated venereal disease. They have reduced the infant mortality rate, which was 40 per cent in 1945, to 1.2 per cent in 1972. [46] Pham Van Dong, Premier of the DRV, dramatized the importance placed on women's health by founding the Institute for the Protection of Mothers and Children. This Institute and related laws protect women by freeing them from centuries of pulling the plow and from giving birth in fields and at machines in factories. The Institute is the national research center and hospital which specializes in treating the most complicated gynecological and obstetrical cases.

In 1945, the 300 hospital beds for maternity care that existed in all of Viet Nam were reserved for the elite. Now, almost every village has its own maternity and gynecology clinic. In 1945, two out of every five women died in childbirth. Today, the maternal mortality rate has dropped to less than one per cent. [47] All women get two months paid maternity leave before and after childbirth and special meat and milk allowances while pregnant and nursing.

Vietnamese health workers emphasize preventive health care— concentrating on educating as many people as possible in maintaining good health. No doctors make a profit by maintaining the state of medical ignorance. The population is now totally immunized against malaria, cholera, TB, and other diseases that used to claim the lives of thousands. The same law of 1967 that provides for women's advance-ment in factories and co-ops, also makes provisions for regular gyneco-logical check-ups for women workers by doctors who are on duty in work centers.

One woman from the U.S. who visited Hanoi had a chance to com-pare Vietnamese and U.S. attitudes toward gynecological problems. During her tour, she had severe menstrual cramps. Her guides insisted on taking her to the hospital. The hospital had modern x-ray equipment, but no flush toilets. They took an x-ray to make sure her IUD was not causing the problem. To prevent infection, they gave her vitamin C, iron pills and antibiotics. A nurse bathed her before the doctor gave her a pelvic exam, which she said was very gentle. All this was standard procedure. They told her that if they decided to remove her IUD, she would have to follow the usual practice of remaining in the hospital for two days to make sure there were no complications. She also learned that acupuncture is used to regularize menstruation and eliminate cramps. There was no hint of contempt for women's bodies that one finds among gynecologists here.

The seriousness with which women are treated comes from the high value the Vietnamese place on every human life—especially on the lives of women, the producers of new generations. Vietnamese traditions and a new revolutionary optimism about the future, combined with the effects of U.S. genocidal policy, make childbirth a celebrated event. A doctor from the Institute for the Protection of Mothers and Children recently told a visitor that family planning wasn't very popular in the spring of 1973 because everyone wanted to celebrate the signing of the **Paris Peace** Agreement with the birth of a child. But leaders of the Women's Union insist that "family planning is a must" to insure the health of women and children, and give women time for study, rest and amusement. [48]

The Institute dispenses birth control pills to women in the cities, and, assuming there are no medical complications, they distribute IUD's in the countryside. They are continuing experimentation to perfect the use of a regional plant, reportedly used by Meo tribes, to induce abortion or temporary sterility. The Women's Union has a special committee to disseminate birth control information to both women and men. They organize study groups only for married women, but pamphlets, photo displays and magazine articles are available to everyone.

During the "Three Postponements" campaign everyone was encouraged to use birth control. Now two children is considered the ideal family size and birth control is considered a collective social responsibility. Trade unions, for example, impose moral sanctions on men who violate agreed-upon plans to limit family size. Some men use condoms and a small minority in the cities have had vasectomies.

Abortions are available free of charge to any woman who wants one. But the Vietnamese prefer that the decision for a woman to have an abortion be a careful one arrived at by both husband and wife. Very few women who are not married become pregnant and there is no public discussion of this situation.

The tragedy of Doctor Ngo Thi Ngoc Trung summarizes the major health problem of Vietnamese women more dramatically than statistics. After her father died of malnutrition in 1946 in the South, she and her mother went North. There she became an outstanding student and was the first woman doctor to specialize in x-ray work in the DRV. She was 23 years old when she was killed by a bomb dropped on Bach Mai hospital during the Christmas Bombing, 1972. [49]

The war has created new health problems—never before experienced on such a massive scale in medical history anywhere. Living for months in underground bomb shelters—never being exposed to sunlight—deprives humans of essential vitamins. A variety of new nervous diseases have appeared since the war. The Institute for Protection of Mothers and Children issued a special plea to women's organizations, individuals and mothers all over the world to help heal the wounds created by U.S. genocidal policies.

Continuing struggle

Bui Thi Cam, a leader of the Viet Nam Women's Union, recently told an American woman in Hanoi,

We have equality, but we are not yet equal. [50]

Although women have made fantastic gains in the revolution, they recognize that many problems remain to be overcome. For example, their goal is to have women hold more than three per cent of the places on the Central Committee of the Lao Dong Party. They're working for more women to be in higher-level leadership positions everywhere.

At the 1974 Women's Union Congress, the Central Executive Committee of the Union drew the delegates' attention to additional problems for the women's movement. Here are highlights from that Report:

Owing to the influence of the old regime and of the atrocious war, to the fact that our work of education and training has been neither all-round nor systematic, and to the still inadequate efforts of the women themselves, their sense of being collective master has not been truly high. . . .

Women still suffer from inadequate living and working conditions. . . . The birth rate is too high. This has a had influence on women's health, life and family happiness and hampers their progress in all fields.

The law on marriage and the family is still being infringed. In some instances, violations of the democratic rights and family happiness of women have not been duly sanctioned in time. . . . [In outlining their tasks the Union later resolved:] The Union should educate and persuade everyone to respect the law on marriage and the family so as

CHÀO MỪNG ĐẠI HỘI PHỤ NỮ V.N LẦN THỨ

GIỎI VIỆC NƯỚC, ĐẢM VIỆC NH
PHẤN ĐẤU THỰC HIỆN NAM NỮ BÌNH ĐẲ

Ban Tuyên huấn Hội Phụ nữ Việt Nam và
Hương trình cổ động Trung ương phái hành

This poster greets the 4th National Congress of Vietnamese Women and affirms women's capacity to
in the Three Responsibilities Movement.

*to involve the whole society in opposing and criticizing violations of this
law. . . .*

*The organization, leadership and guidance by the Union at various
levels have not kept pace with the growing women's movement. . . .
The organization, leadership and guidance by the Union authorities at
various levels still bear a bureaucratic character and fail to fully relate
to the feelings and aspirations of the masses of women. . . . Coordina-
tion still lacks a consistent and constant character. . . .*

*The women's movement has made much progress, but the
machinery of the Union and its cadres is not yet equal to their tasks. Its
executive committees at various levels cannot yet claim to be truly
representative of the broad masses of women engaged in production
work and combat activities in every field. . . .*

*We must work out policies and adopt measures which allow them
[cadres] to attend full-time residential training courses. . . . They must
be fully conscious of their responsibility towards the cause of women's
emancipation, strive to overcome all obstacles, ceaselessly seek to
raise their standards, be modest and learn from the masses. . . .* [51]

After exploring these and other problems, the delegates discussed
many ways to resolve them. They agreed:

*To strengthen the organization from top to bottom, so the Union will be
able to know the wishes and opinions of its members . . . a given policy
should always be accompanied by measures for organizing and
guidance to get it carried out. . . .*

In this book, we have noted instances of inconsistent application of
policies favoring women's emancipation. As the process and struggle
continues, we assume that implementation of these policies will be
stronger and more effective. Meanwhile, some men continue to hold
contemptuous attitudes toward women. Others, while they respect
women, don't fully accept them as equals. Some make jokes about men
being hen-pecked or afraid of women since women have become
fighters. The writer, Cam Thanh, told me she made a speech to the
National Congress of the Writers' Union exposing these problems:

*In Dong Lac District, for example, where nearly all political leaders are
women, men joked: "the frogs jump and sit on the altar." But that was
much more common in the sixties than it is now.*

Nguyen Thi Thap, past President of the Women's Union, also
wrote about the problem of some women not understanding how best
to defend their own rights:

*They think women's role is to look after the children and work in the
kitchen. They advocate that women should not be politically involved,*

*since politics is a man's task. . . . Obviously such a viewpoint is com-
pletely wrong. Every big or small question related to the interest of the
class and nation is directly or indirectly related to women's interests.* [52]

Uneven progress dramatizes the long road the Vietnamese
people—especially the women—have traveled. It also gives us a sense
of the texture of the continuing struggle ahead. For example, in Quang
Binh Province, just north of the 17th parallel, 460,000 people survived
the daily bombing by relocating their homes and work in an elaborate
network of caves and tunnels. After six years of life underground,
villagers are relieved to be breathing fresh air again in their new
thatched homes. The leaders of the Women's Union in that province
are proud of their members' anti-aircraft record. They responded,
"Never," when I asked them if women would return to being housewives now that there was peace. Nevertheless, a few minutes later, one
said,

*Girls in secondary school do worse than boys because they're more
interested in love. It's natural.*

Another disagreed and pointed out that this was a "feudal attitude
towards women." The others weren't sure.

In Hanoi, on the other hand, editors of the Women's Union magazine have launched an "offensive" against feudal underestimations of
women's capacity. They have devoted entire issues to publicizing the
achievements of women students. Their articles also urge that men
share the housework on an equal basis in order to eliminate women's
disadvantage in studying.

Nationally, the post-war Three Responsibilities Movement gives
the struggle for women's liberation added prominence. While Vietnamese women fight for full equality, they affirm women's special
qualities and responsibilities. Vo Thi The, member of the Central
Executive Committee of the Viet Nam Women's Union, told me:

*We are very proud of women's special sensibilities: patience, tender-
ness, patriotism, love of family and faithfulness. With these feelings,
we have a particular contribution to make to the revolution. Our special
role is clear in the new Three Responsibilities Movement which
organizes all women to work actively in (1) political and economic life
(2) in the family and (3) in the struggle for equality between men and
women.*

Yet some questions of women's liberation in the DRV have yet to
be considered. There is no public discussion of alternatives to marriage, even though both married and single women are economically
independent and secure. While it's clear that they plan to expand the

number of child care centers, there don't seem to be any plans for men to take responsibility for running the centers. This may change: the Vietnamese conception of women's emancipation is an evolving one— neither abstract, nor fixed. It reflects their resources, needs, experiences and struggles.

The Vietnamese have no fixed conception of human nature. Their experience with defeating the U.S. invasion has given them infinite confidence in people's ability to change. Although women still fulfill the traditional tasks of mothers, wives and daughters, the meaning of these tasks has changed. Competition and insecurity in all social relations have nearly disappeared. The progress already made, combined with mutual support, cooperation and unity are firm foundations for continuing the progress towards women's liberation.

Notes

1. Mai Thi Tu. "The Vietnamese Woman, Yesterday and Today," in *Vietnamese Woman* (Vietnamese Studies #10; Hanoi: 1966), pp. 30-31.
2. Nguyen Thi Kim Anh's book was called *Van De Phu Nu* (The Woman Question). It has not been translated from the Vietnamese. Thanks to David Marr of the Indochina Resource Center for providing me with a summary translation.
3. Quoted by Mai Thi Tu (see fn. 1), pp. 48-49.
4. Nguyen Thi Thap, "Women and Revolution," *Viet Nam News and Reports* #14 (March 1973), Supplement on Women, p. 8.
5. "President Ho Chi Minh and the Emancipation of Women," *Women of Viet Nam* #3 (1969), pp. 22-23.
6. Process described by Mai Thi Tu (see fn. 1), pp. 53-55.
7. Le Duan, "We Must View the Women's Question from a Class Standpoint," in *On the Socialist Revolution in Viet Nam*, vol. 3 (Hanoi: Foreign Languages Publishing House, 1967), p. 114.
8. Le Thi Xuyen, "The Early Days," *Viet Nam News and Reports* #14 (March 1973), Supplement on Women, p. 9.
9. Le Duan, "The Vietnamese Women View the Revolution, Love Marriage, Child-rearing at 4th Congress," *Tricontinental New Service*, vol 2 #9 (May 8, 1974) p. 19. At the time of the first edition, this was the only translation available of Le Duan's speech. The complete and official translation is now available in Le Duan, "Role and Tasks of the Vietnamese Woman in the New Revolutionary Stage." *Some Present Tasks*. (Hanoi: Foreign Languages Publishing House, 1974).
10. Report by the Central Executive Committee of Viet Nam Women's Union, *4th National Congress of Vietnamese Women*, Hanoi, March 4-8, 1974; unofficial translation (mimeo), p. 2.
11. Huong Tich, "Wonderful Progress," *Women of Viet Nam* #3 (1971), pp. 11-13. Figures on women's participation in previous assemblies come from personal communication from Women's Union, Hanoi, October 29, 1973.
12. Ho Chi Minh, "Our Party Has Struggled Very Heroically and Won Glorious Victories,"*A Heroic People* (Hanoi: Foreign Languages Publishing House, 1965)p. 12.
13. From personal correspondence from Ann Froines concerning her trip to the DRV in 1970.
14. Unpublished communication from Viet Nam Women's Union, October 29, 1973.
15. Nguyen Thi Thap (see fn. 4), p. 8.

16. For details on land reform and socialist economic transformation of the DRV see Gerard Chaliand, *The Peasants of North Viet Nam* (London: Penguin, 1969), and also chapter 4, "Economic Evolution," in *Viet Nam: A Sketch* (Hanoi: Foreign Languages Publishing House, 1971).

17. Le Dung Trang, "First Visit by a Citizen of the DRV to U.S.," *Indochina Focal Point*, April 16–May 15, 1974, p. 2.

18. Data in this paragraph from the following sources: Vu Huyen and Nguyen Auc, "A Woman Chief Judge," *Viet Nam* #164 (1972), pp. 14–15; Kathleen Gough Aberle, "An Indochinese Conference in Vancouver," *Bulletin of Concerned Asian Scholars,* vol. 3, #3–4 (Summer-Fall 1971), p. 14; "Woman in the Civil Service," article from *Tien Thu* (Saigon), 1961, translated by Chiem T. Kiem; *Women in Viet Nam* (Honolulu: East West Center, 1967), p. 4; Appendix, *Vietnamese Women* (Vietnamese Studies #10; Hanoi: 1966); *Women of Viet Nam* #3–3 (1971); and report and conversations with Dee Donovan on ther trip to Hanoi, June 1973.

19. Chaliand (see fn. 16), p. 239.

20. "President Ho Chi Minh and the Emancipation of Women," *Women of Viet Nam* #3 (1969), p. 22.

21. For details about this law and others see Leo Kanowitz, *Women and the Law* (Albuquerque: Univ. of New Mexico Press, 1969), pp. 88–91.

22. Kiem translations of Vietnamese press, pp. 55–57.

23. "Implementation of the Policies of the Women's Union in Various Services," *Women of Viet Nam* #3-4 (1971) p. 21. For details on the Family Law and its implementation, see *An Outline of the Institutions of the Democratic Republic of Viet Nam*. (Hanoi: Foreign Languages Publishing House, 1974) pp. 156-184.

24. Huyn Kim Khanh, "Vietnamese Communism: The Pre-Power Phase (1925-1945), Ph.D. thesis, Political Science, Univ. of Western Ontario, 1972, p. 438.

25. Unpublished correspondence from Viet Nam Women's Union, Oct 29, 1973, p. 27.

26. Nha Trang, "The Traditional Roles of Women as Reflected in Oral and Written Vietnamese Literature," Ph.D. thesis, Dept. of Anthropology, Univ. of California, Berkeley, 1973, pp. 14 and 27 respectively.

27. *Ho Chi Minh on Revolution,* edited by Bernard Fall (NY: Signet, 1968), pp304-305

28. General Giap, "Stemming from the People," in *A Heroic People* (Hanoi: Foreign Languages Publishing House, 1965), p. 116.

29. Le Duan (see fn. 7), p. 20.

30. Anh Cong and Vu Huyen, "In the Teeth of the Tempest," *Viet Nam* (pictorial) #172 (1972), pp. 18–19.

31. This is a quote from Xuan Dieu, cited in the best available book in English on culture in the DRV; Peter Weiss, *Notes on the Cultural Life of the Democratic Republic of Viet Nam* (New York: Delta, 1970), p. 57.

32. Personal talk with Jill Rodewald, who visited Hanoi in spring 1973.

33. Peter Weiss, pp. 67-69.

34. "The Vietnamese Women and Their Tasks in the New Stage of Socialist Building," speeches from 2nd National Congress of Viet Nam Women's Union, 1960, p. 19.

35. Speeches (see fn. 34), p. 18.

36. Le Duan (see footnote 9) p. 20.

37. Chaliand (see fn. 16), pp. 170-171.

38. Song Ngoc, "How Women Workers Are Cared for at the March 8th Weaving Mill," *Women of Viet Nam* #1 (1971), pp. 21-22.

39. Dinh Phuong Anh, "The Kindergartens of Tan Tien," *General Education in the DRV* (Vietnamese Studies #30; Hanoi: 1971), p. 118.

40. Viet Hoa, "Women's Clubs: A New Feature of Rural Life," *Women of Viet Nam* #1 (1971), p. 18.

41. These statistics on education are taken from the following sources: "Progress," *Women of Viet Nam* #3 (1971), p. 9; unpublished correspondence from Viet Nam Women's Union, Hanoi, October 29, 1973, p. 6; and Reports (mimeo) from the 4th National Congress of Viet Nam Women's Union, March 1974.

42. Tape of interview with Jane Fonda, Hanoi, July 1972.

43. Le Dung Trang. (see footnote 17) p. 2. Other data in this section is from interview by author with Director of General Department of Ministry of Education and Foreign Relations Director of Ministry of Education, October 5, 1974.

44. Viet Hoa, "A Boarding School for Children of War Martyrs," *Women of Viet Nam* #1-2 (1973), pp. 28-29.

45. Unpublished correspondence from Viet Nam Women's Union, Hanoi, October 29, 1973.

46. Unpublished correspondence from Viet Nam Women's Union, Hanoi, October 29, 1973, p. 20.

47. Dinh Thi Can, "Mother and Child Welfare," in *Twenty-Five Years of Health Work* (Vietnamese Studies #25; Hanoi: 1970), pp. 41-45.

48. Unpublished correspondence from Viet Nam Women's Union, Hanoi, October 29, 1973, p. 28.

49. "The Story of Doctor Ngo Thi Ngoc Trung," *Viet Nam* (pictorial) #175 (1973), p. 15.

50. From discussion with Dee Donovan, who visited Hanoi in June 1973.

51. Report of Central Executive Committee, March 1974, pp. 27-35, 52. The following quote on organization is on page 59.

52. Nguyen Thi Thap (see fn. 4), p. 8.

Hanoi, May 1, 1975: Thousands celebrate the complete liberation of Saigon. The poster reads : "Nothing is more precious than independence and freedom."

15.
NO
GOING
BACK

None of the women are prepared to yield what they have gained from the revolution, neither the women who have chosen independent careers after being freed from concubinage, nor the girls at school discussing equal rights.

—Cam Thanh, woman writer in Hanoi

The great majority of women have participated in the revolutionary struggles in both Northern and Southern parts of Viet Nam because they saw that their own survival and liberation depended on gaining two goals: the expulsion of the U.S. invaders from the South and building socialism in the North. The Vietnamese people won complete independence on April 30, 1975. It was what they had been fighting for since 1945. Now there is peace. The people turn towards rebuilding their war-torn country; expanding the revolutionary changes begun during the liberation wars; and working for the reunification of the North and South.

Vietnamese women have moved closer to their emancipation than women anywhere else on the planet because of a particular combination of circumstances: their history and their traditions of endurance and struggle; the political commitment of revolutionary organization and leadership to women's emancipation; the unity and organization of the women themselves; and most important, women's extraordinary participation in production and political and military action in the long war for national liberation.

Women's Union leaders explain the strength of their movement in these terms:

The stronghold of our movement is the most oppressed and exploited who have a very deep hatred of the enemy and a firm stand in the struggle. They never surrender. . . . We have a firm organization because we are based in the main forces: the peasants and the workers— the enemy could never suppress our movement because we are totally integrated with the people.

Once the ideal Vietnamese woman was passive, frail and obedient. Now popular songs praise women's many-sided strengths. This song is called:

TWO SISTERS

*Ba is a guerrilla in Tra Vinh, down South
And Hai a rice grower in Thai Binh, up North;
Two sisters on two front lines but showing the same virtues:
Heroism, dauntlessness, loyalty and resourcefulness.*

A woman who was a student activist against the Thieu regime took an idea from an old folk tale to give new meaning to traditional conceptions of womanhood:

People usually call us the fair sex and compare our feebleness to water. Don't take offense too early. Who says the water is weak. It is an honor for us to be likened to water, for water corrodes stone in the long run and puts out fires. We women too, despite our frail appearance, are endowed with supernatural strength. [1]

But we don't want to conclude that the Vietnamese experience is unique—that their culture and history has made them some kind of "superwomen," not to be found elsewhere. Each aspect of traditional society and culture has its positive and negative sides. Pre-industrial villagers live in harmony with nature, but when science is not applied, women often die in childbirth. Buddhism encourages both fatalism and charity. Confucianism encourages both obedience and faith in people's essential goodness. Nothing is given. Each step toward liberation has been a strenuous battle that requires conscious decision, determination and unity.

Doan Thi Thanh is one woman who has participated in this battle and gained new strength and independence from it. She is a peasant. A citizen of the DRV. Nineteen years old. Not married. She works in the fields with a production team from dawn to 5:00 p.m., with two and one half hours off at midday. The team meets twice monthly to discuss its problems. She also meets regularly with a youth organization and a militia group. The militia group, all young women, train weekly at the firing range, learn to lay mines and throw grenades. She also has time for reading and cultural activities. She has two sets of clothing: one for work and one for other occasions. She eats three full meals a day, with fish two or three times a week and meat two or three times a month.

Before the revolution, she might have been sold as a concubine to a wealthy landlord in order to buy food to feed her starving brothers. She contrasts the past with today:

We are held in higher esteem today, for we have achieved good results —better in some cases than the men themselves have achieved. . . . The old people say, "In the old days we had to depend on men. Now girls do everything the men used to do." [2]

Part of the success of the Women's Union in organizing for women's liberation comes from its continuity. Leaders—many of whom are women in their fifties and sixties—have experience that spans two revolutions. The strength and confidence of older women in Viet Nam is one of the most dramatic expressions of women's emancipation, as well as a vision of the potential for women everywhere.

When the shooting stops

Even before the 1975 victory, Vietnamese women challenged predictions that when the war was over, women would be forced to return to their old places. In the DRV, a leader of the Women's Union wrote, *The return of men from the front after the restoration of peace can in no way change women's role in work.* [3]

There are many reasons why it seems impossible that the tide towards women's emancipation could be reversed. First, the struggle has continued over the lifespan of more than one generation. Changes initiated in war have had time to take firm root. In addition, in the North, women have assumed a major responsibility for production and technical innovation. As men return from the front, they may have to accept women's leadership and learn new methods of work from women.

In the period of peace between 1954 and 1960 in the DRV, women maintained and expanded their gains. When there is peace, valuable resources spent on defense can go towards expanding child care, schools and hospitals. During the peace of the fifties, women participated equally with men in the tasks of reconstruction and often were leaders of production teams that included men and women—rebuilding railroads, bridges and hospitals. The U.S. government violates the Peace Agreement as long as it refuses to aid in "healing the wounds of war." An enormous job of reconstruction faces the Vietnamese people now and there's no sign that women anywhere in Viet Nam expect to quit their new jobs and go back to doing only kitchen duty. Shortly after the bombing of the North stopped, *Women of Viet Nam* magazine featured an article called "Healing the War Wounds." The photos used to illustrate the article pictured women building new apartment buildings, filling bomb craters, repairing dikes and dams, and returning to work at the March 8th Textile Mill, which had just been rebuilt. [4]

North Vietnamese women celebrated the signing of the Peace Agreement, not only because it forced the U.S. to stop bombing, but also because peace marked the beginning of a new stage of development in the DRV which will allow the people to concentrate their energy on building socialism. In outlining their "tasks for the new stage," the 1974 Women's Union Congress noted:

We will inevitably have to bear some immediate privations in order to have funds for the expansion of production and improvement of living standards in a fundamental and lasting way. . . . [Special] attention should be given to regions heavily devastated by the war and to mountain regions. . . . [Priority also goes to] taking care of women members of families with war invalids, martyrs or soldiers. [5]

In a speech to the National Assembly, the Deputy Prime Minister of the DRV implied that the fight against patriarchal feudal ideas would be accelerated:

One aspect of the problem is that the struggle against the U.S. took precedence over internal development. Therefore, though the people's consciousness in that area was very high, their education has been neglected in the nature of collective ownership, socialist labor behavior and ethics. . . . In the coming years, people must become as aware of the need to build socialism as they were of defeating the U.S. invaders. [6]

Another Vietnamese leader, the director of the Journalists' Association and also a poet, explained his vision of what Viet Nam's socialist society would be like:

If the victory at Dien Bien Phu helped us to educate our younger generation for 25 years, this war will help us educate for 100 years. Our blood is very precious and we don't want it wasted. . . .

Our dream is to turn backward, poor Viet Nam into an advanced, prosperous Viet Nam in the shortest time. The problem is to avoid the mistakes of the industrial countries that have started this process before. For example, . . . we do not want to ruin the air and water and lakes and streams . . . we have no plans to build skyscrapers. . . .

To build the material base is important, but not the most important thing. . . . The most long-term, and the most fundamental thing is how to build people, new human beings. It is a great preoccupation of the Party and government here. In the final analysis, our goal is not how to get refrigerators and TV sets. . . . People have much greater goals . . . future generations will be given large wings to fly into the future. These point to a society where there is no tension, where people can walk the street without being murdered, where relations between people are with confidence and love. . . . We can't be impatient or nervous. Unity is the key to the question . . . the art of waiting for each other. [7]

The long-range goal of the revolution is a communist society where each contributes according to her ability and all people have both their material and spiritual needs met.

The most important guarantee of the continuation of women's progress towards total liberation is the women themselves—women who are strong and well-organized, enjoying a high degree of unity. The political awareness of women who have been fighting for generations is very keen—whether they be peasants or urban intellectuals. Mai Thi Chu, a member of the Central Committee of the National Liberation Front of South Viet Nam and also of the Union of Women for the Liberation of South Viet Nam, spoke for all Vietnamese women when she reported:

At the 1960 Congress members of the Women's Union discussed the importance of making sure that women did fully benefit when victory is eventually won; and the Congress determined to avoid the unfortunate experience of Algerian women, who helped in the fight for independence from the French but were unable to achieve their own emancipation. [8]

Reconstruction and Reconciliation

On May 10, 1969, in his last testament, President Ho Chi Minh wrote:

Our mountains will always be,
our rivers will always be,
Our people will always be.
The American invaders defeated,
we will rebuild our land ten times more beautiful.

The PRG has forced the withdrawal of all U.S. troops and personnel from South Viet Nam and dismantled the structure of Thieu's military dictatorship. On May 15, 1975, five women joined other national leaders on the reviewing stand during the mammoth victory celebrations in Saigon. They, along with many others, will lead the new campaign to make Ho Chi Minh's prophecy a reality.

Reconstruction is a gigantic task. The first priority is to make sure the ten million people in newly liberated areas get food and housing—in their home areas if possible. There are millions of peasants, uprooted and unemployed by the U.S. policy of forced urbanization, who are now returning to the countryside. The PRG expected that it would take six months to stabilize and normalize life and two years to take care of the worst war damage done to the people and land. Three-quarters of the land must be reclaimed; three thousand schools, five hundred hospitals, six hundred churches and pagodas all must be rebuilt. Thieu's economy was totally dependent on the U.S. Now the PRG is trying to make South Viet Nam self-sufficient and erase the influence of the dollar.

The entire population: women and men; old and young; peasants, workers, intellectuals, merchants, and industrialists; veteran liberation fighters and ex-ARVN soldiers, are all needed to heal the wounds of war. After twenty years of brainwashing by U.S. psychological warfare teams, the people will have the opportunity to learn about the real accomplishments of the PRG in areas that have been liberated for a long time. Throughout South Viet Nam, the PRG is administering a

Spring 1975:Women tear down the fence surrounding their village—marking the defeat of the U.S. attempt to make it a strategic hamlet.

policy of national reconciliation and concord. It is a policy which includes general amnesty for all who served the U.S. invaders. It promotes the incorporation of all Vietnamese into the new society.

President Ford's and Henry Kissinger's predictions of bloodbaths have been exposed as slander—last-ditch attempts to justify U.S. aggression. Less partisan observers agree:

It is difficult to find a parallel in history where a victorious army, at the end of a bitter 30 year war, treated its enemy with such leniency as has been seen in Saigon. [9]

All ARVN officers from the rank of lieutenant to general are spending a month in PRG re-education centers. After learning about the nature of U.S. aggression and the PRG program, they are free to return home and participate in rebuilding the country. A national leader told a reporter,

As for those persons who have been working with the U.S. and Saigon governments—we will disarm them, but we will not kill them. We shall let the majority of them go back to their families. We will only detain a small number of people who have killed too many of their compatriots. We will wait until the anger of the people cools down, then we shall release them also.

He did not make political agreement a condition for release, but rather acknowledged:

Those who collaborated with the enemy aren't going to change their attitude overnight. There is no country in the world that has seen the kind of anti-communist war waged by the American imperialists . . . in every field: military, political, social, cultural, economic, ideological. You cannot wipe out those influences in a small number of years. The economic aftermath can be rectified more quickly than those consequences. [10]

More than half of Thieu's army had returned to civilian life in the countryside by July, 1975.

Reunification

The Geneva Accords recognize that Viet Nam is one country. The Paris Agreement affirms the fact. It is the overwhelming desire of the 43 million Vietnamese people, North and South, to end the partition of their country. In 1969, the PRG Program stated:

The reunification of the country will be achieved step by step by peaceful means, through discussion and agreement between the two zones without constraint from either side.

The first step is accomplished. Post, telephone and road communication between the North and South has been reopened for the first time since 1954. Thousands of families are being reunited. In thousands of homes, relatives are appearing on the doorstep after not having been heard from for twenty years.

When Ho Chi Minh first organized the Indochinese Communist Party, he unified revolutionaries throughout Viet Nam. When he declared independence from France, he was speaking for all Vietnamese people. That is why people in Viet Nam refer to Ho Chi Minh as "our president" regardless of where they live. The final campaign to liberate the South totally was called the Ho Chi Minh Campaign and Saigon became Ho Chi Minh City because for most Vietnamese, Ho Chi Minh represents the highest ideals of sacrifice and patriotism. His teaching, *Nothing is more precious than independence and freedom,* became the determination and will that energized the people to defeat the U.S. invasion.

Ho Chi Minh ended his last testament:

My ultimate wish is that our entire Party and people, closely joining their efforts will build a peaceful, reunified, independent, democratic and prosperous Viet Nam and make a worthy contribution to world revolution.

Today, PRG and DRV leaders agree that reunification is certain, but they do not predict the exact time. That depends on the will of the people. The DRV in the North has been building a socialist society for about twenty years. In the South, the people have just begun the task of national reconstruction after years of U.S. occupation and war. They have fought a revolution for independence and democracy and will not begin to create a socialist society until it is clear the people demand it. In the meantime, the people in the North will do everything they can to aid the people of the South in reconstruction because they say, "The North and South are kith and kin." As Viet Nam approaches re-unification, women in the North and South are bound to continue learning from each other and sharing in each other's achievements.

Viet Nam is near

On May 17th, 1975, in a letter to the U.S. women's movement, the Vice President of the Viet Nam Women's Union wrote:

. . . *This great victory is inseparable from your militant solidarity, assistance and support as well as that of all women and peace and justice-loving people in the world. We always remember your beautiful deeds and lofty activities that find full expression in rallies, demonstrations, petitions, leaflets, cables, letters in protest against the U.S. aggressive war in Viet Nam in the past years. Mention should also be made of the many collections conducted in various forms to support the Vietnamese people and women. We remember with deep gratitude your great, precious international support. We think that our victory is also yours. . . . As you know, thirty years of war caused by the French colonialists and U.S. imperialists have left us countless difficulties. We hope that you will continue to support and help us both politically and materially. . . . The happiness of a number of Vietnamese families is still tarnished by their concern for the fate of those tens of thousands of their relatives evacuated by force by the U.S. government, including children from three days old to 14 years old. . . . We now request you to raise your voice and strongly demand that the Ford Administration . . . return these children to their families in Viet Nam. . . .*
May the militant solidarity and friendship between the Vietnamese and American women be ever green.

Yours sincerely, Le Thi Xuyen [11]

The war in Indochina has brought lasting changes to the lives of women all over the globe. Our brothers, sons, lovers or co-workers are no longer drafted and killed. But we are only beginning to feel the effects of the war. The U.S. government tried to export its control and its culture. The people of Viet Nam resisted domination. The war machine built by five Presidents has strained U.S. society to its limits. The war came home as heroin addiction, as Watergate, as gas shortages and economic crisis. The U.S. economy has never been geared to meet people's needs—but military spending has meant that even fewer people can have their needs met. All of us have suffered from the brutality of the war.

The war also comes home as a lesson in the infinite possibilities of human resistance, change, and beauty. The people of Viet Nam, especially the women, would be the first to remind us that they have found no universal formula for liberation. No one strategy could be applied in two countries whose size, people and history are so different. We have seen the many ways that the experience of Vietnamese women is not like our own. Yet the demonic system that attempted genocide in Viet Nam is responsible for the forced sterilization of women inside the United States. As they defoliated in Viet Nam, they use poison preservatives here. As they raped there, they rape here. As they tried to dominate there, they manipulate here.

Because of the heroism of the Vietnamese people, that system of destruction—U.S. imperialism—is weaker. When Ford bemoans "our" loss in Viet Nam, he is actually speaking for a handful of people—the one per cent of the U.S. population who owns fifty per cent of the giant corporations that profit from war. The victory of the people of Viet Nam is also the victory of the overwhelming majority of people in the U.S. We strengthen our victory by participating in the worldwide campaign to help rebuild Viet Nam.

We can be clearer about who are the enemies of humanity. We also have a vision of potential solutions. While we may not proceed exactly the same way as the Vietnamese, it is precisely our differences that enable the Vietnamese to teach us. As victims of U.S. aggression, they have seen the worst of our system. Their uncompromising resistance helps us to see how thorough our own revolution must be.

As we begin to make changes here and our own struggle advances, what we learn from the Vietnamese will take on new meaning. Some themes recur: their strength, organization and determination have shown that a united people, confident that their cause is just, certain of their eventual victory, can defeat the most powerful military machine in the world. Their determined trust in people and their ability to change is an antidote to the cynicism of our bureaucratic, bloated society. The word "liberation" had a different meaning before we began to hear of the National Liberation Front. As women, we've learned that our own liberation is not an isolated process, but inter-

252

woven into the fabric of people's struggles everywhere. We can share experiences with women in Viet Nam; learn from and apply examples of unity; feel sure that we will grow and become stronger.

Notes

1. Lien Nhu, "What Do Saigon School Girls Think?" *South Viet Nam in Struggle* #83 (December 20, 1970), p. 8.
2. Quoted in Gerard Chaliand, *The Peasants of North Viet Nam* (London: Penguin, 1969), p. 156.
3. Unpublished correspondence from Viet Nam Women's Union, October 29, 1973, p. 27.
4. *Women of Viet Nam* #1-2, 1973, pp. 5-7.
5. Report by Central Executive Committee of Viet Nam Women's Union 4th National Congress, Hanoi, March 1974; unofficial translation (mimeo).
6. Terry Cannon, "North Viet Nam Plans the Next Two Years," *Tricontinental News Service,* vol. 2, #5 (March 13, 1974), p. 13.
7. Luu Quy Ky, "Wings to Fly into the Future," *Indochina Focal Point,* August 16-30, 1973, p. 2.
8. Quoted in Sheila Rowbotham, *Women, Resistance and Revolution* (New York: Pantheon, 1972), p. 217.
9. Nayan Chanda reported in *Far Eastern Economic Review* (June 20, 1975).
10. Interview by Linda Garrett with Hoang Tung, May 6, 1975 from unpublished letter.
11. Letter addressed to author.

RECOMMENDED READING, RESOURCE AND POLITICAL CENTERS

Books

Burchett, Wilfred G. *North of the 17th Parallel*. Hanoi: Red River Publishing House, 1957.

——. *Viet Nam: Inside Story of Guerrilla War*. New York: International Publishers, 1966.

——. *Viet Nam North*. New York: International Publishers, 1967.

——. *Viet Nam Will Win!* New York: Guardian Books, 1970.

Chaliand, Gerard. *The Peasants of North Viet Nam*. Baltimore: Penguin, 1969.

Ho Chi Minh. *On Revolution*. (Edited by Bernard Fall.) NY: Signet, 1968.

Marr, David. *Vietnamese Anticolonialism 1885-1920*. Berkeley: University of California Press, 1971.

Ngo Vinh Long. *Before the Revolution*. Cambridge: M.I.T. Press, 1973.

Pentagon Papers. (Edited by *New York Times*.) New York: Bantam, 1972.

Rowbotham, Sheila. *Women, Resistance and Revolution*. NY Vintage, 1974.

Taylor, Clyde. *Viet Nam and Black America*. New York: Anchor, 1973.

Viet Nam Veterans Against the War. *Winter Soldier Investigation*. Boston: Beacon Press, 1972.

Vietnamese Studies. These are a series of books published by Foreign Languages Publishing House in Hanoi. Each volume is devoted to a specific theme: *Vietnamese Woman* (#10), *Traditional Viet Nam* (#21), *South Viet Nam: From NLF to PRG* (#23), *A Century of National Struggles* (#24), *Health* (#25), *Education* (#30). These and other books published by the Foreign Languages Publishing House and Giai Phong Publishing House in South Viet Nam are essential sources of information about Viet Nam. Unfortunately, many are out of print and difficult to find inside the U.S. For a catalogue of those available, write to: China Books, 2929 24th Street, San Francisco, CA 94110.

Viet Nam Resource Center. *Vietnamese Women in Society and Revolution, I. French Colonial Period*. (translations of novels and essays). Cambridge: 1974

We Promise One Another: Poems from an Asian War. (Edited by Don Luce, John Schafer and Jacquelyn Chagnon.) Washington, D.C.: Indochina Mobile Education Project, 1971.

Weiss, Peter. *Notes on the Cultural Life of the DRV*. New York: Delta, 1970.

Magazines, news, pamphlets, resource and political centers

Hunt, David. "Organization for Revolution in Viet Nam." *Radical America*, Jan.-April 1974. (Address: 5 Upland Rd., Cambridge, MA 02140).

Indochina Resource Center publishes a monthly called *Indochina Chronicle* and distributes other feature material on Indochina, including a children's book, texts of the Cease Fire Agreement and translations of the Vietnamese press. (Address: P.O. Box 4000-D, Berkeley, CA 94704.)

Internews publishes a biweekly, *International Bulletin,* which compiles news from radio, teletype from Viet Nam, and other sources. (Address: P. O. Box 4400, Berkeley, CA 94704.)

Newsletter of Union of Vietnamese in the U.S. often has translations of Vietnamese materials. (Address: P.O. Box 495, Berkeley, CA 94704.)

Off Our Backs. Monthly women's newspaper which often carries stories about women in Viet Nam and other international news. (Address: 1724 20th Street, Washington, DC 20009.)

Peoples Press is a center for publication and distribution of all kinds of "peoples' literature," including the following on Viet Nam: *Children of the Dragon* (a story textbook for children), *Spirit of the Land* (photographic essay) and *Viet Nam: A Thousand Years of Struggle* (primer). *We Are Sisters* (letters from women in prison in California to women in prison in Viet Nam) and *Viet Nam: Whose Victory?* (news from independent South Viet Nam and post-war analysis). Address: 2680 21st Street, San Francisco, Ca. 94110).

Second Wave. Women's movement journal that has published articles on women in Viet Nam. (Address: P.O. Box 344, Cambridge A, Cambridge, MA 02139.)

Thoi Bao Ga. Newsletter published by Viet Nam Resource Center. (Address: 76-A Pleasant Street, Cambridge, MA 02139.)

Triple Jeopardy. Newspaper of Third World Women's Alliance. (Address: 346 W. 20th Street, St. Peter's Church, New York, NY 10011.)

Viet Nam News and Reports. Newspaper published by Association of Vietnamese Patriots in Canada. Issue #14 had a special supplement on women. (Address: P.O. Box 220, Station G, Montreal, P.Q., Canada H2M9.)

Vietnamese periodicals: *Women of Viet Nam,* a quarterly published by Viet Nam Women's Union. *Viet Nam* (pictorial), a monthly. *South Viet Nam in Struggle* (weekly organ of NLF). *Viet Nam Courier* (used to be weekly and is now monthly). *Viet Nam Youth. Vietnamese Trade Unions.* All of these can be ordered through China Books. (Address: 2929 24th Street, San Francisco, CA 94110.)

Weather Underground. *Prairie Fire,* 1974. Chapter Two analyzes Peoples War in Viet Nam. Originally published underground, but reprinted and available from: Prairie Fire Organizing Committee. (Address: P O Box 411, Times Plaza Station, Brooklyn, N.Y. 11217)

Women, A Journal of Liberation. Many issues have carried articles about the international women's movement. See especially: vol. 1, #4, Charlotte Bunch-Weeks, "Asian Women in Revolution." (Address: 3028 Greenmount Ave., Baltimore, MD 21218.)

Women's Unions, centers and schools in most cities are sources of invaluable information and activity. The *New Woman's Survival Catalog,* published by Coward, McCann & Geoghegan (New York, 1973), lists the addresses of many centers in each city.